EARLY JESUIT MISSIONS IN TARAHUMARA

Early Jesuit Missions
in Tarahumara

By Peter Masten Dunne, S. J.

University of California Press
Berkeley and Los Angeles · 1948

UNIVERSITY OF CALIFORNIA PRESS
BERKELEY AND LOS ANGELES
CALIFORNIA

❖

CAMBRIDGE UNIVERSITY PRESS
LONDON, ENGLAND

PRINTED IN THE UNITED STATES OF AMERICA
BY THE GILLICK PRESS

TO

FATHER CARLO ROSSI

ONETIME PUPIL

EMINENT LINGUIST

AND DELIGHTFUL TRAVELING COMPANION

OVER OLD MISSION TRAILS

AUTHOR'S PREFACE

THIS STUDY of another unit of the Jesuit mission system in northern Mexico is the third made by the author for this series of volumes on the activities of the Jesuits in Spanish North America. It follows in logical sequence the second monograph: Pioneer Jesuits in Northern Mexico (1944). That volume dealt with the missions of the Sierra Madre Occidental among the Acaxée and Xixime Indians, with the tribes of the plains east of the divide in modern Coahuila, and especially with the trouble-torn missions established among the Tepehuán Indians who resided chiefly on the eastern slopes of the Sierra Madre in what is now the state of Durango. The present book describes the extension of the Jesuit mission system north of the country of the Tepehuanes into the territory of the Tarahumares in modern Chihuahua. The facts herein have historical significance, for they form a chapter in the northward advance of Spain's colonial frontier.

The Jesuits, expelled by the King of Spain from his dominions in 1767, were suppressed as a religious order by Pope Clement XIV in 1773. The order was restored by the papacy in 1814, and in the latter part of that century the Jesuits returned to Mexico to take up again their ancient mission work among the Tarahumares. Here they are still working in the 1940's.

The author is indebted to the courtesy and coöperation of many people in the preparation of this study. Dr. Herbert E. Bolton, editor and inspirer of this series, has given the author generous privileges in the use of his collection of documents. Father José Martínez Cabrera, superior of the Jesuits in the city of Chihuahua in 1940, was most helpful in facilitating a journey through northern Tarahumar country, and Señores Silvestre Terrazas and Lorenzo Arellano Schetelig were cordial and coöperative in the indication of local historical sources. Señor José G. Rocha, custodian of the archives of Parral, kindly placed this rich depository of documents at the disposal of the author. Finally, gratitude is due to Mrs. Richard Jones of Los Angeles who went over and over the manuscript and with infinite pains prepared the index.

P.M.D.

University of San Francisco
March 19, 1948

CONTENTS

ILLUSTRATIONS

MAP

Chapter I

THE LAND AND THE PEOPLE

A CROSS THE yellow-flowing Río Grande from El Paso in Texas lies the city of Juárez in Mexico in the state of Chihuahua. From there a journey of more than two hundred miles, by rail or road, almost directly south takes the visitor to the city of Chihuahua, capital of the state. It is dry and dusty travel, for most of the district is desert country and its broad reaches sweep off to the horizon in a seemingly illimitable plain. This does not say that there is no pleasurable relief to the eye, for bold and rocky sierras lift rugged shoulders from the desert floor, and in the clear atmosphere rise up far away in lavender and blue. As the sun sets they are flushed to rose and in the far distance they seem to float upon the horizon's edge like argosies of mystic promise. From Chihuahua southwest, and south is the country of the Tarahumar, an ancient race which still lives upon the land.[1]

The visitor from the United States thus enters the region where the Tarahumares dwell.[2] Not so the ancient missionary. He trudged into the land from the south, from Mexico the capital of New Spain, passing through Zacatecas, famous for its mines of silver, and then on to Durango where the Jesuits had a house and college. From this base the padres used to travel north and a little west through mountainous country where the already established missions of the Tepehuanes lay scattered in the glens and valleys. Soon the borderland between Tepehuán and Tarahumar was reached very near to what is now the southern boundary of the state of Chihuahua. The first missionary among these Indians, Father Juan Fonte, went north into Tarahumar country through a delightfully rolling valley which he called the Valle de San Pablo, where is now situated the town of Ballesa in south central Chihuahua. Later when Parral was founded not many miles east, the missionaries used the frontier town as a base for further penetration into the country of the Tarahumares.

These places lie on what is known as the Mesa Central or central tableland of Mexico. Two long and lofty cordilleras, one on the east and one on the west, lift up this plateau like a great canvas stuck up

[1] For notes to chapter i see page 241.

with points and peaks and ridges, and hold it high and taut. These are called the Sierra Madre, the Mother Range, Occidental and Oriental, respectively. From Zacatecas north and northwest the range, more than eight thousand feet in elevation, gradually declines until it reaches the broad plains of north Chihuahua and Texas. Around Parral and the Valle de San Pablo the country is mild in aspect. It rolls in gentle hills and spreads in vales and valleys. North and east the hills straggle out into the great plain of the Mesa Central which spreads to the Río Grande. These high levels of the Mesa are watered by rivers which carry down to the Río Grande the waters of the Sierra Madre Occidental. The central and main stream is the Río Conchos. To the south are two main tributaries, the Río Parral and the Río Florido, and north is the Río San Pedro. Here, in the seventeenth century, on the banks of the streams of east central and southeast Tarahumara, the Black Robes organized many thriving missions of Tarahumar Indians. Northward lies the city of Chihuahua, capital of the state, close to the northeast boundaries of ancient Tarahumara. Roughly speaking, a line drawn from a point somewhat south of Parral north to Chihuahua marks the eastern limits of the old Tarahumar country.

In the west the aspect of the country is different. Northwest from Parral or southwest from Chihuahua lie the eastern spurs of the Sierra Madre Occidental. This great range extends northwest along the coastline of the Gulf of California and reaches a height in southeastern Chihuahua of more than eight thousand feet. Westward from the more open land of eastern Tarahumara the traveler comes upon broad and level uplands with wooded mountains in the distance. These distant peaks are the eastern spurs of the Sierra Madre. In the level and slightly sloping uplands and in among the wooded mountain spurs dwell many Tarahumares. In southwestern Tarahumara the summits of the Sierra Madre Occidental reach their greatest elevation. Most of the sierra here is of volcanic origin. The rock is composed of soft tufa so that wind, rain, and melting snows have wrought curiously and sometimes savagely upon this part of the earth's outer crust. Wind erosion has in places cut the rock into fantastic shapes, weird cliffs and buttes, and needle-pointed pinnacles. Streams have bitten deep into its easily yielding surface so that the rivers have cut formidable barrancas and precipitous gorges to a depth often of three thousand feet.

Amidst the gorges, where the mountain Tarahumares live, the climate varies in summer from the coolness of the summits to a tropical heat where mountain walls shut out the wind, and the sun of the semitropical belt beats down with unprecedented heat. Vegetation of course differs too. The cool summits are fringed with pine and clothed with oak, down in the barrancas grow the flora of the warmer zones, cacti, the century plant, the *palmilla,* and the *sotol* from which the Tarahumares obtain the fibers for their basket making. In summer clouds of glossy gnats swarm upon man and cover his body with stinging welts. Malaria and tropical intestinal diseases are common in this country. Relief comes in the winter months.

Most of the Tarahumares are not exposed to these inconveniences of life in the gorges and barrancas, for they live in the folds of the wooded hills or along the broad savannas of their northeastern district, or are scattered in villages farther westward on the great plain of the Mesa Central. Western Tarahumara lies over the divide where the rivers flow in a westerly direction after they have zigzagged their way out of the barrancas and gorges. Ultimately they water the corridor between the mountains and the sea and drop into the Gulf of California. These streams, which have various names among the ranges, contribute to the waters of the coastal Fuerte, Mayo, and Yaqui rivers. The last named is enlarged by the inflow of the Río Papigochic. This stream gathers its waters from the eastern slope of the sierra, flows northwest through a broad and beautiful valley, turns west, struggling with many a wrench through the Sierra Madre, and finally on the western slope joins the Río Batuc to form the Yaqui. The old missionaries found here a rough divide over which they passed from one group of missions to another.

The gorge of the Río Uriqui is particularly famous for its sheer and craggy walls. Juan María Salvatierra in 1684, previous to his labors in Lower California, while working on the western fringe of Tarahumar country, descended into the "stupendous gorge." About halfway down, according to his own account, he got off his mule "on the side opposite the precipice, sweating and trembling all over from fright. For there opened on the left a chasm the bottom of which could not be seen, and on the right rose perpendicular walls of solid rock."

On the eastern watershed the branches of the Río Conchos run far up into the land and take the waters from the wooded eastern spurs of the sierra. Thus the upper waters of the Conchos run close to the sources of the streams of the western divide and they are augmented lower down by the Río Florido and the Río San Pedro. These waters ultimately find their way to the Gulf of Mexico via the Río Grande.

The Tarahumares are today among the most compact and unmixed of any of the Indian tribes of Mexico. The men are swarthy and stalwart, fleet of foot and strong of limb; this last characteristic the missionaries noted three centuries ago. At the present day you can still see the Indians in the market places of Parral and Santa Bárbara wearing only a breechcloth; you meet them along the roads which lead into Chihuahua, and as you watch you will see them suddenly break into a run, an ancient habit. Swift and tireless runners they were always regarded. Today they can still run down the deer and the coyote. The old missionary, Herman Glandorff, left his name in legend because of his own reputed qualities of fleetness on the trail.

The origin of this tribe is lost in the twilight of prehistory. Perhaps thousands of years before the time of Christ the Tarahumares were part of a great migration from the north, their ancestors having crossed from Asia. Perhaps early in the Christian era they descended with the Aztecs who settled farther south. Some ethnologists include the Tara-humares with the Uto-Aztecan tribes, which according to one classi-fication include ten groups with subdivisions. Of these, besides the Tarahumares, the best known from the annals of the Jesuit missions are the Pimas, the Mayos, the Yaquis, and the Tepehuanes. The lan-guage and many of the customs of these tribes are kin to the Ópatas and Cáhitas. To the latter belong the Mayos and Yaquis. South of the Tarahumares live the Tepehuanes, north and east of the Conchos. On the west the most numerous neighbors of the Tarahumares are the Lower Pimas and smaller and less distinct groups such as the Varohíos and the Tubares.

There is some difference of habit and dress between the Tara-humares who live in the high sierra and barranca country and those who dwell in lower regions. The former groups are more primitive and almost completely untouched by modern civilization, whereas the inhabitants of the lower vales and plains have become somewhat

Mexicanized. The costume of the highland men is of the simplest: breechcloth, made more secure by a decorative girdle which is wrapped twice about the body; headband, which keeps the long black hair from falling over the face; and sandals for the feet. In winter the men wear a blanket which they deftly carry flung over the left shoulder. The women wear sandals, a coarse shirt, and an ample skirt with a girdle somewhat like those of the men. To these articles they add a shawl which is tied over the breast and hangs over the back. The folds of the shawl serve to carry corn and vegetables and more often a baby. Caves in the mountains and barrancas, or in the palisades which frame some of the rivers such as the upper Papigochic, have served from time immemorial as the dwellings of some of the tribe. However, since the coming of the white man and the missionary three centuries ago, the Tarahumar has learned to build for himself rude primitive huts made of planks and timbers.

Besides the customary diet of corn, these people, especially those of the highlands, eat fish, birds, and mammals of various kinds, lizards, horned toads, snakes, and sundry insects and their larvae. Mention has been made of how they can run down a deer. For two days they will keep upon the animal's track with unfailing eye, but seldom catching sight of the quarry. Finally the pretty beast has spent its energy, its hoofs are worn away, and it collapses. When the creature thus falls from exhaustion it will be throttled by the Tarahumar Indian or killed by his dogs. Sometimes, however, the deer is snared. The Tarahumares formerly used the sling in hunting, now they trap the gopher and the coyote, but in the country of the headwaters of the Río Conchos they still shoot with bow and arrow. They will fell a great pine to capture a squirrel which perches on its upper branches and they are a sure hit in throwing a stone. Bird or animal within range will fall. In more modern times the Tarahumar uses the rifle, a dangerous luxury he never knew as a charge of the missionary or of the colonial Spaniard. This weapon was introduced during the revolutions of the nineteenth and twentieth centuries.

Many of the influences of the seventeenth- and eighteenth-century missionary still persist among these people in the mid-twentieth century. Local or village groups of Tarahumares still have their *gobernador* (the cacique or chief of ancient pagan days) whose prestige and authority were increased by the early missionaries. The gobernador has his court to assist him in a criminal trial, but he is the final judge of the guilt of alleged misdemeanors, and of the punishments which should be meted out to the wrongdoer. Thievery is a common crime and punishable by whipping. Drunkenness, as in the time of the padres, has persisted into modern days and is looked lightly upon. In a Tarahumar court it is a mitigating circumstance in any crime. The Tarahumares still hold to monogamous marriage. Desertion and irregular sex relationships are punishable in various ways. A straying husband may be forced back to his wife. A single man may be forced to marry a girl who has conceived by him or he may be whipped, which is the more usual punishment for seduction. Charges of assault and battery come into court, but the punishment is usually light.

It is a commonplace in mission history that when the missionary departed and the mission was secularized or broken up, the neophyte, even though he had long been a Christian, reverted to many of his old practices of superstition and magic. The rosary was introduced by the missionaries as an article of devotion and a facility to prayer, but the habit of wearing it as an ornament around the neck passed through all the tribe and today is worn by Christian and non-Christian alike. Many of the men still wear the rosary around their necks at the present time. The beads were often made out of Job's tears, a product of the plant *Coix Lachryma-Jobi*. There is also a suspended cross often used as decoration or amulet. The well to do and the medicine men (wizards, shamans, or *hechiceros* as the missionaries called them) wear a large crucifix which they buy from Mexicans. Though the rosary has often been turned to superstitious use, as for instance in the cure of the sick, many Tarahumar Christians wear the beads as a symbol of religious devotion.

The manner in which ancient custom has crept into religious observance or religious celebrations is seen clearly in the native dances, called the *matachines,* which are not necessarily superstitious and have been permitted by the missionaries. The Tarahumares perform the dances on the feast of Our Lady of Guadalupe, at Christmas time, and at the Pascua de Reyes, or what Anglo-Americans call Little Christmas, the feast of the Epiphany. On such occasions the natives dress up in gaudy and sometimes weird attire with bandana handkerchiefs, colored stockings and shoes, and bizarre headdress. Facing each other they go through motions which somewhat resemble the Virginia reel, shaking rattles and waving fans to the tune of the musicians who play on native-made violins and guitars. Formerly they painted their faces for this dance and carried skin bags of fox, squirrel, or opossum. The days of Holy Week are of particular importance to the Christianized Tarahumares of the plains and the lower mountains. The painted and plumed *fariseos* (pharisees) make their appearance some time before Holy Week begins. During the holy days the festal equipment consists in whirl-rattles, painted swords, and plumed crowns. There are the Judases and the pharisees wearing crowns decorated with chicken or turkey feathers. Small boys are painted from head to foot in stripes of red, white, and black, and the dancer of the *pascol* or Easter dance, is adorned with belt and ankle rattles and daubed with paint on face, hands, and head. In the barranca, during Holy Week and other fiestas, appears the garbed clown and jig dancer who performs a rapid shuffle with his feet to the music of cocoon rattles and violin. During Holy Week in the lower country the guitar and violin (which the Tarahumares make with surprising skill and accuracy) give place to the flute and the drum. It is during this time in the organized missions that, under the supervision of the padre, the *gobernador* and other officials are elected, couples properly married, and children baptized, for it is during the festivities of Holy Week that the Indians come into the mission centers from far over hill and dale.

The bee has become an object of superstitious regard (not the bumble bee which sleeps in the ground and stings, but does not work), but the honey-gathering bee which labors and produces sweet honey and useful wax. Unlike many of their fellows, the Tarahumar Indians esteem work and therefore they esteem the working bee. One may therefore never kill a bee. Its honey is used for food; its wax at the burial services often held without benefit of Christian clergy. Fruit trees, introduced of old by the missionaries, have become long since incorporated into the Tarahumar economy, but have not been made objects of superstitious regard.

The Mexican Jesuits, expelled by the king of Spain in 1767, have in modern times come back to their ancient charges, and they have organized a group of modern missions among the Tarahumares. In the mid-twentieth century at such ancient mission centers as Cárichic, Sisoguichic (the great Neumann's old mission), and Píchachic, the Black Robe is again sustaining or spreading Christianity and looking to the education of the youth.[3] The modern missionary has introduced nuns for the education of the little Tarahumares. The girls learn to read and write in Spanish and to cook and sew. The boys become at least literate, and are given a training in the dogma and morale of Christianity which it is hoped will endure through life. But beyond Sisoguichic in the high Sierra Madre, and in the well-nigh inaccessible barranca country and among the gorges, the modern Tarahumar roams and lives his primitive existence practically untouched by Christianity or by modern civilization.

How the black-robed missionary first came to these people in the 1600's and how he worked among them for a century and a half, Christianizing, organizing, and educating, is the story which the following chapters unfold.

Chapter II

THE FRONTIER CREEPS NORTH

A<small>T THE END</small> of the Middle Ages a New World appeared before the eyes of Christian leaders and Christian workers. Since Queen Isabella, who made possible the sailing of Columbus to the New World, was an an ardent Christian, and since the interest of Pope Alexander VI had been from the start definitely engaged, it is not surprising that Christian missionaries came speedily in the wake of discovery. Four friars of three different orders were companions of Columbus on his second voyage to the New World in 1493; with Cortés in his Conquest of Mexico was the Franciscan, Fray Bartolomé de Olmedo, as desirous as Cortés himself to make Christians of the native populations.[1] Furthermore, it is well known from various documents issuing both from the papal curia and the Spanish court that the leaders of Christendom were equally as anxious for the spiritual as for the material conquest of the Americas.[2] As for Cortés, his ardor for the immediate Christianization of the Mexican Indians was so impetuous that it had to be restrained by the Franciscan Olmedo.[3]

No sooner was the conquest of Tenochtitlán, the capital of Mexico, achieved in 1521 than the missionary work, already begun during the course of the Conquest, was permanently established in Mexico City and a stabilized organization was soon set up. The Mercedarian, Father Juan de las Varillas, and the Franciscans, Fray Pedro Melgarejo and Fray Diego Altamirano coöperated with Fray Olmedo even before the end of the Conquest. Two years later three other Franciscans entered the capital, of whom the best known is the famous Pedro de Gante, not priest, but lay brother, founder of education in New Spain. Stabilization and methodic organization were formed with the arrival of "the Twelve" in 1524, Friars Minors all, led by the illustrious Martín de Valencia.

Then began the absorption of the Mexican Indian into the Catholic faith and the process was rapid indeed, so rapid that misgivings were felt as to the advisability of conversion almost *en masse*. Martín de Valencia in a letter to Charles V writes of one million two hundred

---

[1] For notes to chapter ii see page 242.

thousand brought into the Church between 1524 and 1532; Pedro Gante in a letter of June, 1529, speaks of fourteen thousand baptized in one day.⁴ What defects there were in the Christian education and correct indoctrination of such wholesale numbers would, it was thought, gradually and naturally correct themselves in the course of the next immediate generations, for the children could then be instructed from the beginning and possess the doctrinal completeness of one born in the Faith.

The Franciscans did not long enjoy a monopoly. In 1526 twelve Dominicans arrived in New Spain led by their superior Tomás Ortiz, and in 1533 came seven Augustinians with Father Francisco de la Cruz at their head.

Speaking of the Church, an enthusiastic prelate has written: "Where armies and explorers stop, she goes forward, often enough armies and explorers find that she has gone before them."⁵ This was frequently true in the first century of the history of Catholicism in Mexico. With the captains of Cortés, with Alvarado southeast, with Orozco south, with Olid east, with Nuño de Guzmán north and northwest went the missionaries into Chiapas, Oaxaca, Michoacán, Jalisco, and Sinaloa. The Dominicans established houses and missions south, the Augustinians chiefly north, while the Franciscans spread to the west and far to the northwest and northeast. Sentispac, on the coast near the mouth of the Santiago River, was the farthest western Franciscan mission established in the sixteenth century, and Topia in the rugged heart of the great Sierra Madre became their farthest mission northwest. Into these mountain fastnesses the missionary preceded the explorer.

So far as missionary activity is concerned, the work of the religious orders of the half century from 1522 to 1572 forms a distinct period. In 1572 the Jesuits came and introduced an era of somewhat different form. In the first half century, especially from the 1540's, the frontier of Mexico and of Christianity advanced north at a rather rapid pace. The discovery of silver mines was the compelling factor. Silver was discovered in Zacatecas in 1546 and two years later the town of Zacatecas was founded. During these years there was a rush to the north. Soon the metal was discovered in other districts still farther north, and Fresnillo, Sombrerete, San Juan del Río, Durango, Indé, Topia, and

Santa Bárbara, the latter founded in 1567, became within these twenty years the "Mother Lode" country of Mexico, which in sheer extent of geographical surface exceeded the Mother Lode country of modern California. From Zacatecas to Santa Bárbara it is, as the crow flies, three hundred and fifty miles.⁶ These were exciting "gold-rush" days according to the slower tempo of the sixteenth century, and as the frontier moved north a great new province was organized as a distinct unit of New Spain. It was called Nueva Vizcaya and was given its own organization, governor and inferior officers, subject to the Viceroy of Mexico, the highest colonial authority.

The first governor of the new province was Francisco de Ibarra, nephew of Diego de Ibarra, one of the mine-owning millionaires of Zacatecas. This Francisco was fitted for his job. He had opened up the new country in the 1560's by a series of explorations which took him up to Indé and Santa Bárbara, across the rugged Sierra Madre to the coast of the Gulf of California, and then north along that fertile corridor between the mountains and the sea as far as the Sonora River and the Casas Grandes of modern Chihuahua. Famed in Mexico's frontier history as Indian fighter and mine developer, Ibarra was yet a close friend of the Franciscans and always had the friars with him in his various expeditions. When they did not precede him, as in Topia, the friars accompanied him, and they remained in many a newborn town to found a mission.

Thus it was especially with the town of Durango. Before the Spanish town was founded Fray Jacinto de San Francisco, who had been one of Cortés' soldiers, together with Fray Pedra de Espinareda, worked north from Nombre de Diós and preached Christianity to the Tepehuán Indians in the country which bordered on the Guadiana Valley in which Durango was founded. Here sometime later Espinareda founded a mission named San Juan de Analco near the spot where in 1563 the town of Durango was established by order of Francisco de Ibarra.⁷ The enduring Mexican city of Durango, then, was set upon the spot in the lovely Guadiana Valley where the Franciscans had planted a mission for the primitive Tepehuanes. Thus during the half century from 1522 to 1572 the Franciscans not only established many centers of spiritual influence, in and about Mexico City, but spreading their labors far north they accompanied or preceded the secular explorer; they stood at the birth of a province and of a city, the city of Durango in the Province of Nueva Vizcaya.[8]

As the Franciscans aided in the birth of the capital of Nueva Vizcaya, so were they the mothers and the nurses of San Juan del Río, Sauceda, Guatimapé, Topia, and San Juan de Carapoa west on the Fuerte River. They had their martyrs too. This last town was no sooner founded by Ibarra in 1564 than it was destroyed, and Fathers Azevedo and Herrera were slaughtered with the rest. Father Juan de Tapia and his companion, Lucas, were slain while returning to Zacatecas from a missionary expedition in Guadiana. And in 1562 in the heart of the Sierra Madre Occidental in the sequestered vale of Topia two unnamed friars met death at the hands of the wild Acaxées.

Thus the first half century closes an epoch in the ecclesiastical annals of Mexico: the numerous and more cultured Indians for hundreds of miles in and about the capital had been Christianized, and the national foundations of a church had been laid. Then, in more distant provinces, the first permanent missions *entre infieles* had been started among the more primitive nations of the west and northwest.

The arrival of the Jesuits in Mexico City in 1572 began an activity, both educational and missionary, which was to continue for two centuries. The men of this religious order introduced a note of greater organization and system into the mission field, and their missionary exploits, here as elsewhere, have caught the especial notice of historians. It was not for nineteen years after their arrival in New Spain, however, that the Jesuits inaugurated a permanent system of missions among the primitives of the northern wilds. The story of these missionary exploits is becoming better known, for, like the Franciscans, the Jesuits endured their trials and their dangers, torture and death, all the while that they were baptizing hundreds of thousands of natives of various tribes and tongues.[9]

It was good that the Jesuits came to New Spain when they did for the cause of education needed them in the capital. It was good for the missions that nineteen years later, in 1591, Gonzalo de Tapia and Martín Pérez began their missionary labors at San Felipe on the banks of the Sinaloa River, for the number of Franciscans was not sufficient even to hold in continuity what mission stations they had begun. Thus it was that although the mild Tahue Indians in and about

Culiacán on the coast had been Christianized by the friars, there was in the late 1500's no missionary to continue to care for them. It was the same with the Zacateco Indians near Cuencamé and in the country of the lagoons.[10]

Though the Jesuit Tapia was slain by Indians in 1594, others came to take his place, and with the succeeding years the missions spread north along the coast of the Gulf of California and became famous in the missionary and historical annals of the New World. The missions were the beginning of a long period of missionary endeavor and of frontier expansion which reached ultimately the fair province of Alta California and its Bay of San Francisco. The Jesuit Black Robes did not, it is true, carry these missions so far, for King Carlos III of Spain expelled them from his domains in 1767. It was the Franciscan Gray Friars with Junipero Serra at their head who again stepped into the breach to carry the cross to the mission site of San Francisco in the famous year of 1776.

East of the Sierra Madre Occidental, Durango, founded by Ibarra and nursed spiritually by Franciscans, became in time the center of a great Jesuit missionary activity. Residing here in the capital of Nueva Vizcaya since 1593, the Black Robes began their missionary work east among the Laguneros with Juan Agustín de Espinosa in 1594 and north among the Tepehuanes by Gerónimo Ramírez in 1596. By 1598 Ramírez was beginning his baptisms on a large scale, and by that year he was in permanent residence among these sullen primitives at a pueblo he had founded eighty miles north of Durango and which he called Santiago Papasquiaro. That same year Santa Catalina was founded thirty miles farther north, later Zape, and an organized community of Indians at Guanaceví. In 1600 a helper came for Ramírez—Father Juan Fonte. Still others arrived in 1603. Juan Fonte became the first apostle of the numerous tribe of the Tarahumar Indians.[11]

Chapter III

FONTE, FIRST APOSTLE OF THE TARAHUMARES

FATHER JUAN FONTE holds the distinction in history of being the primary apostle and protomartyr of the Tarahumares. The early career of the missionary, as is usual with the Jesuit, was undisclosed and uneventful. Fonte was born in Barcelona in 1574 and at the age of nineteen entered the Society of Jesus in 1593. In Spain he passed through the customary spiritual and intellectual training of a Jesuit, and six years later, in company with Father Pedro Díaz, former Provincial of New Spain, he crossed the Atlantic, already a priest, a young man of twenty-five. On his arrival in Mexico the young Black Robe was sent immediately to the Tepehuán mission to aid Gerónimo Ramírez, and he was there and with the Tarahumares from 1600 to his death.[1] In 1604 Fonte took his last vows, four of them, becoming a professed member of the Society. During the years immediately following the missionary's arrival in the Tepehuán mission he gained valuable experience which, added to his native ability, was to serve him well with the Tarahumares on the northern Tepehuán border. Baptism of the Tepehuanes continued after 1600 at Santiago Papasquiaro, at Santa Catalina, and farther north at Zape, which Gerónimo Ramírez was able to found shortly after the arrival of his helper Fonte.

As the years passed, Father Fonte was assigned to these northern pueblos, Zape, thirty miles north of Santa Catalina, and the community of Christians at the mines of Guanaceví, fifteen miles beyond Zape. Then he was sent east to another mining center, Indé, where between 1603 and 1607 another community and mission of Christian Tepehuanes was established. Some sixty miles north of Guanaceví begins the country which was a border between the Tepehuanes and the Tarahumares. Here were three districts comprising the fringes of the two tribes frequently mentioned by Fonte and his successors on the mission. They were Ocotlán, the Valle de Águila, and the Valle de San Pablo. The last of these places can be identified today in the region lying west of Santa Bárbara. The Valle de Águila was the farthest

---

[1] For notes to chapter iii see pages 242-243.

north of the lands of the Tepehuanes; the Valle de San Pablo was already on the fringe of the Tarahumares.

Father Juan Fonte made his first *entrada* into this border country in 1607. The immediately practical motive of his apostolate among the Tarahumares, besides the general desire to bring Christianity to still another people, was the cessation of the all but continuous border warfare which had existed between the Tepehuanes and the Tarahumares. The Jesuit fathers were accustomed to such perpetual conflict between tribes and whenever possible they strove to put an end to it. This same situation was present in another part of the vast area of Jesuit missionary activity, for southwest in the mountains the Xiximes and the Acaxées were constantly on the warpath. Their Christianization, completed finally in 1610 by the conversion of the Xiximes, brought peace to a border and to a province.

By the year of his entrada, 1607, Fonte had penetrated as far north as Ocotlán and the Valle de Águila, and had evangelized the Tepehuanes. Some of these Tepehuanes were already Christians, and Fonte was but rounding out the work of Father Gerónimo Ramírez, who had come close to this region some years before. While Fonte was in the Valle de Águila some pagan Tepehuanes came south to seek the aid of their Christian tribesmen against the common enemy. One of the Christian caciques, listening to this plea for aid in warfare, proposed that the decision be left with the missionary. Fonte, of course, counseled peace, and his advice was accepted. He was able to meet some of the Tarahumares on this occasion and he gave them the same counsel. Both the pagan Tepehuanes from the north, as well as the Tarahumares, were impressed by the wise kindliness of Fonte's personality and through his benign influence an enduring peace for the first time in years placed its quiet hand over the border. Fonte with a companion now proceeded north to the Valle de San Pablo.[2] Here, through a trusted Tepehuán cacique, Fonte was able to visit in friendly conference eight hundred and forty-two braves of the Tarahumar nation.[3]

Here was Fonte's chance to fulfill a desire of many years. He had a great eagerness to go north among these people. Once while he was at the mines of Indé there came to see him a group of savages, most probably Tarahumares, traveling six or seven days' journey. Their number was large, and they invited him to come to their country. It was impossible for him at the time to do so, the formalities of the Spanish government and of the *Patronato Real* not permitting such independent freedom of movement. He wrote at this time: "I feel keenly my inability to go back with them as they were pressing me to do. I said to myself: 'If only I could, without dependence upon the Viceroys and without listening to them, go forward like our Father St. Francis Xavier[4] to present the gospel of Christ even though it would be at the risk of my life.'"[5]

Such were Juan Fonte's desires a few years before the event we are relating. No more propitious set of circumstances had ever before offered themselves for the beginnings of the Tarahumar mission. The border was at peace, and Fonte had met hundreds of Tarahumar braves and found them ready for the gospel. The Jesuit made up his mind to loosen the official bonds which restrained him from opening a new mission and from admitting a new nation into the pale of the Church. In the early spring of 1608, therefore, he went south to confer with Francisco de Urdiñola, Governor of Nueva Vizcaya, and through him to influence the Viceroy himself in Mexico City, at this time Luis de Velasco II, serving his second term.

Fonte himself informs us what happened at Durango. Since certain caciques of the Tarahumares were requesting the gospel and baptism, he urged Governor Urdiñola to ask Viceroy Velasco not only for permission to extend the missions into this new nation, but likewise for three additional workers, one for Ocotlán, the newest of the Tepehuán missions which had been inaugurated the year preceding, and two for the proposed new mission in the Valle de San Pablo, which would open the Tarahumar country.[6]

Fonte was satisfied with the success of his negotiations. The Governor had evidently told him he would obtain the necessary approval from the Viceroy, for just two days before departing for the north again, Fonte wrote from Durango under date of April 22, 1608: "I am in a happy and enthusiastic state of mind, seeing the door now opened to us for numerous conversions, especially since these developments can go forward without the aid of captain and soldiers. This I have always avoided and shall continue to avoid, for when progress is made without extra expense the ministers of the King more readily concede workers for the new fields, and the natives themselves are happy to see us in their lands unaccompanied, for at the sight of soldiers and other Spaniards they flee."[7]

Fonte added some reflections on the profound change which had come upon the former rebellious and warlike Tepehuán nation as a result of the spread of the gospel and the influence of the fathers.[8] He evidently hoped for the same fruit from the prospective Tarahumar mission. Fonte now left for the north again, for the district of Ocotlán, taking with him as fellow worker Father Juan del Valle. Here he would keep in touch with his Tarahumar neophytes of the Valle de San Pablo and await official permission to make a second entrada to establish closer contact with the nation. "I will take this mission upon my own shoulders," Fonte writes in his enthusiasm, "and since the good Lord has given me health and I am not yet old [he was thirty-four] I should suffer a scruple of conscience in shunning anything even the most difficult and laborious."

Two years later all this constructive work was threatened with collapse by the atrocity of a Tarahumar hechicero, as the Spaniards called these Indian wizards or medicine men. This fellow persuaded a band of ten of his henchmen to descend south into the Valle de San Pablo and murder a cacique who was undergoing instruction for baptism. The deed was perpetrated, with the result that the relatives of the murdered neophyte were furious. The one circumstance which gave pause to their desire for revenge was the fact that the fathers were in the Valle, and to stir up war would endanger their lives. They therefore persuaded the missionaries to retire to the more secure pueblos in the south. The Tepehuán avengers then made war upon the Tarahumares. At the same time they sent south to Durango an embassy, headed by the murdered chief's son, to seek out Governor Francisco de Urdiñola and ask his aid against the criminals. But since the Governor was absent on a campaign against the Xiximes the delegation had to return without definite promise of assistance.

Whether, however, the murderous Tarahumar hechicero underwent a change of heart, as the historian of these missions avers[9] or whether the fear of the Spanish arm led him to relent, the fact is this leader of evil went south on a mission of peace, sought out Juan Fonte, apologized for his offense, and requested baptism.[10] Such a step on the part of one so important affected others of the Tarahumares, who now came to San Pablo seeking baptism. War was definitely over, the baptism of a new nation had begun, and the Valle de San Pablo was become the gateway to the Tarahumares.

But our missionary had to wait two years before fulfilling his desire for an entrada deeper into Tarahumar territory. In December of 1610 Father Rodrigo de Cabredo, himself an old missionary in Nueva Vizcaya and Jesuit Provincial of New Spain,[11] showed his interest in the conversion of new nations by sending Fathers Juan del Valle and Bernardo Cisneros southwest over the mountains to visit the isolated Hinas and Humis. Cabredo also commissioned Fonte to go a second time into Tarahumar country and to set the mission upon a solid basis. Our knowledge of Father Fonte's missionary enthusiasm would lead us to suspect that his eagerness would send him immediately to the north, to the Valle de San Pablo and beyond.

Fonte started in December of 1610 or possibly early in January, 1611. The season is cold at this time of year, but it is usually dry. It is fortunate that Fonte's letter telling of the happy advance and adventure is extant.[12] Our narration therefore can be highly authentic. Fonte, seeing that his first contact with the Tarahumares had been made in the Valle de San Pablo, the border where Tepehuán and Tarahumar met, now planned to penetrate their territory and to persuade as many of them as he could to migrate south and to take up their homes in the valley, for it was a propitious spot and there they would enjoy prosperity and peace.

Fonte in this design was following the customary practice of the missionaries. It was practically impossible to influence and instruct the natives in their primitive state, scattered as they were far over hill and dale, precipice and crag. They must be brought together, thought the missionary, to live in groups in more level and accessible spots. This is the genesis of the formation of the mission pueblo.

With this purpose in mind, then, Fonte set out for the north accompanied by four Tarahumar chiefs, two of whom were Christians, and a few others. One Christian Indian boy went along as the father's servant and to assist at Mass. North from the Valle de San Pablo the Black Robe traveled over low hills and along winding valleys, more than fifty miles into Tarahumar country. The success of the advance was reassuring for the padre was everywhere well received. The element of adventure too was enjoyable, since Fonte missed nothing which was distinct in the personal habits of the Tarahumares and in their mode of living.

These primitives, Fonte reported, were more docile than the Tepehuanes. Instead of huts, many of them lived in caves large enough to comprise several ordinary dwellings.[13] They buried their dead in cemeteries apart, and alongside the corpse they placed food and all his clothes and possessions which were considered necessary for the journey into the great beyond. All other things belonging to the deceased were destroyed and his dwelling was burned or razed. The women were good weavers, making their clothes of the fiber of the agave or century-plant. They were retiring, thought Fonte, and shy in the company of men.

The Black Robe thus introducing himself to new peoples was evidently impressed by his first contact with the Tarahumares deep in their own country. (The welcome they gave him undoubtedly aided in his sympathetic report.) When Fonte and his group were nearing the first Tarahumar pueblo, scouts descried him from a lookout and sent word of it to the village. The men, women, and children came out a great distance to welcome him, and as he approached they stood in good order arranged in rows, and they greeted the padre and escorted him to the pueblo. The cacique, decorated all in feathers, carried his lance; the others held their hands over their heads in token of esteem and respect. Arrived at the pueblo the Black Robe made them a speech. "I am most happy at last to be here with you," he said in part, "for it is only for love of you that I come into your country. . . ."[14] Fonte said not much more on this occasion. Introduction into the truths of the Faith would come at a later opportunity for such development.

These Tarahumares seemed to have been completely won over. Their pleasure at having the padre among them was manifest, and their hospitality would have done honor to more civilized peoples, for they brought food and refreshment for Fonte and his party. Many returned a second time to visit him and to tell him of their joy at seeing him in their land. Fonte writes: "The women at first shrank away in bashfulness, but later seeing their men in free and easy converse with me, and myself speaking with them as with my sons, they too finally came up to speak with me as with their father. And they, as well as the men, asked that I might return to see them in their country once again."[15]

The Black Robe spoke to them of the necessity of baptism and of the worship of the one God. They assented and told him of a child dying in the vicinity. Fonte baptized the infant before death and later on, to the contentment and even pride of the Tarahumares, he baptized five other children, including a boy who was very ill with smallpox. The father and mother had petitioned Fonte that he bless their son with this Christian rite.

It had been understood from the beginning that Juan Fonte could not tarry indefinitely at this time with these new friends. But before departure he took cognizance of the fertility of the spiritual field and left provision for its partial cultivation. Inquiring as to the number of Tarahumares in this the most southern district of their nation, he was told that there were three thousand one hundred and seventy, besides certain isolated groups who could not be reached. Encouraged at the prospect of so fine a harvest the missionary before departure left an organization behind, so that the field might be made ready through cultivation for eventual sowing of the seed.

In other words, in that mature way of those who are at the same time intelligent and stable, Fonte provided for the continuity of this his present influence. He appointed four men, called fiscals in the ecclesiastical or mission parlance of the period, who, possessing already a certain tincture of Christianity as the result of Fonte's earlier contacts, would gradually instruct their people in the fundamentals of the Faith. To each fiscal was assigned a certain district. The padre, acting as a primitive normal school teacher, instructed them how best to introduce to their tribesmen the basic truths of the Christian religion and pointed out the proper psychology in the carrying on of so delicate a work. These fiscals would come from time to time to the Christian pueblos to report to Fonte concerning the progress of their work. Thus leaving behind him something that would grow and develop in his absence, Juan Fonte prepared to return south to the Valle de San Pablo.

Besides this contact, opening wedge for later apostolic endeavor, and besides the organization just described, Fonte was able to accomplish a work of definitely concrete development. We have seen that the padre had set his mind on populating the Valle de San Pablo with Tarahumares, inducing numbers of them to migrate south for this purpose. Here they would mingle in a friendly manner with the Tepehuanes and the border rivalry and warfare would become permanently a thing of the past. Fonte was now able to accomplish his purpose. Fortunately he had gained the admiration and confidence of a prominent hechicero (it was these leaders the fathers set out primarily to win over), a man who was half Tepehuán and half Tarahumar. This leader knew both languages and he agreed enthusiastically with the missionary's plan for the settlement of the Valle. He used his influence to successful purpose and it was chiefly through him that the Valle was peopled with enough Tarahumares to form a goodly pueblo. This town was called San Pablo. It has enjoyed a continuous existence and lies today in a valley framed partly by rolling hills which straggle off from the Sierra Madre. This ancient Christian settlement is today known as San Pablo Ballesa.[16]

These newly won Tarahumares who had moved to the Valle would not allow their attentions to their newly found spiritual father to cease. For his journeys and visitations to various districts of the vicinity, his Tarahumar neophytes furnished Fonte with an escort of eight or ten men, placing over them a captain to whom they owed obedience. It was shortly after his return to the Valle de San Pablo that Fonte had opportunity to pay a needed visit to the mining center of Santa Bárbara. It was necessary that the Spaniards of the mines be made aware of the recent developments among the Tarahumares in order that they might be sympathetic to the movement and, above all, be careful not to afflict these people with atrocity or oppression.

Father Gerónimo Ramírez did exactly the same thing in 1598 when, upon founding the new Christian Tepehuán pueblo of Santiago Papasquiaro far south of Tarahumar country, he visited the Spaniards of the mines of Papasquiaro some miles up the Río de Santiago to gain their coöperation and to be able to assure his Tepehuán neophytes that the miners would not molest them.

Fonte then for the same purpose and under much the same circumstances paid a visit to Santa Bárbara. But his Tarahumar neophytes would not let him go alone. Not only his usual escort of loyal Indians, but an augmented body must accompany him on this especially important visit to the workers and owners of the mines. Fonte endeavored to decline such attentions, but the Indians insisted that at least thirty braves with bow and arrow should escort him to Santa Bárbara. They desired, they said, to demonstrate to the Spaniards the quality of their esteem for their father. They shrewdly desired too, of course, to demonstrate to the Spaniards that the Jesuit was their protector. Nor was this all. The new residents of San Pablo contributed provisions for the journey, food and blankets for the father's comfort. It happened that while they were on the road a terrific rain pelted down upon them. The Tarahumares were attentive to their padre manifesting by various kindly offices their true quality of sons.

Ramírez' mission twelve years before to the mineowners of Papasquiaro had been successful, so now in 1611 did Fonte's bear fruit with the miners of Santa Bárbara and lead to an enduring settlement. It is true that the Spaniard had often oppressed the Indian in various ways, kidnapping his women, enslaving him to domestic service or to enforced labor in the mines. Such treatment had led to revolts of no small proportions, such as the great Mixton rebellion of 1541 in Nueva Galicia or the lesser uprising among the Acaxées in 1601. But by the influence of the Black Robe the Spaniard also was induced to better his ways. Besides, it was not difficult to persuade him that in addition to the motive of Christian charity and religion, there was the more immediate and concrete argument of self-interest. Certainly a rebellious tribe was no advantage to the Spaniard, whether he be miner or stockman; the frontier could be safe and prosperous only with the Indian at peace. Thus Father Juan Fonte was able to persuade the Spaniards of Santa Bárbara to respect his children new-born to the Faith, and to promise to refrain from all molestations of the Tarahumares of San Pablo.

The accomplishment of all of this work for the safe advancement of the frontier and the expansion of Christian civilization and culture consumed probably several months. When it was completed Fonte undertook again the long journey south to Durango, capital of Nueva Vizcaya and head of this mission system. Just as he had provided on the ground, by means of the fiscals, for the continuance of his Christian influence and teaching, so now, intelligent apostle, he had to provide with his superiors and with the Spanish high officials for future augmentation of workers in the field, lest this sowing be neglected and the promise of fruitage die before the blade had barely sprouted from the ground.

Down to the valley of Guadiana then, to the capital Durango (at that time also called Guadiana), Fonte went again to consult with Francisco de Urdiñola, Governor of the Province of Nueva Vizcaya. This able official by this time well appreciated the advantages of a peaceful frontier. In office since 1603, he had to deal from the start with the Acaxée revolt. Later in 1607 and again in 1610 he had trouble with the cannibal Xiximes. The Governor shortly after his entrance into office had visited the flourishing Sinaloa missions on the west coast and witnessed the tremendous advantages accruing to this part of his province from the peaceful and coöperative attitude of the Indians of the valley of the Sinaloa. Now in 1611, with the promise of the conversion of a new and numerous tribe, Urdiñola would be enthusiastic in his representations to the Viceroy in Mexico City and to the Jesuit Provincial for additional workers for this northern vineyard.

Father Fonte was successful. Additional missionaries were now sent to augment the personnel of the Tepehuán missions. By 1612 six Black Robes were working in this field.[17] Two years later there were seven.[18] An experienced missionary could now be released from the south to help Fonte in the north. This man was an old co-worker with Fonte, Gerónimo de Moranta. He was a kinsman of Ignatius Loyola's intimate friend and secretary, Father Jerome Nadal. Entering the Jesuit Order in 1595 at twenty years of age and coming to the New World under the influence of the Jesuit saint, Brother Alphonsus Rodríguez, who had also been the inspiration of the labors of St. Peter Claver among the Negro slaves at Cartagena in South America, Moranta came to the Tepehuán mission in 1605 and on repeated occasions had been Fonte's companion among the Tepehuanes.[19]

It was always a more or less patient wait for missionaries. They could not always be sent immediately from Mexico City and other southern centers where their services were likewise in demand. Unfortunately, too, in 1615 the north Tepehuán country lost one of its missionaries, Father Juan Pérez de Córdoba, drowned while trying to ford a branch of the Río de las Nazas in flood. He was buried in Guanaceví where he was beloved.[20] Nevertheless, by 1614 Fonte and Moranta both could work in the north.

After 1611, as is evident from the records, Fonte was giving more and more of his time and presence to the Valle de San Pablo, where by the hundreds Tepehuanes and Tarahumares continued to migrate into the valley and to live together in peace. Progress was the note during these years in the Valle.[21] Fonte reported in 1615 that more and more Indians were coming to him from the back country. A hechicero, however, at Indé tried to cause some trouble. He told the Indians that Fonte was a murderer and would kill their children with baptism. The Indians laughed at the wizard and showed still greater confidence in the padre. When a woman, after giving birth to a still-born offspring, ran to a hechicero for help, Fonte taught her to go to God in prayer, thus to obtain real solace. When the crops were ruined by pest Fonte introduced the neophytes to the prayers of the Church composed for just such vicissitudes. These people were consoled and asked for baptism.[22]

Here, then, was another border brought to peace by the Christian spirit and Christian civilization, a border which in the past, like others in northwestern Mexico, had been ripped continually and torn with war. The Tepehuán-Acaxée frontier had for some years enjoyed an enduring peace; and just recently the Acaxée-Xixime border had been brought to constructive development; and now, finally, the problem of the Tepehuán-Tarahumar fringe was being solved in a friendly blending of the two nations to the exclusion of frontier raids and the alarms and atrocities of war. Juan Fonte had been the angel of peace and under his beneficent influence the Tepehuán tiger rested with the lion of the Tarahumar.

Chapter IV

FONTE IS SLAIN

WHILE ALL THINGS seemed to be ready for a deeper penetration into Tarahumar country, with new men arriving in the Tepehuán mission and releasing others for work exclusively among the northern Tepehuanes and the southern Tarahumares, a great setback occurred which was to delay further progress in the conversion of the northern tribe for more than twenty years. This calamity occurred in the year 1616, and is known in mission history as the Tepehuán Revolt. In this maelstrom of violence and massacre not only were the Tepehuán missionaries slain, but there likewise fell two Jesuit travelers from the west, and the two who were working among the Tarahumares in and about the Valle de San Pablo, namely, Juan Fonte, and Moranta. The violent elimination of these two men and the near ruin of the Tepehuán mission put a stop for two decades to further advance of the Tarahumar mission.

The Tepehuanes had never been so generous and enthusiastic in their acceptance of the Faith as some of the tribes over the Sierra Madre on the west coast, the Ahomes, for instance, and the Mayos along the Mayo River. Moreover, the hechiceros or medicine men, always and everywhere a thorn in the side of the missionaries, seemed to be more numerous and more powerful among the Tepehuanes. The hechiceros were always the leaders of opposition against the padres, since the missionaries on their entrance among the nations deprived the hechiceros of their wonted leadership and prestige.

It was a hechicero, one Quautlatas, who went about the different pueblos and missions of the Tepehuanes with a small stone idol, and this rude divinity spoke to the Indians of revolt. The god was displeased with the Tepehuanes, said Quautlatas, because they had admitted the Spaniards among them and had become followers of the God of the Christians. They would do a good and pleasing thing to the divinity did they slaughter all the Spaniards, the missionaries included. Those Indians who fell in the fight would enjoy resurrection within seven days, and with the Spanish yoke shaken off, fresh

---

[1] For notes to chapter iv see page 243.

blessings and all the old joys of paganism would return. The god would even see to it that no more Spaniards would be able to cross the seas; storms churned up in the Atlantic would make shipwreck of all their boats.[1]

Christianity did not keep the native Indian from remaining a child; it did not prevent the Tepehuán from remaining credulous and fickle, open to almost any stupid or extravagant leadership. Quautlatas, therefore, beginning at Tenerape on the Río de Santiago, and passing with his idol through the other pueblos and missions of the Tepehuanes—Santiago Papasquiaro, Santa Catalina, Zape—and to other villages nearer Durango, such as Sauceda and Tunal, was able to gain so substantial a following that the bulk of the tribe agreed to join in the conspiracy against the Spaniards.

We can understand the success of the hechicero. With many of these Tepehuanes, Christianity had not gone beneath the skin. For many, Christian morality was an abominable restraint and the discipline of the mission pueblo was irksome. They longed for their old-time liberty and their wild, disorganized life. They had not asked for the Spaniards who were, after all, intruders. Though the padre was kind, the more serious breaches of mission discipline were punished by flogging at the hands of Spanish soldiers. Spaniards had often exploited the Indian cruelly. Thus it was not difficult for Quautlatas to whip up a spirit of discontent and rebellion.

The plan of the rebels was to strike at Zape on November 21, the Feast of Presentation of Blessed Mary the Virgin. A statue of Our Lady brought up from Mexico City was to be dedicated at Zape on this feast, and all the Tepehuán missionaries, including Fathers Fonte and Moranta from the north, were invited and expressed their intention to be present. Other Spaniards, with their slaves and servants, from the vicinity, from the mines of Indé and Guanaceví, would likewise grace the occasion. These arrangements were known to the rebel Tepehuanes. If at Zape on the twenty-first of November, a concentrated and successful attack could be made, many of the Spanish miners and frontiersmen and all the missionaries could be felled at one blow. Such was the plan gradually worked out among the rebels.

The Tepehuanes could not hide entirely their evil intent. The missionaries noted a growing coldness among their neophytes, and Father

Andrés Pérez de Ribas, passing through the country on his way to Mexico City from the thriving missions of the west, noted a sort of sinister aloofness to which he was not accustomed among his devoted Ahomes and loyal Suaquis of Sinaloa. Ribas made known his impressions to Bernardo de Cisneros, missionary at Santiago Papasquiaro, and the latter replied: "Who knows what demon of an idol has come into this nation to render it changed and restless."[2]

Indeed, it was not only Cisneros who had noticed the change in these Christian and formerly obedient and docile Tepehuanes. His companion at Santiago, Diego de Orozco, and the two Jesuits working at Zape, Luís de Alabez and Juan del Valle, experienced a vague trouble in the altered attitude of their charges, and notified the new governor, successor to Francisco Urdiñola, Gaspar de Alvear. The missionaries sent repeated warnings, but without effect. Alvear in his inexperience attributed the worry of the fathers to nervousness and an over-stimulated imagination.

But the conspirators could not wait for the assigned day, November 21, and thereby spoiled their plans for total extinction of the Spaniards in Durango. Five days before the set date, the rebels' smouldering anger burst into flame on the morning of the sixteenth at Santa Catalina. The occasion was the presence there of two travelers on their way from Topia to Durango, over the ancient trail from the west through the Sierra Madre. Santa Catalina is a natural stopping place after the long trek down the backbone of the sierra into the upland vales of western Durango. One of these travelers was a merchant with his wares carried on the backs of a couple of burros; the other was a Black Robe missionary, Hernando de Tovar, on his way from San Andrés on the western slope of the divide to the mission center of Parras far out on the plains to the east. These wayfarers arrived together at Santa Catalina the evening of November 15.

The presence of the merchant with his wares, which they might spoil, and of the padre, whom they might kill, was too much for the rebels. Dissembling their sinister intent that evening, the hostiles fell upon the travelers the next morning as they were ready to depart, striking down Tovar, the first victim of this uprising, and endeavoring to slay the merchant. He escaped however, and, fleeing down the Río de Tepehuanes, gave the alarm at Atotonilco. He found the Spanish residents of the mining town prepared for defense, for the padres of Santiago had warned them of the probabilities of trouble.

But their preparations were in vain. The settlement was attacked on the morning of Thursday, the seventeenth, and, except for two who managed to escape, the seventy inhabitants together with their priest, the Franciscan Fray Pedro Gutiérrez, were slain. That same day Santiago Papasquiaro, eight miles south was attacked. Here resided two Jesuit padres and some hundred Spaniards. They took refuge in the church and were able all that day, the seventeenth, to hold the rebels off. But on the following morning, the eighteenth, with the roof of the edifice burning and the besieged suffocating with the smoke, they capitulated on terms of safety to their persons. The promise was vain. They were slaughtered, some hundred of them, including the two Black Robes, Cisneros and Orozco. Only six persons escaped to carry the dreadful news to Durango.

Juan Fonte and his companion Gerónimo de Moranta were included in the massacres of the north. Zape was more than fifty miles north of Santiago, and preparations were being made there for the big celebration of the twenty-first. Fathers Juan del Valle and Luís de Alabez were resident here. On seeing the disturbed state of the Indians they sent a warning to Father Andrés López at Indé not to come; the same warning was probably sent to Fonte and Moranta, but it missed them. A number of Spaniards with their slaves and servants had already arrived for the feast, and the two fathers were slowly trudging their way south. Before they could arrive the fatal storm and havoc had reached the mission, and this on the same day, the eighteenth, that the massacre was perpetrated at Santiago. The very morning that Orozco and Cisneros were martyred, another band of rebels fell upon Zape while Mass was being celebrated in the mission church. The pueblo was taken completely by surprise, there was no escape for those within the church, and as at Santiago, though we know not the details, they were all slaughtered, the two padres and close to a hundred others. All unsuspecting, Juan Fonte and Gerónimo Moranta continued their journey. They were coming in good time for the feast, for on the nineteenth they were approaching Zape, but were destined never to arrive. They were about two miles north of the pueblo when the murderers fell upon them and slew them.

The only one of the seven Tepehuán missionaries to escape was Father López. He had been warned in time just as he was setting out for Zape. He retired to Indé where he spread the alarm, and the Spaniards fortified themselves as best they could, but they were not attacked. López, writing to his superior, bewails his loss of the martyr's crown. But the energetic Santarén, pioneer missionary among the Acaxées, coming in for the celebration at Zape, was slain in a lonely arroyo near Tenerape, in the south. Taking this occasion to add to the destruction of the tempests, two caciques of the Tarahumar tribesmen rose against the Spaniards living near Santa Bárbara, effecting disorder and depredation. They were called Oñate and Oriante. A probably false report was later current that it was Oñate who slew Father Juan Fonte. These two Indians were later captured and slain.[3]

Juan Fonte and Moranta lay for weeks where they fell. The cold and the snow preserved their mortal remains. It was only in January that Captain Montaño, scouring the country in search of the rebels, approached Zape and there beheld the desolation and the hundred corpses lying where they had fallen. His troop discovered likewise the remains of Fonte and Moranta partly covered with snow and lying on the shoulder of a slight elevation which rises west from the banks of the Río del Zape. The corpses of the fathers' two dogs, faithful to their masters even to death, were found near by.

At Zape the bodies of the other martyred padres, Del Valle and Alabez, were identified. The bodies of the four Jesuits were carefully enshrouded and at the orders of Governor Gaspar de Alvear prepared for the long journey south to Durango. The body of Tovar, fallen at Santa Catalina, could not be found, nor could the remains of Orozco and Cisneros at Santiago Papasquiaro be identified amid the universal slaughter, and it was only weeks later that the body of Santarén was discovered. Late in February, when the Governor could join his captain at Zape, the long funeral procession trudged slowly to the capital of Nueva Vizcaya.

This strange cortège made its way painfully over the mountainous country south-southeast to Durango, escorted and guarded by Governor de Alvear and his whole troop. On the approach to the capital, during the first week of March, the funeral procession was augmented by three hundred Indian allies, loyal Laguneros and Conchos from the north and east. The entry was made on Sunday, March 5. Four mules belonging to the Governor, richly caparisoned in brocades which bore his coat of arms, carried the bodies of the Black Robed martyrs. Luis de Bónifaz, superior of the Jesuits at Durango, together with a group of other Jesuits and Franciscans, came out to escort the honored dead. Civic dignitaries likewise participated, and Rafael de Gasque, officer of the King's exchequer, offered his carriage to convey the precious burden. The bodies were taken first to the church of the Franciscans, where that Sunday evening, March 5, a solemn vespers was intoned. All day Monday the bodies lay in state while throngs from the city and the surrounding country came to gaze upon the dead. Finally on Wednesday, March 7, Feast of St. Thomas Aquinas, the martyrs were solemnly borne the few hundred yards to the Jesuit church, preceded by one hundred and fifty soldiers, cowboys in gala dress, loyal Indian allies, the clergy, and a concourse of townspeople eager to honor the missionaries whom they considered martyrs for the Faith. The bodies were laid in a vault under the gospel side of the altar, verses were read over their remains, and the last rites were solemnly performed.

Thus was buried in Durango on the Feast of Thomas Aquinas, 1617, the first apostle of the Tarahumares, Father Juan Fonte, together with his companion, Father Gerónimo Moranta. Fonte was only forty-two years of age and would certainly in the ordinary course of events have seen the gospel carried far into Tarahumar country. But for the time being the costly Tepehuán revolt had ruined all. The Tarahumar apostle himself was gone and five others had been swept from the field by the hand of death. The Tepehuán mission, formerly so prosperous, lay in ruins and would have to be gradually rebuilt. The Tarahumares, therefore, would have to wait many a long year for the men and the organization which could be spared to them. But Jesuits in the meantime would go up to Parral for the spiritual ministration of the Spaniards in those mines. From there in due course, the Black Robe would again go forth, to found the new mission of the Tarahumar.

Chapter V

REBUILDING A BROKEN FRONTIER

OF THE SEVEN missionaries engaged among the Tepehuanes, only one, Father Andrés López, escaped the massacres of the great revolt. It was going to be López' task to rebuild a spiritual edifice upon the scattered fragments of the destroyed mission. Only if the Tepehuán mission were reconstructed could further efforts be made in favor of the Tarahumares. The lines of communication could not remain broken. For the secure and enduring Christian penetration of the Tarahumar country in the north, it was necessary that the long stretch of territory from the base and center, Durango, be made safe for the passage of the fathers.

Andrés López lost no time in his efforts to reorganize the fallen mission. There were, fortunately, materials at hand with which he could work. Not every member of the Tepehuán tribe had joined the rebels. Moreover, among those who did, some were constrained by fear of the consequences of refusal. Many had remained loyal in their hearts and might have returned immediately to the fold had not terror been struck into their souls by the repeated punitive expeditions of Governor Gaspar de Alvear.

Three times the Governor and his captains rode over the land, setting forth from Durango with a repeatedly augmented troop in December, 1616, in March, 1617, and finally in February, 1618. In this final and most successful expedition Alvear led an army of seventy Spanish soldiers and two hundred Indian allies. The Jesuit Alonso del Valle accompanied the troop as chaplain. It was then that Cogoxito —the Little Lame One—the last of the great rebel leaders, was slain in his mountain hide-out near the famous Del Diablo gorge of the Piaxtla, southwest over the mountains from Durango. Quautlatas had been delivered up by the repentant Tepehuanes themselves; Guixiuita had fled so far southwest that he ceased to cause further trouble in the Durango country.[1] Such military activities by the Spaniards, necessary indeed and ultimately successful, struck fear for the present into timid hearts.

[1] For notes to chapter v see pages 243-244.

Father López began his work of reconstruction from Indé, whither he had fled at the news of the uprising. There lived an old and abandoned Tepehuán woman of evil reputation and immoral life. Father López thought that by trying to better her soul he might be able to use her as an instrument for the spiritual repatriation of her fellow tribesmen. The padre's kindness changed her from rebel to willing instrument of peace. He sent her forth with gentle messages and kindly assurances to go among the scattered and timid Tepehuanes and tell them that the father was still their friend; that should they return to the Faith and to quiet pueblo life punishment would not be theirs. These things López said officially in the name of the Spanish government. The message was conveyed in a written note which the woman was to display to the different groups she might be able to reach. Thus it was that numbers of Tepehuanes returned gradually to their old pueblos, to Santiago Papasquiaro, to Santa Catalina, and to Zape.

Andrés López was now the sole worker among the penitent Tepehuanes. The Jesuit *anua* for 1616, in giving the number of missionaries among the various tribes of northwestern Mexico, four or six, as the case might be, reports the lone figure of one for the Tepehuán mission.[2] The necessity of asking for helpers was then an encouraging sign, and the end of 1617 witnessed efforts to supply the need. Father José de Lomas was the first to be sent north. He had formerly worked in the vicinity of Durango and understood Tepehuán speech. The missionary arrived at Santiago Papasquiaro February 8, 1618, and sent a glowing account back to headquarters of his enthusiastic welcome by the local Tepehuanes.[3] After Cogoxito was finally slain it became safer for additional missionaries to take up again the apostolic work. Andrés López did not ask in vain, and a later record gives the number of missionaries in the area as seven.[4]

Indians and Spaniards came gradually back to their old centers. The mines at Atotonilco and at Guanaceví became loud again with human industry. The Indians were grouped, as formerly, into a pueblo with their padre.

What facilitated all of this activity was the advent of a new and strong governor of Nueva Vizcaya. Late in 1620 Gaspar de Alvear was succeeded by Don Mateo de Vesga, called in the records *El Amiral*, the Admiral. He was humane enough to win the peace through his conciliation of the Indians and strong enough to hold it. The vigor and successes of his administration have come down in a series of reports, which, though possibly over-colored, give a detailed account of how the country was recovering in the early 'twenties, not only with respect to the missions, but in the civic life and prosperity of the Spanish settlers, frontiersmen, cattlemen, and miners. Durango was expanding with additional inhabitants, and new homes were being built in the capital by important people.[5] When in 1621 the new Governor made a tour of the districts north of Durango, to the mining centers of Indé and Guanaceví and to such missions as Santiago Papasquiaro and Zape, he was received with loyalty and enthusiasm. At Zape the Indians with their cacique, Don Lucas, rode out to bid him welcome and renew their pledges of peace.[6]

It is not surprising, therefore, that under these propitious circumstances Indians and Spaniards came gradually back to their old centers, that the Indian pueblos returned almost to their former numbers, and that the mines were again worked by the labor of Spaniard and of Indian alike.

San Simón, near Zape, had formerly been a small village of scarcely more than a dozen families, but it began to thrive in the early 'twenties and to become, for that province and for the missions, an important center. The place of most encouraging improvement was Zape itself. This pueblo became more populous than ever before and more ardent in its faith. It was renamed Santa María de los Mártires, because of the hundred people, including the four Black Robes, who had been slain there. Near Zape, besides San Simón, were the lesser pueblos of San Ignacio and San Pablo. These four settlements were organized into a unit called a *partido,* with Zape as its head.

The spirit of reconstruction was carried on still farther north into Tarahumar country. Shortly after 1616 two of the missionaries of the group which had been sent to reëstablish the Faith among the Tepehuanes, Juan de Sanguessa of Navarre and Nicolás de Estrada, born in Mexico City, penetrated into the Valle de San Pablo and remained among the Tepehuanes and Tarahumares for several months. But a disturbance among the Tepehuanes forced them to retire. These two Black Robes were the immediate successors of Fathers Fonte and Moranta. Father Sanguessa returned to the Valle de San Pablo in 1630.[8]

In the meantime Zape was further honored by the installation of a statue of Blessed Mary the Virgin. It was such a ceremony which had offered the occasion, as we have seen, for the outbreak of the revolt in November, 1616. This same statue of the Virgin Mary, mutilated during the atrocities of the rebellion, was sent back to Mexico City to be remade and refurbished and then reinstalled at Zape in commemoration of the martyrs. This at the expense of a pious army captain of Guanaceví. Four fresh missionaries had come to the Tepehuán mission in 1620; two of them had been stationed at Santa María de los Mártires, or Zape. Conditions were therefore propitious and settled for the celebration of the Feast of Our Lady and the installation of her statue. The continuity of purpose is seen by the fact that whereas seven years had elapsed since the revolt, the fathers and the Spaniards resolved to hold now in 1623 a feast which should surpass in enthusiasm and in splendor the originally planned fiesta of 1616. The Feast of the Assumption falls on August 15; the vigil of the feast was set for the dedication of the statue.

The tragedy of 1616 gave background and offered poignancy to the celebration of 1623. A procession of Spaniards and Indians marched the fifteen miles from Guanaceví to Zape. Triumphal arches were built at intervals along the road set off with foliage and fragrant herbs. A mile and a half north of Zape, at the place where Fonte and Moranta fell, there was placed an *enramada* or bower shrouded in flowers to serve as the first stopping place of the procession. Here prayers were said and a benediction given. Then the procession marched into the town itself, which lies just across the freshly flowing Río del Zape. There was a solemn Mass, a sermon, and a benediction. The following day, the fifteenth, Feast of the Assumption, celebrations and ceremonies continued. Santa María de los Mártires became a place of devotion and of pilgrimage, and for more than a century after these events the statue was still revered. Even well into the twentieth century the memory of the fallen Jesuits still clung to the countryside, and the portraits of the four who were massacred at Zape still adorned the walls of the ancient church.[9]

Thus progressed the recovery of the Tepehuán mission, which was the necessary condition for the reopening of the missions among the Tarahumares. Seven fathers lived among the Tepehuánes in 1624.[10]

An official list of 1625 tells us that Fathers Nicolás de Estrada and Guillermo de Solier were at Indé ministering to 514 Indians, that at Santa Catalina Fathers Andrés López and Burgos cared for 634 neophytes, and at Guanaceví Fathers Martín Larios and José de Lomas watched over 264.[11] This looks as if the number of missionaries had been increased to eight, for both Zape and Santiago would each have at least a padre.

All this activity was building up a foundation for the renewal of the Tarahumar mission and was bound to lead to certain preliminary contacts with these northern tribes. Just as formerly Juan Fonte had prevailed upon certain families of the Tarahumares to migrate south into the Valle de San Pablo, so now during this reconstruction work after the revolt, some of them continued the migration south to live at San Simón near Zape.[12] Furthermore, José de Lomas was now able to get in touch with the Tarahumares of the Valle de San Pablo. Lomas praised their political instinct and their skill in weaving and building. They were industrious too, reported the padre. They bred Spanish fowl (aves de Castillo), raised sheep, and with the Spaniards they bartered wool for cloth and other objects.[13] Lomas seemed enthusiastic about these Tarahumares.

It was during this period of reconstruction that the rebel chief Oñate, who had risen with the Tepehuanes in 1616, was taken and slain. Oñate was a Tepehuán and the reputed murderer of Father Juan Fonte. Ever since the uprising he had been a source of trouble on the border in the Valle de San Pablo and had lately caused a rebellion there, forcing Father Lomas to retire. Twice expeditions from the newly organized presidio at Santa Catalina had been sent north for the purpose of capturing Oñate. The second time the captain was successful. Oñate was taken alive and was executed. Father Martín Larios accompanied at least the second expedition and prepared the rebel for his last end. He died exhorting his fellow tribesmen to lead a good life and to live in peace and harmony with the Spaniards.[14]

Good effects followed the removal of this thorn which had for so long a time been lodged in the body of the missions. The southern fringes of Tarahumara settled down more solidly to peace, and both Tepehuanes and Tarahumares who were living in or near the Valle de San Pablo evinced a desire to move closer to the highway by which the Spaniards traveled to the mines of Santa Bárbara. An attractive spot, therefore, was chosen in this year of 1623, for the foundation of a new pueblo. A finer location did not exist, wrote Larios, for it was delightfully situated on a junction of the Río Florido with one of its tributaries. The place had been known as Las Bocas del Río Florido, but now the padres and Indians called it San Miguel de las Bocas, or simply, Las Bocas.[15] The name perpetuated itself for centuries in the annals of these missions and it remains still upon the land, another example of an ancient mission site gathering to itself a population which grows into a permanent village, town, or city. Although this new mission was more than forty miles southeast of the Valle de San Pablo and well into what was considered Tepehuán country, Tarahumares came to live here, and the Jesuits always considered it part of the Tarahumar mission.[16]

Father Martín Larios reports enthusiastically in a letter to his superiors of these recent developments in the north and he expresses the desire to spend all his life near the Valle de San Pablo. He was not in permanent residence there, however, and soon had to depart south to join his companion, Julio de Sangueza, at Indé or Guanaceví.[17] It was just at this time that Gonzalo de Hermosillo, the first bishop of the newly created diocese of Durango, in visiting all the missions east of the Sierra Madre mountains went north through Tepehuán country and penetrated as far as the Valle de San Pablo. He was a great admirer of and on intimate terms with the missionaries in whose work he took an extraordinary interest. So enthusiastic did he become over what he saw in the north, a repetition, be it said, of what he had witnessed in the missions of the Laguna country far to the east and in the plains, that he wrote to the General in Rome, Father Mutius Vitelleschi, a letter of warm congratulations on the heroic work his sons were doing away out on the very rim of the world's civilization. "I am able," the Bishop writes in part, "to proffer a thousand congratulations to Your Paternity because of the excellent results which the fathers of the Society have attained in those districts."[18]

By 1626 the Tarahumares of San Miguel de las Bocas showed themselves such ardent neophytes that they were thought by the missionaries to put to shame the "tepid Tepehuanes," who were somewhat of an obstacle to the conversion of the Tarahumares. They were anxious to serve the Mass of the fathers and to aid about the church; also, desiring to have a chapel all to themselves, they built one near a settlement which consisted entirely of their tribespeople.[19] Some of their chiefs made the long journey to Durango to ask both civil and ecclesiastical authorities for permanent missionaries.

As a sequel to this touching gesture on the part of the Tarahumares, Father Juan de Sanguessa returned to the Valle de San Pablo, while Father Juan de Heredia was designated to keep in touch with the new pueblo of San Miguel de las Bocas, though he does not seem to have been permanently resident there. Heredia made an entrada at this time, accompanied by Captain Juan de Barrasa, who had been named by the Governor at Durango. These two, captain and padre, with their men went as far north as the Río Conchos, where at Nonoava they entered into friendly relations with the Tarahumares who were living in the vicinity.

Returning south to San Miguel de las Bocas on the Río Florido, Captain Barrasa and Father Heredia went through ceremonies which were a sort of official recognition of the Christian character of the pueblo. This may be considered the official founding of San Miguel de las Bocas. The year was 1630. Though the reported numbers were small, only four hundred in all, this foundation with that of San Pablo Ballesa in the Valle de San Pablo was a real beginning for the entrance of the missions into Tarahumara proper.[20] After a few months Juan de Heredia was replaced by the Portuguese Gabriel Díaz, who founded a second pueblo of Tarahumares on the same Río Florido not far from San Miguel, and they called the new foundation San Gabriel.[21] Father Nicolás de Estrada soon replaced Díaz. This same year of 1630 Estrada reports the result of his labors to his superior Diego de Cuellar.[22] The fruits of the new pueblo of San Gabriel were immediately evident. Five hundred pagans came into the new settlement and into San Miguel; they had for eight years petitioned in vain for missionaries. Among the Tarahumares baptized in 1630 were three caciques. One of these, however, soon relapsed into paganism. The lapse did not aid his morals. He murdered an enemy, cutting out his tongue.[23]

The following year, 1631, mines were discovered at a place called Parral, fifteen miles northeast of the old mining center of Santa Bárbara. Another "gold rush" set in. Spaniards came up from the south, others moved from Santa Bárbara, and a new settlement of Spaniards was formed. This new community would serve as a protection for the missionaries working on the Río Florido and would lead eventually to increased interest in the conversion of the Tarahumares.[24] Conversion would become now almost a necessity, for the Spaniards working the mines were always safer among Christian Indians than among pagans. Before this decade was out, therefore, the mission system was to enjoy further extension and a new district, Baja Tarahumara, was to be organized.

Chapter VI

A NEW MISSION UNIT

MINES HAD BEEN discovered at Parral! It was not the first time such a discovery had stimulated the formation of a mission. Over the mountains, on the western slope of the sierra Father Santarén had been offered the occasion to found a new mission, and had begun the evangelization of a new group of Acaxée Indians, through the newly opened mines in the sierra of Carantapa. A miniature gold rush had taken place there in the first decade of the 1600's, making it safer for the missionaries to venture farther north, while the presence of Spaniards to be spiritually administered to and of new tribes to be converted created the occasion and offered the motive for the Christianization of the ragged Acaxées northwest of Topia.[1]

So it was with the discovery of the mines of Parral in 1631, and the evidence of this appears clearly in the record. The interaction of mine and mission seems to have been mutually advantageous. The missionaries reported that the previous conversion of numbers of Tarahumares rendered them friendly to the Spaniards, while the concentration of the latter in the district made it safer for the fathers to advance farther into Tarahumar country, since in case of trouble help would be at hand.

Although the 1630's formed a decade of general slowing down of activity in the mission field, yet this period shaped the events which were to lead to the definite founding of the mission unit called Baja Tarahumara or Lower Tarahumara at the end of the decade. In 1632, the year after the discovery of the mines in Parral, a development took place in Durango, which would encourage and strengthen the desire for progress among the Tarahumares. The Jesuit school for boys which had long existed in the capital was endowed by a wealthy churchman of Nueva Vizcaya so that it could now increase its faculty, augment its courses, and take in without tuition an increased number of boys. The donor or founder of the college was the licentiate Don Francisco Rojas de Ayora, canon and vicar-general of the diocese of Nueva Vizcaya. The Vicar-General's gift was generous. He made over to the fathers at Durango his estate of San Isidro de la Punta and a cash sum

[1] For notes to chapter vi see page 244.

of fifteen thousand pesos. When he died a few years later he willed to the college still other amounts. The *hacienda* or ranch of San Isidro comprised many acres of cattle country well stocked, together with fields and meadow land fit for agriculture.[2]

It had always been the desire of the first bishop of Nueva Vizcaya, Gonzalo de Hermosillo, great friend of the Black Robes, to found a Jesuit college in his episcopal city of Durango. But before this could be accomplished he died in 1631 in Sinaloa while making an official visitation of those flourishing missions in that part of his diocese. But under his successor, Bishop Alonso Franco y de Luna, the happy development now took place. The institution of the Jesuits now became a secondary school, teaching grammar, literature, and Latin.[3]

It is true that the year 1632 registered a setback west of the divide in the mountains of Chínipas. This happened on the first day of February when the Guazápares and Varohíos led by a rebel chief rose up against their two missionaries, Julio Pascual and Manuel Martínez, and slew them.

But no repercussions of this revolt were felt east of the divide, and the fathers there quietly continued their work among the Tepehuanes and the Tarahumares in the district of Parral. Later, however, there was trouble at Zape. In April, 1638, a cacique named Don Felipe and his brother, Don Pedro, a popular leader with the Indians, tried again to stir the sleeping cinders of revolt among the Tepehuanes. Pedro had a wider influence for evil, for he was medicine man or hechicero. The two brothers fled the pueblo of Zape with a number of followers, and, as always with such evil-doers, hid out in the hills, robbing, stirring dissatisfaction, and persuading other malcontents to join in a rebellion against the fathers. Rebel Don Pedro threatened with death all who would not run away from their pueblos. This was a cause of worry to the missionaries, especially to Father Gaspar de Contreras, who had just this year in July been named superior of the Tepehuán mission by his Provincial, Andrés Pérez de Ribas. Captain Juan de Barrasa at first tried diplomacy. He sent a group of friendly Indians into the mountains after the rebels, proposing reconciliation and promising forgiveness on the part of captain and missionaries. But the leaders remained obdurate, and they accused the missionary at Zape, Father Martín Suárez, of cruelty toward them.

However, in the early fall, rebel Don Pedro was murdered by one of his own tribesmen, while Don Felipe fled north to Parral, where the Governor of Nueva Vizcaya happened to be staying. Don Felipe abjectly begged the Governor's pardon for his evil deed, blaming again the cruelty of Father Martín Suárez. But the Governor discovered that whereas the rebel had fled from Zape in April, the father had not arrived there until June; he discovered moreover that Suárez enjoyed a wide reputation for kindness and generosity of behavior. Don Felipe was confounded with his lies, but was reprieved by the Governor from hanging, the usual fate of rebels. By the middle of September with the ringleaders removed or dead, the trouble was over and the mission quiet. The superior Contreras speaks his satisfaction in a letter to his provincial.[4]

In the two Jesuits just mentioned, Andrés Pérez de Ribas and Gaspar de Contreras, there was a combination of personalities which held great promise for pushing forward the Tarahumar mission. Pérez de Ribas, Provincial of the Province of New Spain from 1638 to 1641, had been a missionary for sixteen years, from 1604 to 1620, and was one of the most famous of the Black Robes of the missions on the west coast, or in all America, for that matter. He had worked first on the Río Fuerte among the Suaquis and the Ahomes down near the sea, where the river throws its clear waters into the Gulf of California. Then in 1617 Ribas had gone north to the newly subdued Yaqui tribe and had experienced a splendid success in their complete evangelization. It was during the final years of his labors in Sinaloa that he witnessed the beginning of one of the most extraordinary increases in converts and in territory of all of the mission history of the Americas.

When Ribas was called south to be given offices of trust in the capital of New Spain he did not forget his former confrères or his former neophytes. He set himself to write a history of these missions, which he completed in the 'forties and published in Madrid in 1645. He entitled the great book the *History of the Triumphs of Our Holy Faith (Historia de los Triunfos de Nuestra Santa Fee)*. By the time he was made provincial he had probably completed parts of the first draft of an important work on the history of Sinaloa which still exists in the Jesuit Archives in manuscript.[5] Surely, Andrés Pérez de Ribas, as highest superior of the province of New Spain, would not be backward in aid-ing the advance of the missions which he had learned to love so well. As a matter of fact, the history of the 1640's shows a gain all along the line of the missions both east and west of the Sierra Madre.

So far as Father Gaspar de Contreras is concerned, his experience in the missions had been long and successful. He had come to the Tepehuanes in 1627, at which time he was one of seven working in the mission. During the eleven years which followed he had experienced the trials and vicissitudes of missionary life. He had seen the number of padres reduced, had experienced the trouble caused by the rebel Don Felipe, had witnessed the rush to the mines at Parral, and had been the companion of Gabriel Díaz and Juan de Heredia. Gaspar de Contreras was well seasoned then to become in 1638 the head of the whole Tepehuán unit.[6] This Black Robe's appointment as superior of the mission by Provincial Ribas, shrewd observer of men, demonstrates, therefore, both the interest and good judgment of Ribas and the capability of the new Tepehuán superior.

Appointed in July, within a month Gaspar de Contreras was writing to his provincial, reporting on the habits and customs of the Tarahumares, on their spiritual condition and readiness for the Faith, and urging that a permanent and well-organized mission be set up among them.[7]

The picture here offered, probably slightly overdrawn, is an attractive one, and it becomes evident that from the time of Fonte's contact with the Tarahumares more than thirty years before, much progress had been made by them. They had tamed a great deal from the olden days when Fonte had found them so wild and they were showing themselves docile and submissive to the Spaniards of Parral. The Spaniards could pass unarmed through Tarahumar country and trade freely with the natives. The Tarahumares profited by barter with the miners, trading corn for wool, articles of clothing, and other wares. The Indians were good weavers too, but especially were they excellent workmen, as the Spaniards discovered to their joy. It was not only the drudgery of the mines to which they subjected themselves (and it looks as if the labor went for the most part unremunerated) but they were put to digging canals for the improvement of the land which Contreras reports was very fertile. Indeed, Parral and its surrounding valleys are called a granary. The Tarahumares were likewise good fishermen, and the fish were the finest in Nueva Vizcaya, avers the enthusiastic padre. The cackerel caught in the streams (*bogre:* cackerel) ran sometimes to five *arroba* in weight or approximately a hundred and twenty-five pounds. Game was as abundant as fish.

When the Superior Contreras writes of three pueblos he is speaking of San Gabriel and of San Miguel de las Bocas, founded under the direction of Díaz and Heredia in 1630, and of a third, Tizonazo, formed since that time. It was of set purpose, wrote the missionary, that the southern Tarahumares thus lived in their formed pueblos in such delightful and easily accessible places, for they eagerly desired that missionaries should come to them. These Indians were but imitating the eagerness of their primitive brethren on the other side of the divide. Those unbaptized wanted baptism, but especially did they desire Christianity and the fruits of the spirit which the Christian culture would produce. For it had always been the experience of the Tarahumares that whenever the fathers were among them they lived more peaceably among themselves, and ferocious wars with their neighbors ceased. Such is the rosy picture painted by Contreras.

And he knew well how to touch the conscience and stir the activity of his Provincial in Mexico City. He informs Ribas, who may not have known the facts, that in 1629 Franciscan missionaries wanted to enter the Tarahumar country. There was danger of a clash of jurisdiction or the disturbance of contrary interests, and the Viceroy, the Marqués de Cerralvo (Contreras mistakenly refers to him as the Marqués de Salinas), was appealed to and decided that this field should belong to the Jesuits. But neither Viceroy nor Provincial had provided Jesuit missionaries of permanent residence for these Indians, and so they had been neglected. Ribas would know, of course, the background of Franciscan activity in or near this same country, as we have narrated it in an earlier chapter. It will be recalled that there was a Franciscan convent in Durango and that in the massacres of the Tepehuán revolt one Franciscan was slain in the mining center of Atotonilco.

It so happened that at the time Contreras was writing thus to Provincial Ribas, a plague was raging among the pueblos of the Tarahumares, one of those deadly epidemics which so frequently at the coming of the Spaniards decimated the primitive population. The Black Robe gives it the usual name, *viruelas,* probably typhus. Muleteers coming every day into Santiago Papasquiaro on their way south to Durango reported the wretched plight of the sick, dying without baptism or, if baptized, without the sacraments. "This flock is ours," presses Contreras, "and we are responsible for their baptism." The padre begs that the number in the Tepehuán mission be again increased to seven as formerly, for now there were only five. With two more missionaries the Tarahumares could at least enjoy from time to time a temporary visitation.[8] Added to this appeal was a letter to Ribas from a Spaniard of Parral, a layman, who begged the Provincial that more missionaries be sent to the Tarahumares.[9]

Now the Provincial Andrés Pérez de Ribas was the very last man upon whose ear such an appeal would fall without leaving an impression. We have already sketched his former activity in the missions and his subsequent interest in their progress. As Provincial it was to be expected that he would use his power in the promotion of that which seemed to be closest to his heart and uppermost in his mind. As proof of this Ribas had written a letter to Father General Mutius Vitelleschi in behalf of the missions, probably asking for additional men to be sent from Europe to labor in them. It became plain that with the accession of this Provincial in 1638 the period of slower movement in the mission field would be ended.

We do not possess Ribas' letter, but we have the General's reply: "I have that appreciation of the missions of the Province, and especially of those of Sinaloa, which they deserve. And not once only, but often have I spoken of them in a spirit of especial esteem. I know well the need they have of many ministers of the gospel and so far as I am concerned I shall lend aid in procuring them. I ask Your Reverence that on your part you come to the assistance of the missions with all care and diligence, sending from other sections of the Province laborers who, as I am informed, are superfluous in some colleges, but are deficient in the missions. Likewise I beg of you that you supply to those who labor in so holy a work what is necessary for them with all charity and generosity. . . . In conclusion I ask Your Reverence with all possible earnestness to look toward a new spirit and enthusiasm for that province, which I shall expect from you, since as an old and tried missionary there, the project touches you with an especial interest."[10] Thus General Vitelleschi to his Provincial Ribas on October 30, 1639.

And Ribas was not slow to act. Indeed, he had already taken steps in the direction indicated by the Father General in Rome, expecting undoubtedly aid and encouragement from Europe. For that same year of 1639 saw the definite opening of the Tarahumar mission upon a permanent and organized basis. This was effected by the arrival and permanent residence among the Tarahumares of two Jesuit fathers, José Pascual and Gerónimo de Figueroa. Pascual was a young Spaniard from Valencia, just ordained priest. Figueroa was a veteran of the Tepehuán mission. The two Black Robes arrived in Parral in June, 1639, eager for the new mission.[11]

The Governor of Nueva Vizcaya, Don Francisco Bravo de la Serna, was sojourning in Parral when the missionaries arrived. This official ordered some of the Tarahumar chiefs to report to him at Parral, which they did. He then introduced to them the two Black Robes and exhorted them to great respect toward and veneration for these men of God, representatives to them of the Almighty. And further to impress the chiefs, the Governor did what two decades before his predecessor, Urdiñóla, enacted in presence of the Xixime chiefs—he fell to his knees and kissed the hands of the two missionaries.

Pascual before joining Figueroa was sent south to learn the Indian language, residing with Gabriel Díaz at Las Bocas. But Figueroa made a bold gesture. He penetrated north into absolutely new country traveling through the small valleys and around the low hills which lie north of Parral, until he reached the Río Conchos, about thirty miles north as the crow flies. Here in a beautiful spot on the banks of the wide and shallow Río Conchos, just on the fringe of the rolling country to the west and on the edge of the immense stretches of dry and level plain to the east, near a mining settlement, Figueroa founded San Felipe, destined to be the center of the southern missions of the Tarahumar.[12]

Thus was the mission among the Tarahumares set upon a permanent basis by the Provincial in Mexico City, the old missionary Pérez de Ribas; thus was a new unit organized, a fresh link in that chain of establishments with which the Jesuits were encircling the whole of northwest Mexico. The new unit was called Baja Tarahumara.

Chapter VII

FOUR CACIQUES REBEL

W ITH THE founding of Baja Tarahumara in 1639 there was created
a continuous system of missions from Durango in the Valle de
Guadiana to San Felipe on the banks of the Río Conchos. This line
of missions extended two hundred and thirty miles. North from Durango through the Tepehuán country there were, with their *visitas,*
Santiago Papasquiaro (eighty miles above the capital), Santa Catalina,
Zape, Guanaceví, and Indé, the last two being mining towns with
adjacent missionary Indian pueblos. A few miles northeast of Indé
was Tizonazo founded before the entrada of Figueroa and Pascual.
Here dwelt Cabesa and Salinero Indians. Northwest thirty-five miles
was San Miguel de las Bocas on the banks of the Río Florido. North
northwest another forty miles lay Parral and thirty miles beyond was
San Felipe. West of Parral some forty miles was the Valle de San
Pablo with its old settlement begun by Juan Fonte long ago, the present San Pablo Ballesa. With San Miguel de las Bocas began the Tarahumar missions as distinct from the Tepehuanes, so the Río Florido can
be called the boundary separating the two mission groups.[1] It is evident
that in the beginning these Tarahumar missions were few and far between. So it was at first with the Tepehuanes, before the visitas helped
to fill in the intervening distance. The new missionary lived alone in
a far isolated district.

Father Gerónimo de Figueroa at San Felipe on the banks of Río
Conchos would win from the start some encouraging successes.[2] Arrived at Parral early in June the Black Robe would be on his way north
before the month was up, and though we have no reports to confirm
the details of his travel and of his arrival no doubt Figueroa's welcome
was warm and affectionate, for the Indians had been asking and waiting for permanent missionaries.

This guess is confirmed by the report of his first activities at what
was to become the important San Felipe near the mining settlement. Having baptized the younger children and begun instruction of
the adults, Figueroa had such success that by the middle of August

[1] For notes to chapter vii see pages 244-245.

he judged that large numbers of his neophytes were sufficiently prepared for baptism. He fixed as the day for this event the fifteenth of August, Feast of the Assumption of Blessed Mary the Virgin. José Pascual in the south at Las Bocas was learning the language and proving himself a valuable assistant to Gabriel Díaz.[3] Pueblos de visita or visitas were soon formed near San Felipe, and when new missionaries arrived San Gerónimo de Huejotitlán, San Pablo on the Conchos, and San Francisco de Borja were formed. In the meantime José Pascual went to San Felipe, and Figueroa, superior of the unit, was sent to organize San Gerónimo.

In May, 1642, Luis de Valdés, the new governor of Nueva Vizcaya, was ordered up to Tarahumara to inspect conditions at Parral and to visit the new group of missions. Arrived at Figueroa's pueblo of Huejotitlán, the Governor was pleased with the fine assemblage of natives from the outlying hills, which Figueroa had been able to collect for him. With a solemnity which impressed the simple mind of the savage Luis de Valdés formally appointed Indian governors and captains of Huejotitlán and of the near-by pueblos.[4]

Cornelio Beudin, often referred to as Godínez, was one of those sent up to Tarahumara shortly after the arrival of Figueroa and Pascual. By 1646 two more missionaries, one being Nicolás de Zepeda, went into the country, giving this new unit five padres, equal number with the older Tepehuán foundations.[5] Cornelio Beudin seemed happy and contented in his mission for he wrote a pleasant letter to a Jesuit friend of his in Belgium, his native country, dated May 18, 1646, stating that his health was good and the mission progressing.[6]

Down at the mother house at Durango there was material disaster, for as the result of heavy rains in 1647 the Jesuit church collapsed and the tower fell. But no one was injured, and the tabernacle protected by a covering supported by four pillars was not crushed. Alms immediately poured in and soon a new church was rising on the site of the old, built of stronger materials than the poor rubble of stone and mud of the pioneer fabric.[7]

Nevertheless, in the north there had been disturbances even prior to the writing of Cornelio Beudin's placid missive to Belgium. There was a nation bordering on Tarahumar and Tepehuán country to the east. This group is known to history as the Tobosos, and they were at this period, and repeatedly later, a scourge to these missions and to the Spaniards of the mines and ranches. What the Apaches of the following century were to the mines and missions of northern Sonora the Tobosos were to mines and missions of what is now southern Chihuahua.

Late in 1644 these savages went on the warpath. They came into the country of the newly formed Tarahumar missions and into the neighborhood of Parral, and for many months from late in 1644 through 1645 were a plague and a pest to Spaniards, neophytes, and missionaries alike. Father Nicolás de Zepeda was at San Miguel de las Bocas during this period and he has left us a full account in a letter to his superior dated April 28, 1645.[8]

These untamed Tobosos, joined at times by other groups called Cabesas and Salineros, broke over the traces in the fall of 1644 and invaded the fertile Valle de San Bartolomé, which lies just northeast of Parral. They attacked a hacienda, killed a Spaniard and a Christian Indian, and drove off the horses and cattle. Then, in the hope of further plunder, the Tobosos attacked Parral itself, thinking to get loot of silver together with other booty. Silver they got none, but they murdered a Spaniard and took some animals, and though pursued they were able to escape unharmed. Soon after this foray the hostile Indians attacked Indé, south of Parral, where they drove off fifteen hundred mules and two thousand head of cattle. They also committed murder. When messages of these depredations were being hurried south to Durango that the Governor, Louis de Valdés, might send assistance, the runners themselves were intercepted between San Miguel and Tizonazo and killed. These Tobosos preferred to decapitate rather than to scalp their victims. Even when the Governor, finally notified of the havoc wrought in the north, was reporting events by letter to the Viceroy in Mexico City, these messengers too were attacked. They were able to escape, but the letters were lost.

This northern country was at this period insufficiently protected, for there existed no presidio north of Santa Catalina among the Tepehuanes. Governor Valdés drew upon the soldiers resident here and ordered their captain, Juan de Barrasa, to march northeast in a punitive expedition against the hostiles. The Captain left October 6, 1644 with a force of seventy soldiers and two hundred Indian allies of the Tepehuán and Concho nations. But even while he was penetrating their country the Tobosos eluded him to make another incursion—this time into Indé—and make off with a herd of sheep. Captain Barrasa was, however, this time not to be fooled. Though he had penetrated as far as the Río Grande, he learned from his scouts the whereabouts of the raiding Tobosos, attacked them, and recovered the stolen animals. Infuriated by this setback, the Tobosos now initiated a campaign of propaganda against the Spaniards and missionaries and were able to persuade a group of three hundred families, prospective neophytes who were in the course of preparation for baptism at Tizonazo, to pull up stakes and join the Tobosos in the wild life of the eastern plains.

Further trouble ensued. A loyal Christian chief, either Tepehuán or Tarahumar, one who had been baptized in his youth by Gerónimo de Moranta, was sent by Governor Valdés into the Salinero country, bordering on the Tobosos south, that he might break the ground for the eventual conversion of these Indians. His name was Don Alvaro, and Father Zepeda himself accompanied him once on a visit to the Salineros. Don Alvaro was murdered by the Tobosos. Then they attacked a great wagon train, owned by the wealthy Marcos Beltrán, threading its way to the mines on the *camino real*. Eleven Spaniards were slain in this encounter, four were kidnapped, and the mules and the goods were stolen. Beltrán himself, though mounted on a fine horse, was wounded with arrows.

When Captain Barrasa was arming to give chase to the savages, orders were sent from Durango that he forego the expedition. The Spaniards made no further effort to apprehend and punish the perpetrators of this latest atrocity. Politics and jealousy were in evidence among the Spanish leaders, with the result that soon Francisco Montaño de la Cueva was appointed by the Governor at Durango to represent him in the north and to have full authority there as his lieutenant.

Nevertheless, the atrocities continued. On March 25, the following year, 1645, a Franciscan mission, San Francisco de Conchos, some thirty miles east of Parral, was attacked by the rebels. Two Franciscans were laboring there among the loyal Concho Indians. The attack came just before Mass on the Feast of the Annunciation. The two missionaries were slain, together with the Indian governor of the pueblo, the church was pillaged and burned and the dwellings of the neophytes set on fire. Another Franciscan mission, San Pedro, was next attacked. Then the Indians of the Valle de San Bartolomé rose. There was evident weakness and lack of ability or energy in the Spanish administration, for in spite of all that had been thus far perpetrated, conditions went from bad to worse.

The Jesuit missionary, Diego Osorio, was resident in the spring of 1645 at Tizonazo. Besides the Christian Tepehuanes and the Tarahumares living in this pueblo there were also some Salineros who, it seems, were not yet baptized. The Tobosos and the Cabesas tried to infect the Christian Indians with the spirit of rebellion.[9] At first they were repulsed, but gradually the virus of evil propaganda began to take effect. Finally these Salineros rose, on April 11, against the missionary and the Christian Indian Governor of the pueblo, Don Ciprián, and forced them to flee to Indé. At this particular time, April, 1645, seven pueblos were either destroyed or depopulated. Six of them were Franciscan missions, the seventh—the pueblo of Tizonazo—was Jesuit. When Father Osorio appealed to Governor Valdés for protection, he was referred to the lieutenant for the north, Francisco Montaño de la Cueva, who gave fifteen soldiers for the protection of the mission. With this help Tizonazo again became habitable and took up the tenor of its missionary existence. The lieutenant dispatched another fifteen armed men to the fathers working near the Río Conchos. This area included San Felipe, where Beudin was laboring, with its two visitas, San Francisco de Borja and Santa Cruz.

Father Zepeda in reporting these matters from San Miguel de las Bocas does not sound an encouraging note for the future. He complains strongly of the Spanish administration and of the attitude of individual Spaniards toward the neophytes. Not only is there no care for or interest in the Indian's Christian state, but the native whether neophyte or pagan, is exploited and despised. He is made to work in the mines for two months with the promise of a wretched pittance and when the time is up he is told he must work another two months with no pay else he will not be paid at all. The civil magistrates take no care to see that the Indians live according to the Christian law. If they go off from the pueblos to the hills to lead a wild and lawless life they are not pursued; if they live in open immorality and polygamy they are not punished. Thus, reports Zepeda, the formerly great numbers in which the Tarahumares used to frequent the Río del Parral are now sadly fallen off and all the pueblos have been diminished. The largest have only fifty or seventy families, some have only twenty.[10]

If all the things which Father Zepeda reports were true the situation at the infant Tarahumar mission was anything but encouraging, and from the foregoing narrative it is evident that something was wrong with the secular arm. The fault seems to have lain with Governor Valdés, since Captain Barrasa was willing and able to bring about some disciplinary measures. This view is confirmed by a royal *cédula* from Madrid, dated November 30, 1647, written by King Philip IV to the successor of Valdés, who was a far different man as we shall see. From this document it seems that over and above the inefficiency of Valdés, he personally had been guilty of the maltreatment of the Indians about which Father Zepeda complained. The royal letter emphasizes the fact that former cédulas commanding mild and just treatment of the Indians be observed. The document complains that *alcaldes mayores* and some who purported to give religious instruction kidnapped the children of the Indians, selling them as slaves or giving them away as presents. "The Governor," continues the King, "Don Luís de Valdés, began to punish them immoderately and without regard to the public faith, for after calling them to attend religious instruction he seized and shot some of them. Therefore they revolted, took up their arms and arrows and made some raids. They broke into my treasury," complains the King, "and it has cost me more than 50,000 pesos to pacify them, although they are not entirely quieted yet."[11]

This indictment of Governor Luís de Valdés, therefore, confirms all the bitterest complaints of Father Zepeda. Surely, had things been no better in the famous missions of Sinaloa the Black Robes would not have been able to advance beyond, or even up to, the Río Fuerte. However, in the first decades of their activity in that area, the padres enjoyed the strong yet prudent and tempered arm of Captain Martín Diego de Hurdaide, who soon had won the fear and the respect of all the surrounding tribes. Hurdaide had died in 1626, and the missions thereafter had never seen his equal nor had the secular arm thereafter worked so harmoniously with the spiritual.

Well did the King, writing in 1647, say that the troubles were not yet over. For after April in 1645, the year of our present narrative, the tumult and turmoil continued. A certain cacique made himself out to be a bishop; pretended to say Mass, to baptize, and make and dissolve marriage. Depredations and murders continued. Hostile Indians attacked Cuencamé, killed the two Rivas brothers and made off with their animals. They stampeded hundreds of the three thousand young steers which Captain Nava was preparing to drive to Parral; they attacked the far eastern Jesuit mission of Santa María de las Parras and also that of San Pedro. In this latter pueblo they murdered seven of the inhabitants. They attacked Santa Ana in the Laguna country, killed eight Spaniards there and made off with everything they could lay their hands on.

Returning from this destruction the Tobosos encountered the family of Antonio Pérez de Molina who with the servants and cowboys were driving a herd of cattle from Mapimí to Parras. They murdered the cowboys, kidnapped the Molinas, mother, sixteen-year-old daughter, and three sons, and took possession of the herd. Later they slew the three sons before their mother's eyes and made slaves of the mother and daughter. In October, running short of supplies, the Tobosos planned to attack the whole of the valley of the Río Florido and especially San Miguel de las Bocas and to slay at all hazards the padre, Zepeda himself. Should he be defended by his Tarahumar neophytes, they too would all be slain, swore the rebels.

At this juncture Governor Luís de Valdés resolved at long last to bestir himself. He made a military entrada into the Toboso country and had the good fortune to surprise the Indians in a council of war. But instead of attacking he treated. The rebels were frightened into submission. They made golden promises which they did not intend to keep and were let off scot free.

When the marauding and stealing continued in spite of fair promises, the Governor ordered Captain Juan de Barrasa to collect arms, provisions, and Indian allies from the Conchos and Tepehuanes for a more serious campaign against the Tobosos. When the rebels saw these preparations they were frightened again and sent ambassadors to treat with the Governor. In the meantime Captain Barrasa entered Toboso country and came upon an important ranchería of the enemy. Probably acting under orders of the Governor, he pardoned some of the rebels, but later hanged five of the ringleaders. The Governor then called a meeting of peace at Atotonilco. The Toboso chief, Don Christóbal Doble, came and was treated well. Again these rebels made empty promises. Indeed, while the very meeting of peace was in progress depredations were being carried on.

Such weak measures, of course, could bring no abiding peace. Father Nicolás de Zepeda closes his long letter and an equally long postscript with the statement of a considered policy according to which the Spaniards of office and influence should coöperate with the missionaries. It is the duty, he says, of the Spanish magistrates to make laws for the newly baptized Indians. There must be discipline strongly enforced. The laws must oblige the Christian Indians to live as Christians and to go to Mass. The neophytes must be regaled and encouraged with presents. When there are disturbances the offenders must be disciplined, for fear is a strong motive in checking the violence of these the poorest of God's children. Rebels must be punished. If pardoned they will fall again. "The others," writes Zepeda, ". . . who have lived in peace see that the rebels who for so long a time have perpetrated such crimes are spared their lives. This is bad. No wonder these districts are only half conquered, for the savages all see that nothing is impossible to do."[12] Zepeda was doing no more than advocating the measures so often contained in the cédulas of the kings of Spain.

The repeated insistence of Father Zepeda on more diligent attention to duty on the part of the Spanish magistrates is especially significant in indicating an important fact about this newly formed Tarahumar mission. Many of the recently baptized Christians did not live continually in their pueblos, Las Bocas, San Felipe, and the others, but went down to Parral, there to work in the mines in hope of some remuneration. Even from far-off Sinaloa and Sonora, Christian Indians went to work in the mines of Parral. Indeed, in 1649 there were one hundred Indians from Sinaloa working there.[13] Since Parral was situated in the territory of the Tarahumares, their numbers must have been proportionately greater.

When the padres had the Indians to themselves the spiritual and cultural formation was carried on in more successful and harmonious fashion; too often the Spanish magistrate or military officer was an exploiter of the neophyte rather than a father, and, as in the present instance, negligent of, or indifferent to, the Indian's spiritual well-being.

Zepeda was right. When the loyal Christian Indians witnessed such soft treatment and the repeated pardons doled out in the wake of atrocious criminalities, they could not be well impressed. They became discouraged and harbored some bitter thoughts on the slight rewards of virtue and the advantages of crime. Evidently, Governor Valdés was an inefficient man, quite unlike his able and vigorous predecessors Urdiñola, Vesga, and that great pioneer Rodrigo del Río y Losa.

With such continuous disturbances afflicting the borders of the new Tarahumar mission and with the dissatisfaction and lowered morale created by a weak administration, it would not be surprising to learn that the infection began to spread and to creep gradually to the Tarahumares, neighbors to the Tobosos and Cabesas. This is what actually took place, for most of the Tarahumares were still pagans, and as so often happened in the missions, especially when they were new, the recently baptized were not strong enough in their Christianity, nor even in their numbers, to set the tone of the districts and to offer a firm wall against the infiltration of grumbling and discontent. The primitives, children as they were and inconstant, were most susceptible to any kind of suggestion or propaganda.

As among human beings in general, but more especially among the native peoples of the New World, it had happened repeatedly that a few disgruntled leaders were able to infect whole groups, newly baptized, with the virus of their rebellious spirit.

An appeal to their ancient liberties and untrammeled moral license would always be a telling argument. To break the shackles of Christian moral restraint was not very difficult for many of the more recently baptized. In such times of restlessness the life of the pueblo would become irksome; then the lure of the wild and of their mountain fastnesses would be upon them. When rebellious propaganda had some basis in the ill treatment of the Indians by the Spaniards the disaffection could spread as flame amidst tinder and dry grass.

The troubles we have been narrating were harassing the new mission in the middle of the 1640's; by the end of that decade the Tarahumares themselves became disaffected and their discontent soon matured into a spirit of rebellion. Soon this spirit would effervesce into acts of open violence, with destruction of their missions and murder of their Black Robe missionaries.

In 1648, when the first Tarahumar revolt broke out, there were five fathers among the Tarahumares, manning, besides San Miguel de las Bocas, three main mission pueblos—San Felipe on the Río Conchos, San Francisco Javier de Satevó north of Conchos on the Río San Pedro, and San Gerónimo de Huejotitlán, south of San Felipe on a tributary of the Conchos. There were other visitas, such as San Francisco Borja. Father José Pascual was now superior of the mission and he has left us a full account of the uprising. Besides Beudin and Figueroa, Vigilio Máez with Pascual was one of the five padres.

The rebellion was led by four caciques with the interesting names of Supichiochi, Tepox, Ochavarri, and Don Bartolomé.[14] They were joined by hundreds of their fellow tribesmen and even by close to a hundred Indians from Sinaloa who were working in the Parral mines. The center of the revolt was a Tarahumar pueblo southwest of Parral called Fariagic. From here the rebels ravaged north, but did not proceed as far as the Conchos; therefore they left San Felipe and Satevó safe, but attacked the visita of San Francisco de Borja, which was in a fertile spot excellent for cattle and grain.

Father Beudin at first word of the uprising sent from San Felipe five Spaniards and fifty Indians to collect and protect the mission herd. But most of these cowboys were attacked and killed and the herd was driven off. The rebels burned the rude church and left the pueblo desolate. The life of the padre himself at San Felipe was in jeopardy, but a loyal cacique, Don Pedro el Colorado, stood by with his men for his protection. Upon receiving word at Parral of Beudin's danger, the *Justicia Mayor,* General Juan Fernández de Carrión, sent up ten armed men for his further protection, and himself took the field against the rebels. But his army was a motley crew taken from among the merchants and miners who had volunteered to serve without pay. The General met the rebels who offered battle. The Spaniards seem to have been repulsed, for Carrión suffered some casualties and withdrew to Parral having effected nothing.

Governor Luís de Valdés at Durango then ordered Juan de Barrasa, now given the title of general, to take the matter in hand. He advanced north from Cerro Gordo with forty paid soldiers and three hundred Indian allies, but having arrived at San Felipe he took no action whatsoever. His hands were tied by two other individuals whom the Gov-

ernor had ordered to accompany him and there was dissension among
the three. Father Pascual journeyed the hundreds of miles down to
Durango to interview the Governor, who as a result recalled the two
officers, leaving Barrasa free to engage in the campaign against the
rebels. He departed, therefore, on his punitive expedition, accompanied
by Father Vigilio Máez.

At this juncture a change for the better took place in the administration of the province at Durango. The ineffective Luis de Valdés
was replaced as Governor of Nueva Vizcaya by Don Diego Guajado
Fajardo, a man of different stamp as we shall see.

General Barrasa, in the meantime, made his headquarters at Cárichic,[15] situated far west and deep in rebel territory. He sent out his
Captain Diego del Castillo to scout for the malcontents. Castillo met
them and was repulsed, and when General Barrasa understood their
strength from the reports of his captain he retired to a safer and
stronger position. The Governor at Durango, hearing of this, resolved
to take the field himself. He set out from Durango December 14, 1648,
and moving with speed and energy he covered the whole two hundred
miles of hilly country to Parral before the month was up. January 13
the Governor set out with forty soldiers and three hundred Indian allies
to join forces with General Barrasa, whom he met after five days' march
in the Valle de Aguilar, far northeast on the Río Papigochic. The
expedition was financed with 10,838 pesos which the Bishop of Yuca-
tán ordered the governor to take from the royal treasury.[16]

After crossing and recrossing the country northwest of the Río
Conchos, the Spaniards captured three rebel spies in the vicinity of
Pachera and Temechic, not far from the headwaters of the Río Papigochic. These captors, loyal to their people, lied when they said they
knew where the two caciques, Supichiochi and Don Bartolomé, lay
in hiding with all their people and that they would lead the Spaniards
thither. The Governor with all his force, now augmented by that of
General Barrasa, followed the guides until the deception was discovered. The three were summarily hanged.

There were marches and countermarches again over rough and
broken country in search of the rebels. Another spy was caught. This
man gave authentic information, namely, that one of the rebel chiefs,
Ochavarri, was fifty miles distant near the banks of Río Papigochic.

Thither the march was now directed, with the fortunate result that the rebel was encountered twenty-five miles northwest of Pachera. The hostiles offered battle, and the Governor engaged with fifty soldiers and two hundred Indians. Victory came to his banners, for ten of the enemy were killed and twenty-seven taken prisoners. The prisoners betrayed the locality of three of the four chiefs, where they had fortified themselves on a hill. The Governor marched thither and discovered them. But he missed his chance, for whereas he deferred his attack until the following morning, the chiefs with their people slipped silently away under cover of night, leaving behind four hundred head of sheep, loot of their rebel raids, and a number of dogs. They fled southwest over the divide into the savage and hazardous country of the Guazápares whither it was impossible to pursue them.

The army now broke into several bands and forayed over the country, wasting it. This brought a delegation of rebels begging peace. It would be granted, replied the Governor, provided the chiefs were given up. They made the promise and were joined by some Spaniards in the search. Don Bartolomé was the first to be taken. They brought his head into camp and all his family as captives. Later a large band of Indians brought in the head of Tepox. Ochavarri and Supichiochi seem to have escaped temporarily, but bands of pursuing Spaniards brought in numerous of their followers as prisoners.

Thus the rebellion frittered out and the Governor was able to depart south to Parral, giving orders to General Barrasa that he follow him within a week. The Governor arrived back in Parral April 16, 1649. The mission San Francisco de Borja had been sacked and ruined, and a couple dozen Spaniards had been murdered and their haciendas destroyed. But one hundred and fifty Tarrahumar prisoners of both sexes had been taken and almost that number had been killed. At long last the first Tarahumar revolt was seemingly over.

These prolonged troubles in or on the borders of the Tarahumar mission bore three good results. A new royal cédula confirmed and strengthened all the efforts of the missionaries for the mild and just treatment of the Indians, the strong and just Don Diego Fajardo replaced the weak and vicious Valdés as Governor of Nueva Vizcaya, and the first steps were taken for the formation of a new presidio for the protection of this more northern country, to be placed at Cerro

Gordo on el camino real or highway between Indé and Parral. Governor Valdés had likewise pressed the Viceroy for a presidio there in 1647.[17]

The King wrote to the Viceroy, the Conde de Salvatierra, January 18, 1648, in answer to the Viceroy's petition of February 26, 1646, for the new presidio. The Viceroy, incidentally, to impress the King with the need, had said that two thousand of the rebels had been brought to peace and one hundred and fifty slain. The King wonders why a new presidio should be necessary now, since for so long a time peace had been preserved without the need for the protection now alleged. He asks for a fuller report, for further specifications, and for a detailed enumeration of arguments for and against the new institution. The extra expense which would be put upon the royal treasury worries the King no little; so he suggests ways and means of creating the presidio without additional strain upon his royal purse. What he desires is that a few soldiers be taken from each of the presidios of old established places to make up a sufficient number for the efficacy of the planned one at Cerro Gordo.[18] The Viceroy's representations evidently satisfied the King and his Council of the Indies, for by 1649 the presidio at Cerro Gordo is an established fact.

Chapter VIII

ANOTHER JESUIT FALLS

THE RIVERS of Mexico are variously and often beautifully named. In the past and up through the frontier history of the country the same stream may have several names in several different periods. The present Río Fuerte was anciently referred to as Río Sinaloa, because on the banks of its upper reaches lived the Sinaloa tribe of Indians. The present Río Sinaloa was variously called Río Petatlán or simply Río de la Villa. But even today, the same stream often bears different names in different parts of its course. The Sinaloa River today, where the mountains narrow its banks, is called Río Petachán and farther still into the Sierra Madre is called by still another name. The Fuerte becomes in the sierra the Río Enrique, and the Río Presidio becomes the Ventana. So it is more particularly with the Yaqui. This delightful stream has a long and winding course for hundreds of miles and if we follow it up from the sea its banks will take us first east, then turn us in a long and graceful curve toward the north whither its direction points for more than a hundred miles. Suddenly the direction turns east again for fifty miles. Then, after winding its way through mountains, the stream finds its headwaters in the heart of the present state of Chihuahua. But in its upper reaches and in the state of Chihuahua the Yaqui is known as Río Papigochic.

This particular change in name is readily explained. Papigochic is a Tarahumar name, whereas Yaqui is a Yaqui name, so that what is Papigochic in Chihuahua is Yaqui in Sonora. Beginning in the land of the Tarahumares and flowing north the river zigzagged through the hills of the Jovas, entered Ópata country, and then turned south through the valleys of the Lower Pimas. Finally near the sea it flowed through the fertile land of the Yaquis. The stream thus pierces the Sierra Madre where toward the north its lofty cordillera descends and breaks into lower and straggling hills. The river forms a natural pass from east to west of the divide of the Sierra Madre, which the missionaries frequently used during later decades of the seventeenth century. It therefore formed a link between the missions east and west of the

[1] For notes to chapter viii see pages 245-246.

sierra. The pass south by way of Topia was over the roughest and through the highest part of the sierra.

The first Jesuit known to thread this pass formed by the Papigochic through the sierra was Father Gerónimo de Figueroa, who in 1641 had gone to the west coast, apparently as official Visitor to the Sinaloa and Sonora missions. Figueroa returned to Tarahumara in the company of Captain Pedro de Perea of Sinaloa. Leaving the west coast to traverse the Sierra Madre, these two went north from the Sinaloa River, passed through the north Sonoran missions of Aribechi and Sahuaripa, and then traveled east along the bank of the Río Papigochic until they reached Tarahumara and the missions of the Conchos and its tributaries. In passing thus through the heart of Tarahumara, Figueroa and Perea found the natives friendly and respectful.[1]

In the land of the Tarahumares the beauty and fertility of the vales and valleys of the Río Papigochic struck the eyes of the missionaries and of the soldiers, beginning with Father Figueroa and Captain Perea. When the newly appointed governor, Don Diego Fajardo, accompanied by Father José Pascual, was in the midst of his campaign against the rebels early in 1649, a certain vale on the banks of this long and winding stream won the admiration of both soldier and missionary.

The attractiveness of this country was first brought to the attention of the Spaniards during the campaigns for the suppression of the revolt among the Tarahumar chiefs which we have narrated in the previous chapter. Governor Diego Fajardo, General Barrasa, and Father José Pascual appear then to have gazed upon that country for the first time and they seem to have agreed from the first that here was an ideal spot for the location of a mission. The valley was thickly populated with Tarahumares. Indeed, this valley seemed to the new governor of Nueva Vizcaya so attractive and the number of Indians so great that even in the heat and dust of his campaign against the rebels he was desirous of founding a Spanish settlement on the spot.

Therefore, at the successful conclusion of his expedition against the four chiefs, Governor Fajardo put into execution his plan, which was another step east of the Sierra Madre in the northward march of the Spanish colonial frontier. The Governor founded a new villa, a settlement which in the course of time would grow into a town, and become populous and important or remain small and unknown according to the future development of mines, commerce, and agriculture. Governor Fajardo called the settlement Aguilar, and contemporaries spoke of the foundation as the Villa de Aguilar. And if it enjoyed permanence, which eventually it did, it was the mission founded near by which gave the settlement its lasting quality. The new villa was not destined to become great. Chihuahua, eighty miles east in a rich mining country and closer to the arteries of commerce and travel to the north—El Paso, San Antonio, and Santa Fe—though founded later grew more quickly, and eclipsed the Villa de Aguilar, which the missionaries called Papigochic, and which is today known as Ciudad Guerrero.

Before departing for Parral and Durango at the successful finish of his campaign, Governor Fajardo left at the Villa de Aguilar a corporal with thirty men and supplies for eight months, giving orders that a church be constructed and likewise a residence for the Royal Justice, for the Captain, and quarters for the soldiers.[2] At Parral he made efforts to enlist citizens or *pobladores* for his new settlement but succeeded in persuading only four families to migrate to this sequestered spot beyond the rim of the frontier.[3]

Between them, José Pascual, now superior of Baja Tarahumara in place of Gerónimo Figueroa, and Governor Diego Fajardo, decided upon a mission near the Villa de Aguilar. A new arrival in the Tarahumar country, Cornelio Beudin, recently stationed at San Felipe on the Conchos, was designated by Pascual to be the founder of the new mission on the delightful Río Papigochic. When Beudin left his native Belgium on his way to the Spanish dominions of the New World he changed his name to one of Spanish sound, Godínez, lest the Government refuse him passport, since at the time of which we are speaking foreigners were not allowed as missionaries in the dominions of the King of Spain. In the ancient records and old histories the padre is most often referred to as Cornelio Godínez, just as the Irishman Michael Wading on coming to New Spain changed his name to Miguel Godínez and thus is spoken of in the ancient correspondence.

Cornelio Beudin came to the Tarahumar mission in 1648, the year before the uprising had been put down by Governor Fajardo. Young, fresh, and energetic, this Jesuit was well chosen to be the founder and superior of the new mission on the Río Papigochic. The Jesuits named the foundation La Purísima Concepción, after the Immaculate Conception of Blessed Mary the Virgin, and fixed its site not quite three miles from the Villa de Aguilar. The new establishment came to be called in missionary annals La Purísima de Papigochic.[4] Both the mission and the villa were placed in a distant, isolated position. They were a full hundred and sixty miles from Parral and one hundred and twenty from San Felipe on the Conchos.

Beudin came to Aguilar from San Felipe in the fall of 1649, and it was he who chose the mission site and gathered the Indians around him. It was a charming spot. High and blue sierras rose miles away to north and to the south, closing in a long valley, the valley of the Río Papigochic. Not far from the stream the great level plain dips a few hundred feet nearly to the level of the river bed. In the fertile river vale thus formed the Black Robe set his mission.

The personality of Beudin was as kindly and attractive as the spot whereon he built his pueblo. His personal charm went far to conciliate and then to attach the soul of the Tarahumar. The primitives began to trust and to love this padre with his mild and charming manner. They became willing to gather around him to form a pueblo not far from their fields of corn and even to build a church for the performance of the exterior rites of Christianity which the padre began to teach them. The neophytes were not at all displeased when Beudin himself took a physical hand in the work of building the church, and they thus became more happy to see him, whom they had begun to love as their protector, settled in a suitable dwelling near the chapel. Not long after his arrival he began to instruct the adults and after what he considered a sufficient period to allow their understanding of the Christian mysteries to mature, Beudin baptized the greater number of those who had come to live near La Purísima de Papigochic.

Thus the year 1649 drew to its close. What spiritual celebrations the padre inaugurated at Christmas time and at Epiphany the record does not reveal. Celebrations and feastings, bonfires and beef for these primitive children of the Faith there certainly were, for the Black Robe never omitted to make humanly attractive these festal days of the Church. Thus the year 1650 was ushered in amidst circumstances which gave promise of happiness and prosperity. Other fathers would come to help Beudin, visitas would be established, and soon the whole

Tarahumar tribe, both north and south, would come happily into the Faith, perhaps repeating those developments which occurred on the west coast years before when Mayo and Yaqui in tens of thousands knew the waters of baptism.

Alas, it was not to be so. The Kings' cédula for the mild and just treatment of the Indians was not obeyed by the Spanish inhabitants of the Villa de Aguilar, who almost from the first began to mistreat the neophytes of Cornelio Beudin. The danger of their isolation, removed as they were from other settlements of any kind, seemed not to prevent the Spaniards from arousing the hostility of the Tarahumares. Don Diego de Lara, alcalde mayor, either did not or could not prevent the injustices and cruelties practiced on the Indians by the Spanish inhabitants of the villa. Indeed, likely as not, he himself gave the evil example. The thing had been done often before as we have just seen from the complaints of Nicolás Zepeda. It was again the old story of Spanish oppression, kidnapping, forced labor, and practical slavery.

Beudin protested in vain. The atrocities continued and the patience of his neophytes began to wear out. This was the more dangerous because the cinders of the revolt of the preceding year were not yet entirely cold. When the Indians saw that the missionary was without power to protect them they began in their simple minds to suspect that he was in league with their oppressors. Beudin was chaplain also of the inhabitants of the villa. He must needs have converse with them from time to time. They too were his spiritual charge. In this contact the neophytes suspected connivance or complicity in what caused their unhappiness and oppression.

It is true there was a small garrison at the villa and Beudin had at the mission a soldier for his protection. But the Spaniards did not mend their ways, the disaffection spread, and three caciques, one who had formerly been very friendly, joined and led the discouraged and embittered Indians. One of these, Don Diego Barrasa, named after Captain Barrasa, just as the Toboso chief, Gerónimo Moranta, had been named after the Tepehuán missionary, was one of the leaders. He came from a nearby settlement of Tarahumares called Iguachinapa. Another was Yagunaque, formerly a Christian, now known as a hardened apostate. Still a third was Tepóraca, an astute and able leader of this and other uprisings.

Yagunaque vowed he would never again see the padre except to slay him, and no other god would he confess but his own person, and that of his wife and children. The third ringleader, Tepóraca, had intelligence and a pleasing personality linked to qualities of leadership. What increased his influence greatly was the fact that he had been formerly on most friendly terms with the Spaniards. The Indians, therefore, felt he must possess very weighty and justifiable reasons for his present rebellious spirit. And all the while their hated oppressors, the Spaniards, kept coming to Beudin with their difficulties and their quarrels so that the Indians thought surely he was an abettor of their persecutions.

An unfortunate event set fire to all this combustible material. The missionaries had always known of their personal danger if an Indian child died after baptism or after having received the last sacraments. The superstitious native mind attributed death in this case to the evil consequences of the sacrament and held the missionary responsible. On May 15, 1650, Beudin had given the last rites to the daughter of one of his neophytes and the child died within two hours. The mother, frantic with grief, went through the mission screeching that the padre had murdered her daughter. This occurrence, added to the ill treatment which the Indians had been receiving and the evil influence of the three chiefs and of certain hechiceros, seems to have been the final drop which made the cup of discontent overflow into the desire for destruction and murder. Commandant Lara at Aguilar warned Beudin, but the latter, overtrustful, did not think his neophytes would forget all his former kindnesses to them.

The storm broke early in the morning of Saturday, June 4, the eve of Pentecost.[5] Two hours before daylight a large group of the rebels stealthily approached the hut where Beudin and his lone Spanish guard, Fabián Vásquez, were sleeping. They set fire to the straw and wooden fabric. Awakened by the smoke and the flames, the soldier seized his gun and the padre his crucifix. When Beudin realized he was surrounded he knew that death was certain and prepared for it. He persuaded the soldier to put away his gun, saying that the hour of God had arrived, and the good man confessed his sins. The two victims then opened the door and went out to take what would come. They both made for the church a short distance away while a hail of arrows poured upon them. Beudin was able to reach the altar before he fell mortally wounded by half a dozen shafts. The Indians then tied a rope around his neck and dragged him about the church, beating him and slashing him with knives. Tiring of this sport they dragged him out to the cross which he had set up in front of the chapel. Here he was finally dispatched with a blow of a *macana* upon his head. On Vásquez, the padre's guard, the rebels perpetrated the same barbarities. They hung the father and the soldier with ropes from the arms of the cross, the missionary to the left. Then they cut them down.

The rebels dressed themselves in the father's clothes, took as loot the ornaments of the altar, and made off with the chalice and the metal container for the holy oils.[6] Frenzied now with blood and slaughter, the rebels ran over the Valle de Aguilar, devastating the farms of the Spaniards and killing a number upon whom they were able to lay their hands. When their work was done, the church burned, its vessels and vestments looted, and the houses of the mission destroyed, they made off to the hills to enjoy the liberties and the license of their former pagan existence. They spread terror far over the country. A pack train was at this time picking its way up the Río Papigochic from the Sonora country and the missions of the west. It was carrying salt, tallow, and some silver. A herd of cattle was being driven before it. The rebels attacked the pack train near Tomochic, killing some of the Spaniards, looting the goods, and driving off the herd. This particular group of rebels was later attacked and defeated by a band of Spaniards from Aguilar. But the country was again up in arms, and unless this new rebellion could be broken neither mine nor mission, pueblo nor Spanish family could live and work securely.[7]

Cornelio Beudin had been but two and a half years in the missions, and his superior, José Pascual, composed an account of his virtues.[8] General Goswin Nickel wrote in 1651 from Rome asking for details of the martyrdom;[9] soon after, the tragedy of his death was commemorated in monographs and pious writings.[10] Beudin was the first Black Robe to fall at the hands of the Tarahumares; soon another would follow him into the posthumous prestige which such a death created in the Latin world of the seventeenth century. Though official Rome was more cautious, the people led by their clergy considered it martyrdom and they venerated Beudin as a blessed martyr.

Chapter IX

APPEASEMENT, NEW REVOLT, MASSACRE

AFTER FATHER Cornelio Beudin's death there followed developments similar to the sequel of each Indian revolt in the missions of New Spain. The alarm was sounded and spread over the country. Some Spanish homesteaders fled to the Villa de Aguilar which had not been attacked; others were able to defend themselves without fleeing from their farms. News of the disaster came immediately to the villa only a couple of miles away. The Captain and *Justicia Mayor*, Diego de Lara, hurried over to the mission with some soldiers to recover the bodies of the martyrs and take account of the destruction and the losses incurred.

The Captain found the bodies where the savages had left them, lying at the foot of the cross before the mission chapel. They were naked, for the rebels according to their wont had made off with every bit of personal property they could lay their hands on. The father's gown would be worn by the rebel chief and also his biretta if it could be found. The Spaniards found Beudin pierced with seven arrows, gashed in three places with the crude knives called macanas, and bruised and torn in various other ways. But his body was left substantially intact. No limb had been severed, nor had he been scalped. It was otherwise with the soldier. The savages had scalped him and then cut off his head. The Spaniards gathered up the remains of the padre and his soldier guard, collected the scattered and broken remains of the chapel accoutrements, and made their way sorrowfully back to the Villa de Aguilar. The following day, the fifth of June, which that year was Pentecost Sunday, the padre and the soldier were buried near the rude church of the villa.[1]

Meantime word of the disaster had sped to Parral, where fortunately Governor Diego Fajardo happened to be sojourning. He gave orders immediately and wrote a letter. He ordered General Juan de Barrasa and Captain Juan Fernández de Morales to go to the scene of the revolt, the one to the Villa de Aguilar, the other to the destroyed mis-

---

[1] For notes to chapter ix see page 246.

sion of Papigochic. Together they would organize to pursue and destroy the enemy. The letter he wrote was directed to Father Nicolás Zepeda and was dated June 15, 1650. The Governor of Nueva Vizcaya was honored, he wrote, to be in the position to look into the circumstances of the death of a blessed martyr and to be the one who would organize the campaign in punishment of those who had killed him. "And I confess to God," the Governor continued, "that before I return to my capital I shall witness the chastisement of the rebels, effect the residence in the mission of a new Jesuit father, and behold the villa with its environs again richly prosperous, seeing that it has been watered by the merits and the blood of this its protomartyr."[2]

In spite of these noble feelings and good intentions, the Governor at first did not achieve success. Had he sent one able and energetic captain to round up and punish the rebels all might have gone well; but he sent two, as we have seen, Juan de Barrasa and Juan Fernández de Morales. And though Barrasa was now called general, Morales seems on this campaign to have had equal authority with him. Barrasa, well seasoned and able, should have been given the full command; Morales, inexperienced, but self-assured and selfish, should have been kept at Parral where at least he would have been harmless. Marching northwest from Parral, past San Felipe, the two military companies joined forces near the Villa de Aguilar and then went on into the rougher country. Father Vigilio Máez accompanied the expedition. The scouts brought in the report that the hostiles had fortified themselves on a precipitous hill or *peñol*, sharp with pointed rocks, protected by two arroyos, and covered by a thick garment of trees and brush. The rebels had chosen well. When it was evident the Spaniards were approaching the fortified position, Morales insisted on an immediate attack, even before he had made certain the force of the enemy. Barrasa would remain behind with a few men to guard the provisions. Morales had not taken pains to ascertain the force of the enemy. As a matter of fact he was far more seriously outnumbered than he had dreamed, possessing only fifty Spaniards and less than two hundred Indian allies. The rebels, well fortified as they were, numbered around six hundred. The arroyos had to be crossed in the face of enemy fire while rocks and trunks of trees fell against the Spaniards as they began the assault of the sharp and tangled flank of the peñol. Morales found it to be an impossible task. All day the attack continued and the hostiles could not be dislodged. At sundown Morales retired leaving the rebels in proud possession of their well-chosen position. That night upon the precipitous peñol other Tarahumares arrived to join their rebellious tribesmen.

The Spaniards made camp and fortified themselves as best they could a short distance from the hill. The next morning the rebels, swollen with victory, came down from their strong positions to harry and attack the Spaniards in their own camp. This attack occurred for six days successively. Since the Spaniards had guns and the Indians only bows and arrows, the latter could thus be staved off, although not without some loss to themselves. It was plain that the Indian forces were constantly augmented. The rebels were even blocking retreat toward the Villa de Aguilar. On the seventh day Morales allowed himself to be drawn into an ambush, thinking he was pursuing a fleeing enemy. He had got himself and his men involved in great danger and only some horses sent up by Barrasa saved the situation. As it was the rebels captured one Spaniard alive and a few hours later slew him within sight of the Spanish camp.

A new contingent of a thousand men which had come to the successful rebels forced the Spaniards to devise plans for a more or less shameful retreat. They accomplished it by a ruse, favored by a dark and stormy night. The camp fires were lighted as usual and the Indian allies shouted and sang. In the meantime the main group of the Spanish soldiers silently and unperceived threaded the passes and the vales which led back to Aguilar and to comparative security in the valley of Papigochic. The Indian allies came up safely later, but the whole affair was a wretched admission of failure.[3]

Governor Fajardo was furious at this fiasco and, as in the uprising of 1649, he determined to take the field himself. Since Father Vigilio Máez had gone back to the recently founded Satevó, his mission,[4] Father José Pascual, still superior, met the Governor on his way into the rebel country to offer his services. The Governor asked him to accompany the expedition.

Fajardo with his men, arriving at the fortified peñol, saw that it was still held, but by a much smaller force. The Governor thought of surrounding the hill, but this was impossible, for the number of his men would not permit it. He attacked therefore. The rebels retreated to the strongest position on the mountain and evidently were determined to sell their lives as dearly as possible, aided by their women. When the Spaniards and their allies attacked from two positions at once, and when their chief, said to be the very one who had slain Father Beudin, was felled with a ball from an arquebus, the rebels lost heart and fled under cover of night. They had lost heavily, while three Spaniards had been killed, as well as a number of Indian allies, and many had been wounded, including the Governor.

Fajardo pursued the rebels as far west as Tomochic. Here the going became exceedingly difficult because of continuous rains and swollen streams. A council was called by the leader. Father José Pascual persuaded the Governor, suffering from a wound, to give up the pursuit, return to Aguilar for rest and care, and to bring about peace through a negotiated settlement. The counsel was accepted and the Spaniards retired to Aguilar where the Governor recovered from his injury.

To offer peace to the rebels Governor Fajardo chose a trusted Indian ally, probably one of the Christian and loyal Tarahumares. He was well received and the rebels on the Governor's terms agreed to cease their depredations and resettle in their former pueblos. This the Indians were the more willing and even anxious to do since they had lost several of their leaders during the interval when the able General Barrasa, though the Governor had retired, continued his activities against them, not by direct attack, but by harrying their flank and wasting their country. The rebels even sent a delegation to the Governor, at Parral, and there was brought about a mutual settlement of peace. The Tarahumares returned to their pueblos and to their accustomed work in the mines. Appearing full of good will, they were easily persuaded to return to Papigochic, the ruined mission and scene of Beudin's martyrdom, there to rebuild the chapel and a dwelling for a missionary who would again be sent among them.[5]

This new missionary was a Neapolitan by birth and had come to New Spain in 1642 in company of the well-known and high-born Pedro de Velasco, son of the Viceroy Luis de Velasco II. Father Velasco, former missionary and later Provincial, had been sent to Europe as procurator of the Jesuit Province of New Spain. As was often the case, then as today, the procurators sought for young Jesuits of energy and ability who had vocations for the missionary life. Such was Jácome Antonio Basilio. The young Black Robe spent his first years at the novitiate at Tepotzotlán, learning the Mexican language, in which he became an expert, and teaching in the school for Otomí Indians which the fathers had administered for many years.[6]

When news of the death of Cornelio Beudin reached Mexico City many of the ardent spirits among the fathers begged to be sent to take his place, hoping no doubt they too at some future time might be able to achieve martyrdom. No one begged more insistently than Jácome Basilio, and though reluctantly because the padre was also a valuable man in the capital, his superiors acceded to his request and off he went to the Tarahumar mission arriving, as it seems, early in 1651. He was assigned immediately to Papigochic to fill the place left vacant by Beudin.

On his way northwest from Parral to his mission, in passing through the Villa de Aguilar, he tarried to offer the benefits of religion and of the sacraments to the Spanish and Indian inhabitants of the settlement. Arrived finally at Papigochic he inaugurated a fruitful spiritual activity which went on for months and which met with extraordinary success.

Basilio divided his time and his labors between the villa and the mission, though it was the latter which claimed his most continuous residence and the expense of his most earnest energies. He taught the Tarahumar children the catechism, he prepared adults for baptism, he encouraged the gathering in or near the mission of groups of Tarahumares scattered through the valley of Papigochic and along the river banks. The mission was once again growing into an Indian pueblo and gave promise of becoming a flourishing Christian settlement. Indeed, the energies of the new padre led him farther afield and he traveled miles into Tarahumar country, going as far as Temechic twenty miles south of Villa de Aguilar.[7]

Thus there passed for the young Black Robe a fruitful year. But when March of 1652 arrived the father was to see the ending of all his work and to receive his desired reward. It soon became apparent to the Spaniards of Aguilar that the peace promised by the rebel Tarahumares who had slain Cornelio Beudin was not in full measure sincere. Chief Tepóraca was among the dissemblers and he showed himself persistently disaffected. He was a born leader of opposition. Restless, energetic, and shrewd, his arts of persuasion were difficult for the simple primitive to resist. Moreover, because of his activity in the former rebellion and his bravery in the field, his prestige was high among his tribesmen. So that even while Father Basilio was carrying on his work in the midst of his people, this leader was planning and plotting the downfall of mission and pueblo, of Spaniard and missionary alike.

The revolt, though suspected by the Spaniards, came suddenly, led by Tepóraca, whose name signified *El Hachero,* which means "Woodcutter" or "Backwoodsman." The Woodcutter had worked well. Secretly and silently he had begun to stir up the embers of the preceding revolt. It began to be clear that the peace with the Governor of Nueva Vizcaya, Diego Fajardo, was made insincerely in dissimulation. Affairs were then already prepared for the rebel leader Tepóraca. Upon the warm embers he blew silently but intelligently and persistently. He blew for months until the coals of revolt were hot enough to burst into flame.

The fire actually broke out on March 2, 1652. On that day Captain de Lara saw Chief Tepóraca scouring about the vicinity of the Villa de Aguilar with a large group of Tarahumares, all armed. This action boded no good. The number of the group, the bows and arrows, meant trouble. Captain Lara sent out a band of soldiers to speak with the Indians and to assure them of continued friendly feelings. It was a weak movement on the part of the Spaniards and could not possibly have settled anything. As the soldiers after the parley were returning to the settlement the Indians strung arrow to bow and let fly upon the retreating Spanish soldiers a rain of arrows. No Spaniard fell, but they wheeled about, unlimbered their clumsy guns, and spat a hail of leaden balls into the now fleeing group of savages. Thus was war declared and the fight was on: another uprising of the savage against the Spaniard, another murder of a missionary.[8]

The sound of the volley from the arquebuses reverberated far out upon the valley of Papigochic and almost as rapidly Dame Rumor sped upon the wings of Mercury. The Spaniards of the outlying farms of the Villa de Aguilar, noting these signs of a fresh uprising of the savage, left their work and their domiciles and fled into the town for protection. Then Tepóraca and his band attacked the settlement itself.

This was an exceedingly clever move and Tepóraca thus proved himself to be an astute leader. His attack upon the town this second of March, 1652, was not intended to be anything other than a ruse; the real attack would come later. At the moment all Tepóraca wanted was to keep the Spaniards busy and to hold the ranchers who had fled to the settlement well occupied with defense within the town limits. For while the villa was being defended by the soldiers and ranchers, bands of rebels went from farm to farm, now vacated by their owners, and drove off without any resistance the herds of cattle and sheep. These they conducted into the folds of the surrounding hills in order that with this provision they might be able to sustain, if necessary, a prolonged and possibly a permanent resistance.

So it was done, and when sufficient time was given for the accomplishment of this important robbery and looting of the Spanish farms, Tepóraca called off his men and the hostiles retired from the environments of the Villa de Aguilar. Their ruse had succeeded: the Spaniards had fled from their homes and farms of the countryside and now their cattle and sheep were in the possession of the rebel Indians. It was all very easy. The planned attack in force would come the following day when all the rebels would have had time to concentrate their number upon the town. It was murderous and ruinous. It effected the extinction of this isolated frontier settlement for many years to come.[9]

Father Jácome Basilio was away when the crisis came to a head. He had gone off to the south on one of his missionary excursions to the Tarahumares deeper in their country and was at Temechic when a loyal Tarahumar chief, Don Pedro, who raced all of the twenty miles, brought him news of what was taking place at Aguilar and stated the intentions of his tribesmen to slay all the Spaniards and to wipe out the settlement. Don Pedro offered to lead the father to safety, either to San Felipe or to some other mission or town, even to Parral. When word spread among the loyal Tarahumares of Temechic they became greatly disturbed, for they had come to love Basilio after his repeated visits to them. They begged him either to remain there with them in security or else to flee with Don Pedro to some safer refuge.

In this crisis it is not difficult to understand the psychology of Jácome Antonio Basilio. It was the news of the murder of Cornelio Beudin two years before, which had led him to seek residence in the wilds of

Tarahumara. Having volunteered for the New World and then begged for this particular mission he certainly was not going to run away from the death which was to be expected and which was even desired provided duty demanded his presence. Duty did so demand, for the Christians at Aguilar in their hour of danger needed his spiritual ministrations. Did death come in such circumstances it would be offered in what he considered the golden form of martyrdom. Basilio's mind was made up on the instant; no reflection was needed. He would hasten to the Villa de Aguilar and lend his spiritual aid to the Spaniards there who were in danger of their temporal and perhaps their eternal lives.[10]

The Black Robe consoled his Tarahumar neophytes of Temechic and quieted them. He wrote a hasty message to Governor Fajardo and to José Pascual telling of the pressing danger, and then mounted his horse and sped toward Aguilar and into the midst of the fracas. So great was his haste that he left behind in his hut at Temechic an opened letter he had just received from his confrère, Father Vigilio Máez, who was working at Satevó. After giving the two messages to Don Pedro, charging him with their safe delivery and bidding farewell to his weeping neophytes, he mounted his horse and sped into danger and death.

Basilio arrived at the Villa de Aguilar during the lull which followed the first attack, coming into the settlement probably in the afternoon or early evening of March 2. Here he found bustle and excitement among soldiers, other Spaniards, and loyal Christian Tarahumares, and clamor and fear among their women. Basilio began his holy work of spiritual consolation, quieting troubled spirits, advising on measures of defense and taking the confessions of the many who came to him, for they realized that death might soon be upon them. Well might the women weep and fear and the men be busy with measures of defense, because before the darkness of that night was spent, in the early hours of March 3, the rebels launched their final and their fatal attack.

When the alarm was given, the inhabitants rushed to the only strong and fortified protection, a sort of fort with towers which served also as the Captain's residence. Near to this and enclosed in palisades were the principal houses of the townspeople. Many cowered here for safety as they listened to the terrifying war whoops of the savage and to the blows of his strong club against the palisades.

The padre retired to the church with his faithful interpreter, Don Felipe, to await what fate might bring. For long that morning in the darkness the rebels labored in vain to breach the protecting wall, but at break of day succeeded in forcing an entrance. They were able at the same time to set fire to the fort and to some of the other houses. This drove the inmates into the open where a horde of rebels was ready to shoot them down as they emerged from the protecting walls of the burning stronghold. The Captain and many soldiers fell with scores of Spaniards and loyal Indians of both sexes.

The church whither Basilio and his interpreter and many others had fled went thus far unassaulted. But the padre could not remain thus in cover with the cries of the afflicted and the whoops of the rebels sounding in his ears. He rushed out, followed by Don Felipe, to try to stay the fury of the attackers. His action was of one trying with a stick or a straw to stop the fury of a flood. Both he and his interpreter were struck down and killed with the rest. Although felled by arrows, Basilio was seen to be still alive when some Indian dispatched him with blows from his macana. Finally the savages hung him to an arm of the cross which stood before the church. To this rude chapel they set fire and to the rest of the houses, and made their way down to the mission and to the surrounding pueblos and visitas to do the same. Their work done they fled into the hills, sure of sustenance for a long time to come from the flocks and herds they had driven off the day before.[11]

The third of March, 1652, was a fatal day for the Tarahumar mission. When Beudin was slain in June, 1650, it was only the mission which was destroyed, the town, Villa de Aguilar, with its soldiers and inhabitants remained intact. Nor were the rebels very numerous nor well organized. Here was a hurricane which swept away both town and mission, which carried to destruction a captain and most of his soldiers with dozens or perhaps hundreds of the inhabitants of the villa and of the surrounding farms and ranches. Desolation and utter ruin had come to the valley of Papigochic.

It would be long before a beginning of Christianity and of Spanish settlement in these more northern regions could again be made. Thus were the bright hopes of the Italian Jesuit Basilio suddenly and tragically dimmed; thus for the time being was all his work totally undone.

Chapter X

THE PURSUIT OF CHIEF TEPÓRACA

AFTER ALL such uprisings the rebels had to be pursued and brought to punishment. Sometimes it took years to effect this salutary measure of security, sometimes only months. Earlier, and in the missions west of the divide the strong arm of Captain Hurdaide dealt swift and lusty blows so that rebels were speedily brought to punishment and to peace. Nevertheless, in the first decade of the seventeenth century it took even Hurdaide years finally to corral the Ocoroni rebel Babilonio who had fled for security to the Yaquis and who helped to fortify the stout resistance of these people to Spanish penetration. After the Tepehuán revolt it required two years and three prolonged and difficult expeditions finally to stamp out the last embers of revolt and to dispatch the rebel Cogoxito. In 1652, at this Tarahumar crisis, a particular circumstance bade fair to delay any punitive measures and to prolong dangerously the agony of the mission of Baja Tarahumara.

Governor Diego Fajardo had just received orders from Mexico to prepare an expedition against the troublesome Tobosos in the northeast and he had all things ready for the execution of this order when Tepóraca's revolt burst into flame. These Tobosos even after the defeat of 1645 were again on the warpath. Like the Apaches later they could not be permanently brought under the Spanish yoke, nor yet made submissive by the gentle tactics of the gray-robed Franciscan padres. José Pascual considered these turbulent neighbors of the Tarahumares to be in good part responsible for the restless spirit of revolt which was prevalent in certain parts of northern Tarahumara. Now should the Governor choose to be away just this period of the spring of 1652 when Tepóraca was abroad with a couple of thousand followers, when the Villa de Aguilar with the mission of Papigochic lay in ruins, the whole country and the peaceful southern missions would be at the mercy of the rebels. Father Pascual strongly appealed against so foolhardy a move.

The reasons against the Governor's contemplated expedition to the Tobosos just at this time became all the stronger with the evolution of

---

[1] For notes to chapter x see pages 246-247.

the actions of the rebel Tepóraca. After leaving Aguilar a smoking desolation and the mission of Papigochic in ruins the rebels hurried sixty miles east and destroyed the visita of San Lorenzo. Continuing east they fell upon mission San Francisco Javier at Satevó, forcing its padre, Vigilio Máez, to flee. But the rebels did not stop there. They went into the country of the loyal Conchos, and there destroyed seven missions and visitas of the Franciscans.[1]

Tepóraca had then turned south and had endeavored to shake the loyalty of his more southern tribesmen in the missions of San Gerónimo at Huejotitlán, of San Felipe, Santa Cruz, and San Pablo. In this attempt the rebel chief was unsuccessful. The fathers had been in these parts for more than a decade and the faith and loyalty of the primitives had been given time to mature to a loyal stability. So the rebel after ravaging the east and tempting the south, turned north and west into rougher and more isolated regions.

This certainly was not the time for Governor Fajardo to deprive the Tarahumar country of all protection and draw off the military forces for a campaign into the Toboso plains of the east. The Governor inclined to the arguments of Father José Pascual and settled on a compromise. He would leave behind a sufficient force of soldiers under his lieutenant and captain general of Parral, Don Juan Fernández de Carrión. This was only a fraction of the force sufficient to protect a country in time of rebellion. Indeed, Tepóraca soon learned of Fajardo's eastern campaign and was preparing to return south again to try to persuade his tribesmen of the southern missions to join him against the Spaniards. Tepóraca had united his band to others under the leadership of one Pablo, rebel chief of the rancherías near San Pablo, not far from Huejotitlán. This union of forces brought the number of hostiles to more than two thousand. Once this band began to move and harry the country to the south it would spell the ruin of Baja Tarahumara.

At this juncture and in this dire danger to the whole mission system of Lower Tarahumara an unexpected turn of providence brought sudden defeat to the Tobosos and set the Governor with the main body of troops free to turn west and take in hand the Tarahumar rebels. We do not know the details of this success, except that it took place at a hill or mountain called the Peñol de Nonolab. Probably the whole force of the Toboso rebels was concentrated at this stronghold and was surprised and scattered. In any case, Governor Fajardo, achieving with unexpected speed the total defeat of the eastern rebels, was free to lead his forces against the Tarahumares many leagues to the west.

The difficulty under which the Spaniards labored explains the lengths to which this particular campaign drew itself out. The rebels were in their own country and knew every hill and arroyo of the whole extended district. The Spaniards, therefore, in their pursuit of Tepóraca were unable to run him down. He was as elusive as Nacabeba who, years ago in the west, had murdered Gonzalo de Tapia. The rebel kept to the summits of the hills and the escarpments of the mountains and the Spaniards were unable to overtake him.

When the fox could not be trapped, Fajardo marched north to where he had learned the main body of savages had retired. The Indians put up a stubborn resistance and the Governor at first made no headway. A group of forty Spaniards with about a hundred Indian allies found themselves in a trap at Tomochic, which lay over a sierra south of the Río Papigochic. At this place, when deep in an arroyo, they were surprised by many times their number and surrounded on three sides. The only safety lay in flight up the canyon. For two days they thus retreated, fighting almost continually a rear-guard action with the rebels who kept at their heels. Finally the Spaniards were forced to turn and fight.

They prepared to sell their lives as dearly as possible. The rebel leader of the pursuing bands was conspicuous for his shouts and gesticulations urging his men to the attack. But a chance shot from one of the Spaniards, before the order to fire had been given, brought him down. The rest, seeing their leader dead, lost heart, retreated, and disappeared. The Indian showed himself usually a coward in the face of death. Had the rebels attacked and persevered, the Spaniards would have been undone, for they were greatly outnumbered, were exhausted, far from their base, and had run out of supplies.[2]

Providence seemed to continue on the side of the Spaniards, for in a second crisis, in spite of their own mistakes, they emerged successfully through sheer good fortune. The hazard was briefly this: Governor Fajardo imprudently ordered an assault upon a strong natural position called the Peñol de Píchachic, near the headwaters of the Río

Papigochic. The Spaniards were repulsed with loss of prestige and men, forty-two soldiers being wounded in the encounter. Fajardo was furious, and going himself more carefully to reconnoiter the position, vowed that in a second attack he himself would lead the van. He might himself have been wounded or fallen. But here again the opposition melted away. The leader of this group had been a strong personal friend of the Governor and joined the rebels only as the result of the taunts and persecutions of his relatives. It was probably the sight of the Governor and his present danger which led him to a change of heart. Pretending fear and the impossibility of ultimately defeating the Spaniards, he drew his people off in the night and left the field in possession of his friend Fajardo and his men.

The honor and success of the whole campaign was, however, achieved by Captain Cristóbal de Narváez. A large number of loyal Tarahumares followed him. They knew the terrain as thoroughly as did the rebels and the Captain used them to ferret out the hiding places of the enemy and to track them down in their own haunts and fastnesses. In certain minor encounters Captain Narváez had joined diplomacy with military success and gradually eliminated certain numbers of the hostiles. Finally he had the good fortune to trap the major body of the rebels in a place where escape for the larger number was impossible and they had to fight or surrender. They chose to fight and were completly defeated. Many of their bravest were killed, large numbers fell as prisoners into the hands of the Spaniard, and the rest fled.

This slaughter and rout of the rebels brought them generally to a more docile frame of mind. The victorious Captain Narváez made very intelligent dispositions regarding his prisoners. A number of them he had conveyed under guard to the Governor's camp; but certain others were set free with the understanding that they should seek their chiefs and bring back word as to their desires for a peaceful settlement now that they had been so thoroughly overcome. These men returned as the Captain expected they would with answers that signified the end of the present rebellion. The rebels did indeed ask for peace. The Captain, acting for the Governor, made only one condition, that they would hand over to him the chief ringleader, the man responsible for all the recent troubles, Cacique Tepóraca himself. The rebels agreed and in a few days caught their bird and gave him up.

This kind of a settlement—overtures of peace from the hostiles and the Spanish demand for the deliverance of the ringleaders—happened over and over again in the history of these missions. The Indians thus constantly betrayed their own leaders.

Another circumstance which was always present and which contains some humor for the sophisticated modern is the exhortation to baptism of the pagan rebel before execution by hanging. Frequently a captured rebel was thus baptized with the noose already around his neck. To try to bring to repentance and confession the guilty Christian prisoner has been always the benign endeavor of the priest of God. Tepóraca had already been baptized. He is referred to, therefore, in the sources, as an apostate. All exhorted him to repentance and confession—the padre, his relatives, his friends. But his heart was of flint and he would not yield. He was hanged, therefore, to the limb of a tree, cursing the Spaniards as long as he had breath to draw and damning the cowardice of his tribesmen for making peace with the invader. He died hating his own for their treachery and betrayal of himself.

A gruesome custom was now carried out. Both the missionaries and the neophytes were convinced that the soul of the unrepentant apostate had flown downward to eternal perdition. The Spaniards left the corpse to dangle from the limb of a tree. To them it was but the husk or shell of what had once harbored a living spirit. The body was but the empty casing of a spirit that had fled, of a spirit that was damned. As if to punish the body and make it the object of lasting scorn, the Christian Indians, former friends and relatives alike, drew their bows against the corpse and riddled it with arrows. There let it rot.[3]

The missionaries could now go safely back to their pueblos. Father Vigilio Máez trudged his way back to San Francisco Javier de Satevó, on the banks of the San Pedro in the wide plains of the Mesa Central, now the northernmost of all the missions. His neophytes in spite of their northern isolation had remained loyal, and rather than join the rebellion they had gone off to raise their crops in a safer place. They were happy to return and resume their peaceful mission life under the care and direction of their padre. Gerónimo de Figueroa returned to San Pablo, seventy miles south of Satevó. To San Gerónimo de Huejotitlán ten miles northeast of San Pablo went Gabriel de Villar, while to the southernmost of these missions, San Miguel de las Bocas, went

Rodrigo del Castillo. The superior, José Pascual, from whom we have the finest account of all these vicissitudes, went back to his old residence at San Felipe on the Río Conchos. This pueblo was geographically the center of the whole mission group: a little more than twenty miles south of Satevó and some sixty miles or more north of San Miguel de las Bocas.

As for the missions and their visitas which remained standing and where the five fathers resided, conditions continued encouraging enough. In and near San Felipe there lived a thousand Christian souls and there was a church and house for the missionary. Drunkenness, the great vice of the savage, progressively diminished among these loyal southerners. Each successive year as an enduring peace settled down upon the hills and valleys, groups of pagan Tarahumares came in of their own accord from the rugged sierra to live with the brethren in the missions and to be baptized. Every pueblo and visita was able thus to increase its numbers. Trials there were of course. For the length of six years there was a drought which ruined the crops and dried up the Río Conchos at San Felipe. Father Pascual had to devise ways and means of bringing water and planned to have it carried from his visita of Santa Cruz. Other trials doubtless ruffled the even surface of the padres' life though fortunately the plague, scourge of the mission neophytes, this time goes unrecorded.

But the uprising of 1652 and the death of a second missionary within two years acted as a serious setback to the further advance of the Tarahumar missions. José Pascual himself saw the impossibility of continuing at that time the northwest advance of the mission system and his superiors ordered him to abandon the project.[4] The beautiful valley of the Papigochic, therefore, far removed to the west from any other of the mission units, lay abandoned for many a year and the ruins of its mission church as well as of the town of Aguilar remained as mute testimony of the labors which had been accomplished there and of the dead who had fallen there. Decades were to pass before the valley would again be inhabited by Spanish frontiersmen and before the missionary could gather about him in the lovely vales and hillsides happy groups of the simple Tarahumar. Only after more than twenty years had passed would those pueblos again be alive with the hum of Christian life and with the murmur of Christian prayer.

Chapter XI

JURISDICTIONAL DIFFICULTIES

IN THE Catholic Church the age-old rivalry existing between the regular and secular clergy has from time to time through the centuries weakened the drive and lessened the efficiency of this institution's organic strength. In truth, the relation has not been so much a rivalry, as a jealousy of the one group toward the other. This attitude is a manifestation of the human element within the Church, its members being but men, subject to the foibles of human nature.

Throughout most of the history of Christianity the regulars, from Benedict in the sixth century to Loyola in the sixteenth, have constituted that driving force which from time to time has been needed either to reinvigorate the institution or to introduce needed reforms. The expansion of the Church, in modern times encompassing the globe, has been due, after the earliest era, chiefly to the regular clergy, for this group has carried upon its shoulders the chief burden of the missionary labors, sufferings, and martyrdoms. The administration of the Church, apart from the labors in the field, has been rather in the hands of the secular clergy. Although many popes have been chosen from the ranks of the religious, the greater number have belonged to the secular group, and the bishops have for the most part not been taken from the rank and file of the regular clergy, though in New Spain many had been members of the orders. It is well known that Loyola did not wish his men, even forbade them, to seek to be raised to the dignities of the Church and thus to partake in its administration. Two reasons for this are evident. To certain types of ambitious or selfish temperaments the prohibition closed the avenues leading to promotion and to personal prestige or fame, and at the same time it prevented the abstraction of able men from the apostolic labors of the Order.

Because of their closer organization and because of their spiritual success in the first flush of their religious spirit, the various orders of the regular clergy were given special privileges by the Holy See. It was so with the Dominicans, but especially with the Franciscans, in the thirteenth century and it was so with the Jesuits in the sixteenth.

---

[1] For notes to chapter xi see page 247.

These privileges meant exemption in certain particulars from the ordinary jurisdiction of the bishop. The bishop could not dispose of the labors of the regulars, nor visit their houses officially, nor send his own seculars into the work which the regulars were carrying on. However, substantially, the beginnings of a work in a diocese could not be undertaken without the approval and official permission of the bishop. The regulars on their part became very much attached to their privileges. Sometimes, as with the European Franciscans in the fifteenth century, they did not always use them well; sometimes, as with the Mexican Jesuits in the seventeenth, they overstepped the bounds of prudence and propriety in their defense of these liberties.

A great deal depended, of course, upon the attitude of the bishops whether there would be harmony or discomfiture in the working out of the various legalities. In New Spain where the bishops were friendly or favorable to the Jesuits, no disagreement or trouble was recorded. The holy work went on apace and everyone was happy. Such a prelate was the Benedictine, Juan del Valle, Bishop of Guadalajara, who in 1611 visited the missions of the west coast, confirmed eight thousand neophytes at San Felipe, and in letters to the Jesuit Provincial, Rodrigo de Cabredo, expressed in enthusiastic terms his satisfaction with what the Black Robe was doing for the native Indian.[1] Such was the Augustinian Gonzalo de Hermosillo, first Bishop of Durango, who, as we have seen, visited in 1622 the various Jesuit missions east of the divide and, delighted with the progress he beheld, especially in the Laguna region, wrote his appreciation to the Jesuit Provincial Laurencio, in terms similar to those of del Valle. "It has appeared clearly to me," wrote His Excellency of Guadalajara, in 1611, "how much the Church, His Majesty, and the Society owe to these fathers for the noble progress they have made in those districts and for the great sufferings they endure amongst their savage charges."[2]

The first Bishop of Durango wrote to the General Mutius Vitelleschi in 1622 after visiting the missions of Santa María de las Parras: "I am able to offer a thousand congratulations to Your Paternity for the happy results which the fathers of the Society have achieved in these parts. . . . I am very affectionately grateful to Your Paternity and to all the other fathers for the great benefits they confer upon these Indians and for my part I offer myself with all my energy to help them and to serve them in these missions."[3]

These two bishops before their elevation to the episcopal throne had themselves belonged to the regular clergy. This was probably an additional factor making for their sympathetic view of Jesuit missionary endeavor. However, bishops who were not members of the regular clergy, such as in the sixteenth century the great Don Vasco de Quiroga, Bishop of Michoacán, were also strongly in favor of the Jesuits. So were innumerable others. During the 1640's, however, there occurred a famous crisis in Mexican ecclesiastical history, known as the Palafox controversy, between Don Juan de Palafox y Mendoza, Bishop of Puebla, and the Jesuits of his diocese.

Palafox, though friendly and favorable to the Jesuits in the beginning of his administration, became in the course of time as inimical as he had formerly been amicable, and the bitter quarrels and law suits which ensued and which were exacerbated by the imprudence of individual Jesuits themselves, served to accelerate a movement. Individual Jesuits had not always acted prudently with the bishops, nor always in other matters. One Jesuit accepted the invitation to act as judge in a suit against the Bishop of Durango's vicar-general. The bishop was Don Diego de Quintanilla Evía y Valdés, who had the unique honor of dedicating the high altar of the cathedral church of Durango on November 3, 1652.[4] The Jesuit General, Goswin Nickel, in a letter of December, 1652, to the Mexican Provincial Calderón complained of such imprudence in one of his subjects, for the Bishop had angrily stated that the Jesuits had made themselves judges against His Excellency.[5] Another Jesuit in a moment of indiscretion consented to carry to Europe for a friend (thinking thus to evade the customs) a treasure box of silver and jewels. The friend in Mexico wanted it carried to a friend in Spain. But the good padre was caught trying to smuggle in the box. The thing had been done a thousand times; but on this particular occasion a Jesuit had been detected trying to smuggle in treasure. The matter gained widespread notoriety.

The box containing the silver and jewels was sent to the Council of the Indies, and King Philip IV was angered at this scandalous disclosure. General Goswin Nickel took the affair very seriously, as well he might, and wrote to the Provincial of the Province of New Spain, Father Juan Real, the following: "As this imprudent action stirred an uproar and angered the King and his ministers . . . I am obliged to take effective measures lest it occur again and lest the Society again be discredited as it was on this occasion."⁶

So far as the Tarahumar missions are concerned, some pressure and disturbance were felt as the result of the agitations of Don Juan de Palafox, Bishop of Puebla. Then the incumbency of Bishop Evía y Valdés of Durango, 1640-1654, who was never overfriendly, coincided in time with the Palafox trouble.⁷

The general attitude of the higher clergy caused a repercussion in the missions, not only of the Jesuits, but likewise in those of the Franciscans. Bishop Evía y Valdés was not particularly friendly either to the Franciscans or to the Jesuits. He seemed to belong to the same school of thought as the Bishop of Puebla; indeed he had been consecrated by Palafox himself in 1640.⁸ In 1642 Evía y Valdés wanted to interfere in the Franciscan missions, which led Governor Valdés to pen a strong protest to the King under date of December 13, 1642. The Bishop, argued the Governor, had not sufficient men to spare for the missions, and since the missionaries had to live alone his clerics would never persevere in the work. Any such change of mission method would cause great disorder and confusion.⁹

In any case, when the rebellion of the Tobosos first broke out in 1644, the Bishop put the blame of the uprising upon the missionaries, having listened to tales of the fathers' harshness of treatment and cruelty toward their neophytes. Consequently, he had it in mind to take away certain missions from the Jesuits and put them into the hands of his own diocesan clergy. Indeed, he ordered Father Juan de Zepeda from his mission of Tizonazo.¹⁰ The Bishop was shortly disabused, however, and came to learn that it was not the severity of Franciscans and Jesuits which caused the uprising, but cruel treatment from the Spaniards and the instability of the savage under the orderly regime of the missions. Meanwhile, Father Zepeda's absence from Tizonazo made measures of peace more difficult, for the Indian inhabitants of the pueblo joined the rebels. The Bishop therefore allowed the father to return.¹¹

A few years later during the first uprising of the Tarahumares two of the Bishop's clerics accompanied Captain Juan de Barrasa on his punitive expedition. But the credit of these padres with the Indians was not so great as they had thought, and they assumed an authority over the Indian allies and even over the soldiers which caused a disastrous division in the ranks of Captain Barrasa. The Governor, learning of the conflict, ordered that the clerics be replaced by Father Vigilio Máez.[12]

Shortly after the advent of Diego Fajardo as Governor of Nueva Vizcaya the Bishop of Durango returned to his former plan and demanded that the Governor replace the Jesuits at Tizonazo and San Miguel de las Bocas by members of the secular clergy. The Governor, friendly to the Jesuits and with knowledge of their efficient handling of the missions, was nevertheless obliged to yield before the threats of ecclesiastical censure held over him by his bishop. Father José Pascual, superior of the missions of Baja Tarahumara, had recourse for the redress of this grievance to the nearest royal tribunal, the *audiencia* of Guadalajara.

This judicial body decreed by a document of February 7, 1652, that since these districts had been formally made over by the King to the former Jesuit Provincial, Pedro de Velasco, and since there existed no sufficient reason for the ejection of the Jesuit missionaries, these two missions be restored to the Society. This decree was confirmed by the Royal Council of the Indies, and both Tizonazo and Las Bocas were restored to the Jesuit missionaries.[13] The restoration of the two missions was a prudent action, for the Tarahumares were certainly not sufficiently mature in their Christianity to be able to be weened from the spiritual sustenance received from their padres.

The Generals in Rome viewed with concern these indications of changing policy on the part of some of the hierarchy. Just as serious was the intention of certain bishops to withdraw the regulars working in the missions from the immediate jurisdiction of their own superiors and rule them as they would their own secular clergy, selecting their candidate from three names which the Jesuit superior would advance and subjecting them to an examination as to their fitness for the work. The former was against all Jesuit privileges and even fundamentally contrary to the constitutions of the Order. General Mutius Vitelleschi wrote in 1644[14] to the then Provincial, Luis de Bónifaz, to the effect that it would be necessary, were such an arrangement enforced, to give up entirely the direction and possession of such and such a mission or *doctrina,* as the missions were sometimes called.[15]

Concerning Bishop Evía y Valdés, Goswin Nickel, in a letter of 1651, acting at the time as Vicar-General until a new general should be elected (he himself was chosen the following year), gives careful instructions to the Provincial Andrés de Rada, as to how the Bishop should be dealt with. He advises prudence, patience, and humility. He praises the fathers for having shown the Bishop their licenses to preach and hear confessions and advises even the undergoing of an examination should the Bishop insist upon it.[16] Nickel realized that the Bishop of Durango was ill-disposed toward the Society and he deprecated the imprudence of the Jesuit who had angered His Excellency by consenting to act as judge in a lawsuit, the outcome of which went against the Bishop's vicar in favor of Governor Fajardo.[17]

In 1646 a more serious blow fell upon the mission system of the eastern divide of the Sierra Madre, though it affected but indirectly the Tarahumar missions. Bishop Evía y Valdés determined to secularize, that is, to take from the direction of the Jesuits and organize as parishes under the secular clergy, the flourishing missions of the Laguna region southeast of the Tarahumares. The central mission of Parras alone remained under the direction of the fathers.

But the secular clergy were neither so skillful nor so energetic as the missionaries had been. The Jesuits were desolated to witness thereafter the neglect of so thriving a field and the relapse into old barbarities of those who once had been devout and civilized Christians living under the protection of the Black Robes. The superior at Parras, Gaspar de Contreras, writes a saddening report of this desolation to the Provincial Francisco de Calderón under date of May 1, 1653. Contreras has been able through some accidental visits to bring a little spiritual aid to the one-time Jesuit neophytes, but the weeds growing high in the once well-kept field saddened his heart.[18]

Such then were the administrative difficulties which the Jesuits experienced in or near the Tarahumar mission during the stormy 1640's. Things resolved themselves, however, in the middle of the following decade. Evía y Valdés was transferred to another see in 1654, becoming bishop of beautiful Oaxaca in the south. He departed from Durango in January of the following year. His successor was the Licenciado Don Pedro Barrientos y Lomelín, and though we learn from the records of no particular act which would in one way or another affect the missions of the Tarahumara, the absence in the record of trouble on this score would seem to indicate that he coöperated with those who were working so hard to make his vast diocese a fitter place to live in.[19]

By 1654 the whole legal crisis seems to have passed, for Goswin Nickel wrote that year to Provincial Juan Real stating that the Council of the Indies had decided in favor of the regulars. They would not have to be subject to the bishops but directly responsible to their own superiors. The Jesuits therefore could keep their missions.[20] The Tarahumares were assured of the permanence of the Black Robes, and the mission was destined, after an interlude following Basilio's death, to take up again the forward march.

Chapter XII

RECOVERY

THE MURDER of a missionary, considered always as martyrdom, was an event which spiritually consoled the members of the Society of Jesus, although, realistically, it meant the loss of a good man. Indeed, the early Jesuit missions in Florida never recovered from the blow dealt them when eight Black Robes were slain in 1571 by Don Luis, tribesman of Powatán, near the shores of the Chesapeake Bay. The slaughter of the eight who fell in the Tepehuán revolt did not destroy the Tepehuán mission, as we have seen, but gave it a staggering blow. Nor did the death of Beudin and then of Basilio destroy the Tarahumar mission, but these rebellions stopped for the time being all further organization along the fair banks of Río Papigochic, and for two more decades paganism continued to flourish upon its banks.

The southern Tarahumar missions continued on, and even Papigochic would come to life again and enjoy a long and prosperous career in missionary annals. As for the two martyrs, pride was felt in Rome because of their heroism, and we find the Jesuit General, Goswin Nickel, writing in May 1651 to the Mexican Provincial, Andrés de Rada, mentioning the honor to the Society of the martyr's death and asking for authentic details of the event so soon as they could be learned with certainty.[1] Nickel wrote again in August, 1658, that the promised account of the deaths of both the murdered missionaries had not yet arrived in Rome.[2]

For the following two decades, if the Tarahumar mission did not advance geographically, as the missions on the west coast were doing, they nevertheless consolidated their organization, matured in the Faith the Tarahumar nation, and laid the foundations for the advance which was later to take place. During the very time of Beudin's death Governor Diego Fajardo petitioned the fathers for a permanent residence, and eventually for a college of the Jesuits in Parral, as there had from the beginning existed a permanent residence and then a college in Durango. The petition went to Rome. Provincial Andrés de Rada sent it and himself pressed the General for the granting of this per-

[1] For notes to chapter xii see page 248.

mission, expatiating on the fitness for such a foundation in the town and upon the excellent qualities of the countryside. The General assented to the establishment of both residence and college, but the latter should depend on a suitable financial endowment. The residence had to await sufficiently propitious times. By 1668 a new chapel had been dedicated to St. Francis Xavier, but a Jesuit house was not to be set up for some years to come.

We possess today after three hundred years very precise information as to the state of the Tarahumar mission after the abandonment of the Río Papigochic venture. The historian is grateful that the Black Robes wrote letters, that they sent in reports to their superiors, and that they told how things were going in the field.

Gerónimo de Figueroa was an outstanding personality in the Tarahumar missions at this period. He had already labored among the Tepehuanes for seven years. He came to the Tarahumares as superior, as will be remembered, with José Pascual in 1639 when the mission was first organized by the Provincial Pérez de Ribas. Figueroa had held his office fourteen years when he was relieved of the burden which was taken up by José Pascual. Figueroa seems to have weakened somewhat or to have wearied and to have undergone a loss of courage to face the isolation, the monotony, or a dozen other desolations of missionary life on the frontier. After ten years of labor among the Tarahumares he wrote early in 1649 to General Vincent Caraffa, asking to be allowed to retire to a college of the Society. He alleged various reasons, one being that he had already spent seventeen years in the missions. In the same letter he offered constructive observations concerning matters he considered necessary for the good government of the pueblos. Since Vincent Caraffa died before he could answer this letter, Vicar-General Floriano Montmorency took notice of Figueroa's letter.

Vicar Montmorency wrote in September, 1649, to the Mexican Provincial, at that time our old friend Pedro de Velasco, advising that the father be allowed to retire since his alleged reasons seemed to be sufficient, and instructing that the suggestions offered for the better government of the missions be given consideration in the presence of the four provincial consultors. If any suggestion should seem advisable for the better organization and working of the missions it should be actually adopted.[3]

There was one effect of Figueroa's petition to the General: he was relieved of his headship of the Tarahumar mission, but he was not allowed to retire. What his suggestions were to his superiors and whether they were accepted we do not know. We do know, however, that ten years after he had asked to retire he was still in the mission; indeed, twenty years later he was not only not retired, but was active enough and interested enough to write precise and valuable reports concerning his particular mission of San Pablo and about the Tarahumar nation and mission in general.'

The Tarahumar picture for the two decades following the martyrdom of Basilio is not unattractive. It shows a substantial prosperity and continued progress. There remained as formerly five sections or *partidos* each in charge of a missionary. Each partido had one or more visitas; San Pablo, where Figueroa resided, had two, each with a church and house for the missionary. This organization had all been accomplished since Figueroa's entering the mission in 1652 or shortly before. And as we look into the record we find that in various settlements of Baja Tarahumara the Tepehuán was often intermixed with the Tarahumar. The reports constantly bear witness to the fertility of the countryside in and about Parral, and indeed, since it is today still charming, still fertile in its rolling hills and luscious valleys, we can understand the enthusiasm of the seventeenth-century missionary.

San Pablo, particularly, was in a prosperous condition, or perhaps the good Figueroa exaggerates a little for his own. Each mission pueblo owned herds of cows and of sheep, and quantities of oxen, mares, and mules. These pastured in meadows kept green by irrigation, the water being drawn from the streams near which the missions were always placed. With the natural fertility of the land in field, river, and wood, the Christian neophytes were able not only to raise what was necessary for their sustenance, thus making the missions self-supporting, but, tutored by the padres, to conserve in times of abundance what would be good to have in periods of drought or famine. The neophytes were often able to barter a surplus of beans and corn with the Spanish miners for ornaments and articles of clothing.

A medicinal herb, Figueroa reports, was discovered at this time, at least first brought to the notice of the missionaries, which if taken once or twice in *atole* or gruel made from corn, cured afflictions of various kinds including boils and venereal diseases.

It was a distinct help in the encouragement of neophytes that Figueroa was able to provide ornaments of various kinds for his church at San Pablo, which he boasts was the finest in the whole of Tarahumara. By 1668 four new churches had been dedicated, the last being that of San Miguel de las Bocas. Here was Father Rodrigo del Castillo. He had labored hard to get his new church completed, so that as the time approached for its dedication the padre enjoyed a supreme satisfaction. For this new church was decorated with statues, laces and cloths for the altar, and with pictures to adorn the walls. Such ornamentations delighted the childish mind of the poor savage. Being thus attracted, the neophytes, especially the young, were led to take an interest in fitting themselves for taking part in the service. Therefore, as the Jesuits had done from the beginning among the other tribes and nations, so here, too, among the Tarahumares, they taught the youngsters to play on musical instruments and to sing. Those who had learned to sing were then formed into a choir with which to grace festal occasions and to sing for the more solemn Mass which would be celebrated on such feasts. Thus Father Rodrigo del Castillo had trained a choir of Indian boys who became famous in the country and were invited to sing at solemn occasions in the missions and pueblos about Parral. These undoubtedly would give their best efforts at the approaching dedication of their own church. Alas, the dedication was to be a thing of sorrow rather than of joy. Shortly before the glad event, while the missionary and his boys were returning from a dedication near Tizonazo where they had sung, they were fallen upon by a party of savage Tobosos, and five Spaniards and all the choir boys were killed. Castillo himself escaped with his life after being kidnapped and subjected to atrocious treatment.

The feasts of Blessed Mary the Virgin were given an especial solemnity, with the days of such saints as Anna, Mary's mother, Gerónimo, Ignatius Loyola, Francis Xavier, and the apostles Peter and Paul. The training of the boys gave a touch of culture to their savagery, and when to this was added, whenever possible, instruction in the learning of Spanish, both in reading and in writing, we can understand that the Indian must have taken on some tincture of refinement from association with these arts. The padre tells us that the Indians became Hispanicized. True, they did not always live as saints, they might even appear at times to have strayed definitely from the fold of the Church, but it was noticed that even such backsliders, when the hour of death approached, called for the padre and desired through the sacraments to be purified and strengthened for the dread departure.

Figueroa did another service to the mission as well as to future scholarship, for he compiled two treatises in the native languages, one in the Tepehuán speech, the other in Tarahumar. Each treatise consisted of a grammar, a dictionary, a catechism, together with the translation of the principal prayers and the manner of going to confession. The originality of such a work can be imagined. Its value for the incoming missionary was beyond praise, and the good padre had reason to be proud of his work, as indeed he was, for he tells us that through these instruments new missionaries coming fresh into the country were able immediately to begin work among the neophytes in preaching, catechizing, and hearing confessions.[5] Thus it was that years before Juan Bautista de Velasco had written a grammar and dictionary of the Cáhita language, Santarén of the Xiximi, and Oracio Carochi of the Otomí. Thus did many others. Well, then, does Macaulay in a moment of expansive generosity, aver that the Jesuits "preached and spoke in tongues of which no man born in the West understood a single word."[6] Other missionaries, of course, did the same. Many of the Tarahumares understood the Mexican or Aztec language. This knowledge facilitated the work of the missionaries, for the fathers were all adept in this idiom, knowledge of it being required for the missionaries and necessary for admission to the profession of the four vows.[7]

But the fathers had their trials. There were still continuing in the decades of the 'fifties and 'sixties the same complaints which had been voiced years before, namely the Spaniard's lack of interest in the Indian's spiritual and moral welfare. The miners and ranchers continued selfishly to oppress the Indian, forcing him to labor for little or nothing, or actually enslaving him. The government officials looked on idly or engaged in the nefarious behavior themselves. Father Figueroa complained bitterly of the laxity of the officials regarding the external governance of the province at least in the extreme northern parts. Moreover, when depredations were made and crimes committed by unbaptized Indians no punishment was meted out by the Spanish officials so that recurrence became more frequent. The result was that robberies were continually perpetrated and the roads and highways rendered unsafe.

Three invasions of the Tobosos from the east occurred between 1662 and 1672.[8] It was in one of these, late in 1667, that Father Castillo and his party were attacked and his choir boys slain. Indeed, the padre was the only one to escape alive. The hostiles kidnapped him and dragged him along with them in their forays for three or four days over the rough country. When he was half dead the robber band came to the presidio of Cerro Gordo. Only four soldiers were there to guard the place, the rest being off with their captain on an expedition. The soldiers were overpowered, but not killed because of the pleadings of the padre, for whom even these savages had some respect. The Indians took what horses they could lay their hands on and made off, leaving the padre behind with the unhorsed soldiers at the presidio. Fortunately the captain soon came in with his soldiers accompanied by Father Bernabé de Soto.

Father Castillo never recovered from the blow. His own church was soon to be dedicated, but his little choir boys had been killed. Though revealing symptoms of serious illness, he insisted in going on with preparations for the dedication of his new church at San Miguel de las Bocas. He was frightfully weak and dizzy before Mass. While celebrating he was scarcely able to complete the Holy Sacrifice. In fact, he was dying while at the altar and he celebrated his own funeral, for within a few hours of that dedicatory Mass Castillo was dead. A native of Puebla, he had entered the Society of Jesus as a boy and labored for some twenty years on the Tarahumar mission. He was forty-six or forty-seven when he died.[9]

Drunkenness was among the vices which the missionaries had to contend with. From corn the savages brewed a very strong drink. It is likewise well known that they drew powerful stimulants from the fermented juice of the maguey and cactus. In such beverages the Tarahumar indulged to the point of complete intoxication. The Dutch and French at this same period were selling whiskey to the Indians of northeast North America; the Indians of the southwest made their own, yet the evil effects upon the latter seem not to have been quite so fierce and destructive as they were upon the Iroquois, the Hurons, and the Algonquins.

But in spite of trials and vicissitudes of various kinds—drunkenness, raids of wild Tobosos, repeated visits of the plague—the mission work advanced. Groups of Indians came down each year from the upland wilds of the sierra country to join the Christian pueblos and to ask for baptism, and in and about Parral there was being built up a solid bloc of Christian Tarahumares. Figueroa contended that even if the mission declined, it would always be necessary to have fathers in the district. Infant mortality was great. Especially the first born die, said the padre. The adults were not always greatly concerned about their offspring, and often when the little ones were sick they were left to die. Therefore, concluded the missionary, if for no other reason than for the baptism of these abandoned infants and of all the infants, the fathers must never be withdrawn from these lands, in order that through the administration of the holy sacrament the spirits of the very young be prepared for Heaven.[10]

Disquietude continued in this troublesome mission and on the still more troublesome frontier. Father Juan de Sarmiento, working at Satevó, hearing rumors of rebellion and invasion, was about to flee the pueblo, and was already mounted on his horse when conscience struck him hard. He felt that he was running away from danger and abandoning the souls of his poor neophytes. He turned about, returned to his pueblo, and remained.[11] There was a plague in 1666 and again in 1668, and an aversion to the last sacraments was noted by the padres as a remnant of the former rebellion and apostasy.

To help remedy these evils and to gain the protection of Heaven the new Governor of Nueva Vizcaya, Don Antonio de Oca y Sarmiento, resolved to have a chapel built in honor of St. Francis Xavier and to dedicate the town of Parral to him. The Bishop of Durango, Don Juan de Gorospe y Aguirre, was in full accord. It was a happy circumstance that at this time the Jesuit Visitor of all the missions, Father Eugenio López of Durango, was inspecting his Tarahumar pueblos, and in December, 1669, happened to be in Parral. He was requested by the Alcalde Mayor, Don Antonio Joaquín de Sarriá, to officiate at the dedication of the chapel on the feast of the saint, which was December 3. Although the prospective residence of the Jesuits had not yet been founded in Parral, the presence of the Visitor and other Jesuits added grace and prestige to the occasion.

Here on this far northern frontier and in a mining town one of those flamboyant religious celebrations, so dear to the heart of the Spaniard, was carried on for three days. The secular clergy joined with Jesuits and Franciscans in officiating at the services. The first day the Jesuits, the second the Franciscans, finally the diocesan clergy, chanted the solemn Mass. Silver and gold adornments were in abundance. A statue of St. Francis Xavier shone in white and yellow and a painting of him was similarly adorned. The Jesuit superior, Eugenio López, preached with applause from his listeners. Processions marched around the church, soldiers attended in gala uniform, and the townspeople took advantage of the spiritual feast to make merry in sundry secular ways. At night magic lanterns, bonfires, and fireworks illuminated the town and reddened the sky. At such a time the effect of the Jesuit training of the Indians was in evidence, for the missionaries had brought in their choirs of Indian boys from the near-by missions, and at the solemn Mass and Benediction the sweet and silvery voices of young Tarahumares touched the hearts of the devout Spaniards.[12]

By the late 1660's the Franciscans had founded missions in the distant north near those ancient ruins of Chihuahua called Casas Grandes. When the heroic missionary Fray Pedro de Aparicio died there his neophytes asked that he be replaced. Governor Don Antonio de Oca y Sarmiento wrote to the Viceroy, urging the continuance of the mission at Casas Grandes, as a link between the south and those other Spanish settlements which lay to the north beyond a thousand miles of desert in what is now New Mexico. Moreover, some Spaniards were settling in the district and it became necessary, therefore, that the natives be under the influence of the padres.[13]

Thus while the Franciscans were working north and northeast, the Jesuits were laboring north and northwest. This had been for decades the arrangement, rather understood than expressed. Soon the Tarahumar mission would make a great advance. It was being prepared for by the arrival of fresh missionaries: Father Juan de Sarmiento, who was ordered to Satevó in 1665, and Father Pedro de Escalante, who went to San Felipe on the Conchos the same year or near it.[14]

Chapter XIII

TARAHUMARA SPREADS ITS MISSIONS

THAT OLD veteran, Father Gerónimo de Figueroa, by the year 1668, the time of his last report, had labored for thirty-six years in the missions east of the Sierra Madre. Twenty-nine had been spent in Tarahumara since his coming in 1639. Yet, Figueroa was still there, among his Tarahumares, in the early 'seventies, and he witnessed the beginnings of a development which should have delighted his heart. He had grown old in these missions, so that the knowledge that additional Jesuits were being sent here must have gladdened his spirit.

The year was 1673. Two decades plus one year had passed since the slaying of Jácome Antonio Basilio and twenty-three years since the murder of Cornelio Beudin, alias Godínez. In Europe Louis XIV, King of France, was rising to his sun of glory, and James of England, Duke of York, had just united the American colonies by taking New Amsterdam from the Dutch. But Spain's power was on the wane. An infantry, for centuries invincible, had gone down before the legions of Richelieu, and decadence was visible to the eye in the person of the effete Hapsburg, King Charles II.

Not so, however, some of the instruments which Spain had been using for her material advancement. Within the bosom of the Church existed forces which seemed partly beyond the touch of Time's withering hand. In this particular edge of Spain's frontier in the New World the Franciscans had consolidated the frontier of New Mexico and the Jesuits had organized the west coast and the eastern slope of the sierra. Between them these orders had helped to vitalize and stabilize the frontier. The secret of this continued energy was a corporate will energized by ideals which were spiritual. In 1673 the Tarahumar missions became thus revitalized. The city of Parral had been dedicated, as we have seen, in 1668, to the patron of all Catholic missions, St. Francis Xavier, by the pious *teniente del gobernador* of Nueva Vizcaya, Don Antonio Joaquín de Sarriá. His intention was to place Parral, nerve center of the Tarahumar missions, under the heavenly protection of the saint, that the enemies of the missions, ex-

[1] For notes to chapter xiii see pages 248-249.

ternal (the Tobosos) as well as internal, hechiceros and rebels, might weaken before the increasing strength of the Christian Indians. The ancient chronicler and historian of the Mexican Jesuits, Francisco Xavier Alegre, attributes the developments which followed to the special intervention of the saint.[1]

Seeing then that the inroads of the inimical Tobosos from the east had quieted down and that the interior state of the existing Tarahumar mission had for a period of time been prosperous and tranquil, the successor to Don Antonio de Oca y Sarmiento as governor of Nueva Vizcaya determined with his fresh energy to advance the frontier of Spain in the New World by extending the frontier of Christianity and the missions. The name of the new governor was Don José García de Salcedo; his chief interested subordinate, his teniente or lieutenant, alcalde mayor of Parral, who fell in completely with his designs, was Don Francisco de Agramonte. The Governor of Nueva Vizcaya and his lieutenant called a meeting at Parral, which was the most important gathering of notables that the frontier town had witnessed since its dedication to St. Francis Xavier five years before. The purpose was to discuss the advance of the Tarahumar mission.[2]

Let us not be mistaken. Though Governor Salcedo seems to have been a spiritual man, he was governor of a material state, and his concern was not only for the Church but also, and possibly more zealously, for the State. Spaniards, as we have seen, were beginning to settle far to the north, in the vicinity of Casas Grandes. The mines near Santa Bárbara and Parral had been most lucrative. The precious metal, men thought, might be still farther north. It was to the interests of Spain and of the income of the King that the prosperity of the citizens of New Spain increase. This required that the country be settled in enduring Christian peace and order, that the mission advance and be made permanent.

Therefore in such a meeting as the Governor called at Parral in 1673 there was present, representing the mineowners, Don Juan de Siliases; representing the military, Diego de Quiroz and Pedro de Pozo; representing the Church, Don Juan Ignatión Leitón and Don Juan Tello, both sent by the Bishop. Attending these churchmen were other members of the diocesan clergy. Most importantly, perhaps, for the business at hand, were the four Jesuits: Father Gabriel de Villar, missionary at Huejotitlán, Pedro de Escalante, of Las Bocas, Martín de Prado, at Figueroa's old mission of San Pablo, and Francisco de Valdés, from San Felipe on the Conchos. Two new missionaries likewise attended—Fathers Fernando de Barrionuevo and Juan Manuel de Gamboa. Last but not least, mentioned last by way of emphasis, was the scarred spiritual warrior of the Tarahumares, Gerónimo de Figueroa, now again superior of the whole Tarahumar mission unit.

Indians, too, were present, called in by the Governor: Tepehuanes and Tarahumares, since the two nations were mixed in the country around Parral. Among these Indians especially conspicuous was Cacique Don Pablo, known and respected by both nations. It seemed to the fathers then laboring among the Tarahumares that the fidelity to the Faith and loyalty to the Black Robes of this distinguished chieftain was not without especial design of Providence. He had been converted twenty years before and ever since had remained steadfast in the Faith.[3]

It was in this meeting called by the Governor that the prosperous and expansive future of the Tarahumar mission was born. The conference took place September 30, the Feast of San Gerónimo, patron of Huejotitlán, among the oldest of the Tarahumar Christian settlements. The venerable Father Figueroa with thirty-four years of missionary labor to his credit gave the substantial contribution of the whole meeting. He spoke for his highest superior in the Americas, the Provincial Andrés Cobián, uttering the Provincial message to the assembled mineowners, civil officers, ecclesiastics, and Indians.[4] The two new fathers, Barrionuevo and Gamboa, said the Jesuit speaker, had been sent into the north for the sole purpose of laboring among the pagan savages beyond the fringes of the settled pueblos; they had been sent by the Provincial to found new pueblos and organize new Christian settlements. Figueroa reminded his hearers that the sole design of the Society of Jesus in sending valuable men into the pagan wilds was to gain souls for Jesus Christ and that in this purpose the Society was happy in enjoying the encouragement of successive kings of Spain whose minds looked to the spiritual as well as to the temporal condition of their colonies.

Figueroa spoke of the causes which had effected a twenty-year pause in the territorial advance of the Tarahumar mission. The historian

Alegre wrote more than a century and a half ago: "[Figueroa] indicated with sufficient sagacity some of the causes of the past uprising concerning which certain persons tried in vain to place the responsibility upon the natural perfidy and inconstancy of the Indian."[5] Figueroa, we may be sure, was sufficiently pointed in his remarks on the chief cause of the troubles: the dastardly treatment meted out to the natives by miner and soldier alike. The latter apparently tried to disavow responsibility, but unsuccessfully. Since Governor Salcedo was a pious man, and probably honest, he may have realized the significance of the Jesuit argument. The Governor may have deprecated, as was his plain duty, such cruel treatment of the Indians, since the King had repeatedly denounced in royal cédulas the rapacious methods of his colonials. Perhaps the Spanish civilians present were honest enough to recognize the fact and to use their influence, since they were leaders in disciplining the civilian population and the military. At any rate, the speaker painted in vivid colors the sad state of this section of the province of Nueva Vizcaya and let them know the fault was their own. Spanish greed and selfishness were the chief causes of the rebellions.

Figueroa wound up with an exhortation to the civilian population to emulate the desire and zeal of the King for the conversion, reduction, and pacification of the primitives who were included in or who were neighboring on the province of Nueva Vizcaya. With such conversion and pacification, argued the padre, there was intimately linked "the prosperity of the whole Kingdom of Nueva Vizcaya: the safety of the highways, the freedom of commerce, traffic with the mines, and all those more particular interests which the Spanish civil frontiersmen could have at heart."[6]

The modern reader can understand that this discourse on the part of the veteran Jesuit missionary was delivered with some ardor and persuasiveness. Since it is not difficult in the first flush of emotion to lead the Spaniard to generous action, those who were present became infected with the enthusiasm of the padre and expressed themselves as willing and even eager to forward the best interests of Nueva Vizcaya, and they let it be known that since the Governor was strong in his desire for pacification and conversion, they stood ready to coöperate with the Jesuit missionaries in an enterprise so beneficial to themselves and so glorious for Spain and for the Church.[7]

For their part the Tarahumares present, led by their chief Don Pablo, promised complete coöperation with these express desires. Let the Governor rest assured that he, Don Pablo, chief of the Tarahumares, would do all in his power to further the activities of the fathers for the Christianization of his tribesmen. The cacique promised the Governor in the name of the Indians who were present, indeed, in the name of the whole nation, that they would assist the fathers in their travel to the interior of their country, in choosing suitable sites for the organization of Christian pueblos, and in building houses and churches necessary for the missions. Chief Don Pablo himself promised to take an active personal part in the working out of these details. Governor García de Salcedo, in the name of the King of Spain, graciously accepted the proffered assistance of the Tarahumar chief and dismissed the assembly in an atmosphere of enthusiastic good will.

The concluding gesture of the Governor was significant, and to the northern peoples of the New World today, piously picturesque. He imitated the action of his predecessor, Urdiñola, among the Xiximes a half century before, and of Governor La Vesca among these very Tarahumares: the Governor knelt before the Jesuit superior of the missions, Figueroa, and in this position of respect and humility kissed his hands. The other Spaniards present did the same and then the Indians imitated their conquerors and rulers. It was thus exceedingly beneficial, even necessary, to heighten the prestige of the padre in the eyes of the Indian and to let the primitives realize that behind this kindly black-robed missionary stood the whole nation of the Spaniards with their governors and their King.

Thus did a historic assembly end. The impulse given led to the reëstablishment of the broken mission of Papigochic, to the evangelization of the northern Tarahumares, to the founding of Chihuahua, and the creeping of the Spanish frontier north still nearer to the borders of the present United States. We have in this meeting and its constructive spirit the birth of the modern Mexican state of Chihuahua and an important step in the linking of the far isolated region of Santa Fe with the more southern regions of the kingdom of New Spain.

A Spanish convocation, assembly, meeting, junta, or fiesta of the seventeenth century seldom if ever lasted only for a day. When the chapel in Parral was dedicated five years before the celebrations lasted for three days. So now, though the assembly had been dismissed with its work successfully accomplished, the celebrations continued for a three-day period. Parral had never before been the scene of a concourse so great. Its importance as a frontier town was increasing; as an outpost of empire it was thickening its fortifications and strengthening its bastions. The year 1673 should be ever memorable in the annals of the city.

There was no delay in inaugurating the mission activity which had been decided upon in the assembly. After completing the necessary preparations for a continued residence in the wilds of northern Tarahumara, Fathers Fernando de Barrionuevo and Juan Manuel de Gamboa departed from Parral on the first day of November, 1673. With them was the loyal cacique, Don Pablo, a number of his fellow tribesmen, and a group of Spaniards trudging north to make their homes or find their fortunes on the northern edge of the frontier.[8] It is true that Barrionuevo's strength could not stand the first winter's ordeal. His health broke and he had to go south again to be stationed ultimately at Satevó. But he was replaced by a spiritual and energetic spirit, José Tardá, who with Tomás de Guadalajara, soon to arrive, would found new pueblos, reach new Indians, advance the frontier, and, last but not least, leave future generations a magnificent account of their activity.

Indeed, all the Jesuit mission system in Mexico's northwest was to take on a new lease of life, for a fresh stream of its very life's blood had recently been opened to it. Formerly through an ultra-national policy of the kings of Spain, foreigners were not permitted in the colonies, not even as priests for the advance of the missions. The prohibition had been anciently published officially and thereafter renewed. Hence the necessity, in a few exceptional cases, of changing the names of an Irishman like Michael Wading, who came to the Sinaloa missions in the 1620's, to the familiar sounding Miguel Godínez; and of changing our Tarahumar hero's Belgian name of Beudin likewise to Godínez, his first name being written in the Spanish form as Cornelio. It was this restriction which partly explains the lapse generally in the missionary advance which the country suffered in the 1630's and accounts for a general shortage which acted as a chronic disability.[9] The Jesuit Vicar, Floriano Montmorency, governing the Society of Jesus after the death in 1649 of Vincent Caraffa, deeply regrets in a letter to the Mexican Provincial, Andrés de Rada, his inability because of the statute to send more men to the missions. "Certainly," he writes in December, 1649, "the Provinces of Spain alone . . . cannot supply all the subjects which are necessary for the Indies, and it is necessary that we look around for a remedy . . . that the evils which we rightfully fear may not take place." All influence, continues the Vicar, will be brought to bear upon the government in Madrid that the thing be remedied. And he concludes: "I hope that our very strong reasons will force His Majesty and lead him to take compassion on the innumerable souls which will perish for want of evangelical ministers if the gate be not opened . . . for the passage to the Indies of those of Ours who are not Spaniards." [10]

Sixteen years elapsed before the King, or rather the Council of the Indies, was persuaded that the narrowness of their policy with respect to foreigners was a hindrance to the frontier provinces of the Americas, simply because those stabilizers of the frontier, the missionaries, could not reach the necessary man power. General John Paul Oliva writes in exultant terms in a letter of November 29, 1664, announcing the lifting of the ban on foreign missionaries and thanking God for the spiritual favor thus granted the mission system. [11]

Oliva worked out a system for the necessary financing of the men who would travel from the different European provinces to the Jesuit missions functioning in both the Americas, whether these missionaries be Spaniards or not. It amounted to this: the European provinces would supply the men, the provinces of the New World would supply the money. Computing that the yearly expenses for the training in Europe of each individual would not surpass the sum of one hundred Spanish pesos deposited in Spain, and that six years would be required for the spiritual and intellectual training of a man in Europe before he would be ready to leave for the missions, the different Spanish provinces of the New World, namely Mexico, Peru, and Paraguay, should place the amount of six hundred pesos for six years for each missionary they were expecting to draw from Europe. Since the Council of the Indies conceded to Mexico each six years twenty-four Jesuit missionaries, the sum of fourteen thousand and four hundred pesos should be placed in Seville at the end of each six-year period by the Jesuit procurator of New Spain. To facilitate the collection of such a sum the amounts should be paid into the fund gradually each year. The date of this, Oliva's official provision, was 1672, just a year before the beginning of the second great Tarahumar advance.[12]

With the lifting of the prohibition on foreigners in 1664 and the financial arrangement made by Oliva in 1672 the expansion of all the mission system in northwestern New Spain was assured, and indeed, events justified the promise of prosperity. In the west, over the divide, four new missionaries arrived for the Sinaloa missions in 1673. This advent made possible the important pueblo of Babuyaqui in the Chínipas region and missionary activity on the fringes of the country of the Guazápares and Varohíos, where, in 1632, Pascual and Martínez had met death in a rebellion of those two tribes. Babuyaqui would lead to the reopening of the Chínipas missions and this would bring the mission system working through the mountains east from Sinaloa into contact with the missions of the Tarahumares, now on the threshold of their expansion north and west.[13]

To the Tarahumares went as we have seen Fathers Barrionuevo and Gamboa; Tardá and Guadalajara. Another decade and Kino, Salvatierra, Ugarte, Pícolo, would go into the mission world and carry the frontiers north to what is now Arizona and west across the Gulf to Baja California. But among the Tarahumares Tardá and Guadalajara would inaugurate by a splendid career the great advance, and their success would cause still others to be sent into the field.

Chapter XIV

TWO GREAT APOSTLES

THE YEAR 1673, then, marks the period of a new spurt of energy in the activities of the Tarahumar missions as in those of the west coast. The withdrawal of the prohibition against missionaries of non-Spanish blood remedied the long standing shortage of men, and the ever-present desire of the Jesuit General in Rome and of the Provincial in Mexico City for the advancement of the missions combined with Spanish official desire for the advance of the frontier gave the additional push which resulted in the meeting at Parral in 1673.

We have seen that the two Black Robes first assigned to renew the advance north deeper into Tarahumara were Gamboa and Barrionuevo. Unfortunately both of them were soon forced through ill health to drop out of the work they loved so well. That first winter in the wilds, the winter of 1673 and 1674, was too much for Barrionuevo. Food of the rawest and coarsest kind—roots, berries, wild honey, and weeds—though it did not disturb an Indian's digestion, was harmful to the padre. Such a diet, added to the constant exposure he was subject to—nights on the damp ground under the cold stars—began the aches and pains of rheumatism which his body was unable to endure. Therefore, the early spring of 1674 he was recalled from "roughing it" beyond the frontier and placed at Satevó on the banks of the Río Satevó, tributary of the San Pedro. At San Francisco de Javier mission in the sweeping mesas of north central Mexico Father Barrionuevo could still be a missionary, yet somewhat shielded from hardships beyond the limit of his strength.[1]

Manuel Gamboa was able to endure the physical hardships longer than his companion and completed the year 1674 beyond the northern Tarahumar frontier. He worked for a while with the successor of Barrionuevo, José Tardá. On February 13, 1674, these two missionaries, aided by the ever-present and efficient influence and diplomacy of Chief Don Pablo, entered and united three small rancherías called Guitzochi, Corachi, and Cusihuiriachic[2] into one mission which they named San Bernabé, after Barnabas, companion of St. Paul.

---

[1] For notes to chapter xiv see page 249.

Cusihuiriachic, or San Bernabé, still lies near the headwaters of the Río Satevó, where a broad mesa has been broken down with time into a wooded canyon winding southwest. Later, mines were discovered in this canyon, a gold-rush took place and the mission was disturbed. The mines are still there and a railroad from Chihuahua carries out the ore. About this same period San Francisco de Borja was founded, thirty-five miles west of Satevó, and near Santa Ana.

Gamboa before his collapse had been working at San Bernabé. Success was only slight, however, because evil leaders in council tried to persuade the people not to admit the missionaries.[3] Among other activities Gamboa baptized an Indian girl of sixteen years whose body was covered with a loathsome leprosy, the stench of which was so nauseating that even her parents could not endure it. The missionary, true to the discipline of his Order, as St. Peter Claver at Cartegena among the Negroes, and Martín Pérez among the plague-stricken on the Sinaloa, approached the stricken and loathsome creature and spoke to her of Christianity, of the supernatural endurance of pain and disease, and of the possibility of saving her spirit through the waters of holy baptism. The girl was instructed, then baptized, and with health of soul came, miraculously says the old chronicler, also health of body. In any case, the record tells us that the maiden's skin became clean and she stood forth cured by baptism. Such an event enhanced the prestige of the sacrament among the savages, whereas just as the opposite—death after baptism—often caused trouble and sometimes gave an excuse for rebellion.[4]

José Tardá reported on these slight successes to his Provincial, Manuel de Arteaga, by a letter of February 24, 1674. One thing, wrote Tardá, hindering further progress was the devil himself, who at Remaichic, a day's journey from San Bernabé, walked about in the form of an old man persuading the people to have nothing to do with the padres. At least, we can say the old man was doing the Devil's work. But in spite of such hindrances missionaries were able to baptize seventy neophytes and they report that here at San Bernabé the number of baptized reached three hundred and seventy, *poco más o menos*. It consoled Tardá that in other pueblos of the Tarahumares, including far away Papigochic and Pachera, and even the bedeviled Remaichic, there were those who desired the ministrations of the Black Robes.[5]

About a year after his success in the miraculous baptism Gamboa's health, like Barrionuevo's, collapsed under the exposure and lack of all things which civilization had made necessary. Father Manuel Gamboa was replaced by a still greater man, and, it seems, a more successful apostle, Tomás de Guadalajara. By the summer, therefore, of 1675, two great apostles, José Tardá and Tomás de Guadalajara were alone in this distant and sequestered field of apostolic activity. They were a successful team, like Gonzalo de Tapia and Martín Pérez at the birth of the missions on the coast many decades before, like Kino and Campos later in northern Sonora, like Pícolo and Salvatierra in Lower California.

These two Jesuits were responsible for the successes which led to the evangelization of the remaining section of the Tarahumar nation to the west and to the north. This was sufficient accomplishment to give them their niche in history's hall of fame. But these two missionaries did more; they detailed the initial successes of the first year and some months in a most interesting report to their Provincial, Francisco Ximenes, in a letter of February 2, 1676. This letter was in response to the encouragement given them by their superior to go courageously forward into new lands seeking for souls.⁶ History, therefore, is grateful for these reports of their activity.

During this early missionary labor the Black Robes experienced the usual difficulties of the field which were to be followed by the beginnings of success. Cold reception or actual repulsion of the fathers alternated with warm or even enthusiastic acceptance. This encouragement often occurred after the Indians were in a position to observe the padres and to realize that their kindness was genuine and that these were not the men to bring unhappiness and disturbance to the pueblos and the rancherías.

Father Guadalajara seems to have been the leading spirit of the two and, in the summer of 1675 shortly after his arrival, he determined to make an entrada with his companion into Cárichic near the headwaters of a branch of the upper Conchos River, and to revisit that scene of former calamity, ruin, and massacre, Papigochic, in the beautiful river valley. Their starting point was Santa Ana in the midst of the plain on the upper San Pedro and some thirty miles east of Cárichic.

The two missionaries discovered that the inhabitants of the two pueblos, Papigochic and Cárichic, were unfriendly—indeed, that many were inimical. At Papigochic the Indians swore they would have the head of one of the fathers; from Cárichic the natives sent a message that no stranger would be permitted to enter their pueblo. The fathers then took steps to make possible an entrance into Temechic, lying between the other two villages, the pueblo which had been so loyal to Basilio in the uprising of 1652. The son of the Indian governor of Temechic had been baptized and the missionaries had been assured that should they come to the settlement others would receive baptism.

The two Black Robes then made their way south to Temechic and as they entered the village were reminded of past sorrows and warned of future dangers, for they beheld the ruins of the church which Jácome Basilio had begun before his violent death. Guadalajara and Tardá had only slight success. Most of the people were off on a hunt when the padres arrived, and those who remained had suffered their minds to be poisoned by a sower of cockle. This evil one announced to the natives in advance that they should beware of such harmful persons as the black-robed Spaniards. But with patience and kindness prejudices were overcome. The missionaries could always point out to the pagan Tarahumares their happy and contented Christian tribesmen in refutation of any reports to the contrary. The savages could not answer this argument and expressed themselves as willing to receive baptism on another visit of the fathers. So, unsuccessful for this time but not discouraged, the fathers returned to their original mission of Santa Ana, which they called by the double name of San Joachim and Santa Ana.[7]

Shortly after these initial activities of slight success, the fathers determined on another attempt to try to pierce the toughness of the prejudice of the Papigochic Tarahumares. They sent ahead to prepare the way the ever-loyal Don Pablo with twenty companions. The missionaries followed. On the road the fathers' experiences on entering Temechic were repeated: they passed the ruins of the church where Cornelio Beudin had been slain and where Basilio had labored for his few months of enthusiastic ministry.

Don Pablo and his group at first enjoyed success. The men of Papigochic seemed enthusiastic, even enramadas were put up for the reception of the Black Robes. That night, however, at a *tlatole,* or meeting, evil and discontented Indians gained the upper hand and emphasized the fact that they would not become Christians. But this disposition was not general. The Indian governor, the chief of a near-by ranchería, and a group of others said they would receive the fathers and be instructed when the influence of the present discontent should die away. Those well-disposed toward the fathers warned them that the present was not a convenient time in which to press their suit for they feared some violence by the prejudiced.

So, the missionaries retired from the town, and, pretending to lose their way, they created the occasion for wandering about and visiting near-by rancherías. This was the beginning of a grand tour of the Tarahumara country north and northwest. They penetrated almost fifty miles and reached the very northern edges of the nation. In other words, the missionaries and their group of Christian Tarahumares threaded down Río Papigochic, passing Mátachic, up to where the stream turns south on its winding way into Sonora where it is known as the Yaqui. Instead of following the stream, the missionaries faced northwest up a tributary to the village of Yepómera, one of the last of the Tarahumar pueblos.

The pilgrimage was peaceful and successful enough as a beginning of penetration. In the pueblos near Papigochic a certain number were baptized and a few others in other districts through which they passed, including an old man of a hundred years. Consolingly, the travelers met from time to time Tarahumares from the south who had been baptized before the rebellions and these, say the padres, behaved toward them as sons to fathers.

Returning leisurely upstream the party now risked an entrance into Papigochic. They found the spirit friendly, for the baptisms performed in the neighboring rancherías were known, and seeing that no harm was done, rather joy and happiness imparted, those of Papigochic did not resent the action, nor on this occasion did they resent the presence of the fathers among them. Encouraged by the change of heart the missionaries at their departure set up crosses in the pueblo with the intention of returning. They piously gave Christian names to the pueblos they had entered. Mátachic became San Rafael, Yepómera was named El Triunfo de los Angeles, and Papigochic was

called by its olden name, La Purísima, after the Immaculate Conception of Blessed Mary the Virgin. The traveling missionaries then returned to headquarters, one residing at Santa Ana, between Satevó
and Cárichic, the other living probably at San Francisco Borja. Other
pueblos in the meantime began to ask for a visit from the Black Robes.
This missionary work all took place in the early fall of 1675 and a report of it was soon thereafter indited for the Provincial and dated
October 4.[3]

Soon after this tour a remarkable success among the natives of
Cárichic fell to the lot of one of the padres. The men of Cárichic had
been coming over to Santa Ana begging for a visit from Tomás Guadalajara. The padre went on horseback, threading along the level reaches
of the upper San Pedro until he reached beyond a ridge the banks of
another stream running south. It was a tributary of the upper Conchos.
Here in a fertile vale lay beneath him the pueblo of Cárichic, its
rancherías spread along the rich soil of the running stream. The men
of Cárichic gave the padre a royal reception, making a fiesta of the
occasion. They had gathered fruits and had killed two sheep to regale
Father Guadalajara and the Christian Indians who accompanied him.
At the moment of the approach to the pueblo the Indians all came out
joyously to greet him. The father baptized a hundred on that day and,
when the ceremony was over, all—Christians and pagans, many on
horseback—formed themselves in procession carrying two large crosses.
One they planted at the beginning of their line of march and carried
the other to where they would halt and return, which was several miles
distant, for the rancherías fringing the stream were strung along some
distance. They marched then, planted the second cross, and retraced
their steps chanting the classic Christian hymn, *Vexilla Regis,* while
the padre on horseback, when the singing would stop, recited prayers,
especially the *oratorio crucis.*

Toward the end of the march as the enthusiasm rose the crowd was
carried away with emotion and they began to run around and to shout
as if in a riot. The Indians did this, wrote Guadalajara later, to con-
found the hechiceros who had tried to keep them away from the missionary. As they ran about and jumped and frolicked, they kept on
shouting *"Gueua garaucu Pare,"* which in the Tarahumar tongue
means *"Mui bien es el Padre,"* in English: "The father is all right." Those

on horseback did the same. The Black Robe compared the scene to the kind of riot which occurred among university students in Spain when one faction took the lecturing chair away from the other. We would compare it to the antics of high school students in a small town when, after a football game, the victors uproot goal posts and resort to other vandalisms. Here among the Tarahumares was a real but harmless riot, and the father could not repress it. He kept moving about on horseback in the midst of the rumpus reciting psalms and giving thanks to God.

Finally the crowd dispersed singing hymns. The padre says he was moved to tears and promised to come to live with them some day. Father Guadalajara seized the occasion to rename the pueblo. The day was the Feast of the Basilica of Our Savior, Friday, November 9, and the father took his cue from the words of the office for that day from the Canticle of Habacuc, "I will joy in God my Jesus." So he called the pueblo after the name of Jesus, and thus it was known from that time on as Jesucárichic, only a slight change from what it had been in the longer Tarahumar form of Guerucárichic.

The Indians promised Father Guadalajara to build a church and a house for the father. And they were as good as their word. In fifteen days a chapel with straw roof called a *xacal* was completed. Fiscals and catechists were appointed by the Black Robe to assure the continuation of the Christian spirit and the further instruction of the baptized and of those who desired to receive the sacrament. Others who had come from afar departed for their homes.[9] Thus on November 9, 1675, was founded the Christian pueblo of Cárichic, and a new center was added to the list in Christian Tarahumara.

The mission still exists and the ancient church which the missionaries later built upon the banks of the river still remains. Here, today, a Black Robe still attends his Tarahumares. Nuns aid him in the work with the children and on Sunday afternoons as the little Tarahumares, boys and girls, gather for the catechism and the benediction within these ancient walls, we are carried back over the centuries to the day when Guadalajara first carried the gospel to these simple children.

Nothing succeeds like success, it would seem, even with the missionaries. The impulse had been given by their understanding, their kindliness, and their tact. Other invitations came from other pueblos for the fathers to go visit and baptize them. The men of Napabechic went to Santa Ana and invited the padre to go to them too. But the pueblo was small and distant, being some twenty miles north of San Bernabé at Cusihuiriachic. One of the two padres did visit them to prepare the ground, but he thought it best not to begin baptism. Perhaps later, when it could be united with some other community and when a missionary could be free to give them more time baptisms could begin. Indeed, this is precisely what happened, and within two years the record shows that ninety-two Christians were living at Napabechic.

It will be recalled that the reception of Fathers Tardá and Guadalajara at the pueblo of Papigochic had not been unfriendly, although the residents were still influenced by an anti-Christian element. However, the fathers had been able to baptize the chief of the place and this man with nine of his principal tribesmen came to the mission of San Bernabé inviting them to revisit Papigochic. Tardá was most probably in residence at San Bernabé at the time and he accepted the invitation, making of it an occasion to depart again on an extended missionary tour. Unfortunately this second visit to Papigochic was not very successful. The Indians had gone on a drunken carousal and one of them carrying a knife had threatened the missionary. But contact was made with thirty people of the vicinity who had been baptized in the fall of 1675, and certain other happenings and incidents witnessed to the renewed faith of the Christian Indians. Between Papigochic and Temechic, which the missionary next visited, fifty were baptized.

Shortly after this success the two fathers did a daring thing. They accepted an invitation to visit the pueblo of Tutuaca, far to the west. A delegation had come a hundred miles over high mountain ridges and across deep barrancas to see the missionaries of the Tarahumares. Tutuaca lay almost directly west from the mission of San Bernabé. Many of the rebels had fled to this pueblo after the destruction of the Villa de Aguilar and the murder of Basilio. Here they had stored their loot, which the pursuing Spaniards discovered. The pueblo was on the very western fringe of the Tarahumar country, on a branch of the Río Papigochic called Río Tutuaca, which meets the main stream just east of the present boundary between Chihuahua and Sonora.

The pueblo, reports Tardá, was not purely or even chiefly Tarahumar, nor was this language spoken there. Its inhabitants boasted they were neither so indolent nor so wicked as the Tarahumares. These Indians were rather a mixture of Tepehuán and Tarahumar, and the language seemed to be a different idiom. As for the individual inhabitants, some considered themselves pure Tepehuán, others pure Tarahumar, still others a sort of mixture, or just pure Tutuac. An official Jesuit record of 1678 calls them Tepehuán.[11] The Tepehuán-Tarahumar blend in these Tutuacs seems to have been good, for they had among the Tarahumares proper the reputation of being strong warriors, and were enticed on this account to go east taking part in the rebellion which destroyed Aguilar and killed Basilio.

The journey of Tardá and Guadalajara to this western country was interesting. Instead of going directly west from their respective missions which would have been, as the crow flies, between eighty and ninety miles, the padres made a detour south in order to visit on the way some of the recently converted pueblos, and to see what new ones might be organized.

Leaving some weeks before Christmas, 1675, the fathers passed through Cárichic, and then turned north to Tejirachic, passing through Tosaboreachic, Temechic, Pachera, and on down the Río Papigochic to reach the pueblo by Christmas. They were successful, coming to Papigochic on the eve of Christmas, and were happy to celebrate Mass the following morning on the very spot, now covered by a newly made chapel, where Cornelio Beudin had been done to death.

After three days' sojourn in the now settled pueblo of Papigochic the wayfarers turned west with an Indian guide to make the last forty miles across the Río Tomochic and over one of the great ranges of the Sierra Madre down into the valley of Tutuaca. The trek on muleback may have been double the forty miles, for the country here is the roughest to be found in Tarahumara. Nor were the fathers, this time, impervious to the charm, or perhaps to the terror, of the wildness of the scene as they neared the high summit of the range and then began the descent. Like Salvatierra a decade later, a few miles south on the brink of the yawning chasm of the Río Urique, these two fathers stood in awe of the fearsome heights from which they gazed down into the ravines which formed the beginnings of the Río Tutuaca. "The heights from which we looked into the abyss," reported the padres, "were so great

TOP: *Nuestra Señora del Pilar de Norogachic*; left: *the courtyard of Jesús Cári-chic*; right: *the old mission church of San Marcos de Píchachic.*

that objects seemed to fade from view and the pines which are immense in the depths of the canyon seemed from the summit to be but the size of a man." Precipices, rocky declivities, narrow and breathtaking ledges of rock might well have affrighted braver hearts.[12] Though these summits are usually covered with snow in the winter time, fortunately this year there was none. Some of the trails were so perilous that the missionaries suspected their guides of treachery in leading them through unnecessarily dangerous spurs and rocky declivities.

The wildest people lived here in the sequestered folds of the sierra, entirely cut off from any contact with the lower country. At the approach of strangers they usually did one of two things—fly like frightened deer, or hide away in order to attack suddenly from the crevices of the rocks. It was learned that these wild "cimarrones," as the padres called them, were persuaded of the most extreme superstitions concerning the missionaries: that their approach meant their ruin, that all crops would fail and living things cease to grow upon their land. By contrast with this atmosphere, the fathers noted some crosses carved upon a pine, the sight must have stirred their spirits. Spaniards had once trod these dizzy heights in search of fleeing rebels, murderers of the missionaries.

As if to repay Tardá and Guadalajara for the perils and sufferings of the journey, the welcome given them by the Tutuacs was warm and joyous. A hut had been built for their lodging and provision placed there for their sustenance.

But something discouraging transpired. The fathers learned that the inhabitants of Tutuaca had gathered together a great quantity of their strong liquor. That very night they had planned a carousal to celebrate the coming of the Black Robes. The missionaries objected strongly. They declared they would not have entered the pueblo had they known this was to be the outcome. It was not their intention, they said, to encourage by their presence such offenses against God as drunkenness. Sorry, it was too late to change their plans, replied the Indians. Guests had been invited from all around; the liquor had been collected. The fathers could not this time dissuade them from the drunken celebration they had fixed their minds upon.

Realizing to what extremes of ferocious passion the drunken savage can be led, the two Jesuits dared not spend the night in this strange place. Collecting what things were immediately necessary they secretly made their way out of the pueblo after dark and clambered up to a rocky ledge, which they hoped the intoxicated Indians would not be able to reach. They were right on both counts. Near midnight the Indians went to the hut looking for them and finding the padres had fled ransacked the dwelling from top to bottom. The fathers high on their ledge were not molested, and if the howling and crying of the intoxicated ceased in the early hours of the morning the missionaries might have been able to snatch a few winks of sleep.

When daylight broke they had to face the anger of the savages. Why had the fathers fled? Had not the Tutuacs invited them and would they not protect them and care for them? If they had wanted to kill the fathers they could do so at any time. Why had the fathers thought so ill of the Indian and fled from the place prepared for them? They had sought the fathers at midnight only to speak with them. The fathers, nevertheless, did not descend from their protected aerie, considering that the people of Tutuaca were still intoxicated when this committee waited upon them.

Fathers Tardá and Guadalajara high on their ledge of rock refrained from sending a reply back to the people by this drunken committee. The ambassadors went back empty handed, with no padres and no message. All that day the Black Robes waited on their lofty perch and not in vain. The Tutuacs meant well. Nor did they intend to give up pressing their suit with the missionaries. That is what the missionaries desired to ascertain. After the day had passed and the sun was swinging low over the mountains and hills of Sonora another delegation clambered up the precipice to parley with the stand-offish missionaries.

The ambassadors indicated that the Tutuacs were now sober and since the padres had come so far to baptize them why did they not start at once? It was a good time to begin, for many bags and jugs of liquor, the envoys said, had been left untouched for a still greater celebration. The two Jesuits now applied their common sense to this unique situation. Evidently these Indians had good will; did not realize drunkenness was immoral conduct. Better strike now, they concluded, than to wait for another drunken carousal.

So, Tardá and Guadalajara descended from their lofty pinnacle and appeared in the pueblo before a group of the caciques and a motley crowd of the primitives of this isolated pueblo. It was probably Father Guadalajara who spoke. The fathers had not come so far to encourage this sort of celebration; rather they came to do away with so evil a custom. Drunkenness was against God's law. It was not fitting for the Black Robes as priests of God to dwell in a pueblo where God was continually offended. Baptisms could not begin while so great a sin as drunkenness was tolerated amongst these people. The cacique and the rest of the crowd evinced sincere astonishment at this idea. What? Inebriation against the law of Christ? They had not known it. They promised then and there that they would end this practice forever.

They were as good as their word. Dismissing their invited barbarous guests, they poured out upon the ground the contents of the remaining jugs and bags of the fermented juice of cactus fruit which they had held for another grand carousal, and as King David of old sacrificed the water he could not share with his army, so these shaggy Tutuacs poured out their precious beverage, a sacrificial libation to the true God they were beginning to know. With this gesture they sacrificed their barbarous pleasures in order that the Black Robes whom they had invited from afar might consider them worthy of the Christian sacrament. That night there was no disorder in Tutuaca.

The usual thing now happened. Thirty of the best dispositioned were picked from the multitude. These, it was learned, had been so intent upon spiritual things and the impending sacrament of baptism that they had not taken part in the carousal, had retained their sobriety. These were instructed and baptized to become the leaders of the Christian faith among the men and women of Tutuaca. These thirty erected a cross at the entrance to the pueblo and promised to build a church. In this task they would be aided by many others, for the whole pueblo showed good will to the fathers, and by the time of the next visit of the Black Robes still others would receive the saving waters. By the time of the official visitation of Father Juan Zapata in 1678 there were one hundred and twenty-six baptized Christians, and in three other smaller pueblos—Tosanachic, Yepachic, and Moagunia—joined by that time to Tutuaca and forming a unit called a *partido,* there were in all two hundred and twenty-six baptized Christians.[18]

During the days that the fathers remained among the Tutuacs these poor savages gave them much valuable information about the country and the tribes living in the distant ranges and arroyos. It was a day's journey south to the country of the Guazápares and Hios, they informed the fathers. Tutuaca, they said, was an ordinary passage way over the great sierra into the hills and valleys of Sonora. Likewise there was an Indian path from Sinaloa to Parral which led over the sierra into the valleys of Durango, leading first to Cárichic and then passing southwest to Parral. The fathers were told that Tutuaca was the last settlement harboring any of the Tarahumar blood. To the west some pueblos were made up of Tepehuanes of Sonora.¹⁴ Representatives from these villages came in to Tutuaca to see the Black Robes and to invite the fathers to visit them too. The missionaries made what promises they could.

The result of this successful visit to isolated Tutuaca was most encouraging. Following fast upon the conversion of Cárichic and Papigochic, which were added to Cusihuiriachic, Temechic, and Papabechic, this beginning of the conversion of Tutuaca rounded out all the north and northwestern section of the Tarahumar territory and made it ready to be organized into a distinct unit, just as almost forty years before the more southern areas were grouped and named Baja Tarahumara. There was opposition, of course. The good fathers frequently attributed the opposition to the devil, actually it was merely a manifestation of jealousy on the part of the hechicero, or hatred of some for the Spaniard, or dislike of others for the restraints which Christian ethics would harness upon former license. Sometimes opposition came from sheer stupidity or superstition on the part of the Indian who was persuaded he would die as soon as the waters of baptism should touch his brow. The hechicero, medicine man or wizard, did of course try to prevent the work of the missionaries from spreading among the tribesmen, and he was successful sometimes in dissuading an individual or a group from receiving the sacrament.

But in spite of these hindrances, the usual ones in missionary activity, the work given so fine an impulse by the meeting at Parral in 1673 continued rapidly to spread. On the return journey from Tutuaca Don Pablo told the two missionaries that as a result of the success there the remaining pueblos of northern Tarahumara desired to be honored by a visit and to embrace the Christian Faith. However, this could not be done without additional workers in this part of the vineyard. Therefore the faithful Don Pablo took the bull by the horns. He got together fifty-eight pagans from various pueblos and, in company of one of the missionaries, went with them to Parral and showed them to the captain-general as proof and material argument of the thing desired, namely, that official measures be taken for sending additional missionaries.

The captain-general sent one of his officers, Captain Nicolás Caro, with some troops to visit the various friendly pueblos in order to inform himself of the number of settlements and their size, and report on his findings. It was done and the captain-general with the information at hand was happy to pass it on to his superior, the Governor of Nueva Vizcaya. This gentleman, in turn, made vivid representations to the Viceroy in Mexico City, Fray Payo Enríquez Afán de Rivera of the Order of Santiago, who was also Archbishop. In the meantime a Jesuit Visitor to Parral encountered in the mines eighteen Tarahumares from the pueblo of Nonoava. They asked for baptism for themselves and their tribesmen of the pueblo and for catechists. All but one were baptized, included in the group was the Indian Governor of Nonoava. The Jesuit Visitor, with his new Christians, went to the captain-general at Parral and made the same request for missionaries as Don Pablo and his group had made a short while before.

The pressure was to be successful. A new mission unit of the northern Tarahumares was to be organized, and the official name given to it would be San Joaquín y Santa Ana in Alta Tarahumara.

Chapter XV

NEW MISSIONS IN ALTA TARAHUMARA

B Y THE YEAR 1678 the new mission unit, called officially the Mission of San Joaquín and Santa Ana, was completely formed and organized. It might well have been called Alta Tarahumara, since it was an addition to the southern unit named Baja Tarahumara. But such designation nowhere appears in the documents. Four new missionaries arrived from Mexico City in 1677, and the records of the following year show the northern Tarahumar country fully organized and named after the parents of Blessed Mary the Virgin. This new mission unit had been in the process of formation ever since Fathers Barrionuevo and Gamboa entered the country late in 1673 as the result of the council held at Parral earlier that year. We have traced the activities of Barrionuevo and Gamboa; we have seen the splendid work of Tardá and Guadalajara. This was a magnificent advance; it began the rounding out of the whole Tarahumar nation; it resulted in a new group of missions organized into a unit with its own superior or rector. It took five years, from 1673 to 1678 for the new unit to be born.

The pioneers of the upper Tarahumar mission system found in their arduous journey up and down the country a barbarous people, scattered through a country of much fertility and beauty, its valleys watered by the streams which flowed east from the great Sierra or northwest through a divide. Most of the fathers who wrote during this period mention the valleys and the streams. Scattered along the banks of these rivers and arroyos the Tarahumares lived in low hovels built of straw, "which seemed more suitable for catching birds than for human habitation."[1] These huts extended along the river banks often for ten or fifteen miles. The Tarahumares disliked living in groups and seemed to be less gregarious than any of the tribes evangelized in the Mexican northwest.[2]

In the mountains the primitives lived in caves, similar to those which nature has hollowed out of the rocky cliffs and palisades which rise abruptly from the banks of the upper San Pedro or upper Papigochic.

[1] For notes to chapter xv see pages 249-250.

The caves are still there and the modern traveler will find living in them the rude Tarahumar.

It was the task of the earlier missionaries to try to form the Indians along the valleys into more compact settlements which we know as the pueblo. An aid in this task was the fact that families were already grouped fairly closely together, for a daughter would be given in marriage only on condition that the husband would live with the wife's parents and to a degree be subject to them. This seemed to be their only organization: they recognized no other law or jurisdiction. Pueblo grouping seemed to the Jesuit padres to be necessary in order that the neophytes be more easily instructed, baptized as a group, and thereafter live the Christian life together.

By the early 1680's these northern Tarahumares had acquired horses from the Spaniards which they used, however, only for riding. They soon began to raise horses themselves, and by Father Neumann's time some had acquired herds as large as fifty head. They came to possess flocks of sheep, the wool of which they wove into beautiful fabrics.

The men and women went barefooted and bareheaded. The men wore a loin cloth and dropped over their heads a sleeveless garment which came hardly to the middle of the torso, leaving the legs bare. Wrapped around this was the square blanket or *serape*, which they discarded in warmer weather. It is thus these sons of the wild dress today, except that on their feet they wear sandals. After three centuries they have not changed their habits.

For food the Tarahumares planted beans and raised chickens. When Neumann arrived at his mission of Sisoguichic (1681) the Indian governor had some eggs for his repast. Maize, of course, was their principal food from which they made tortillas and a sort of intoxicating wine with which they celebrated their carousals. On any occasion of rejoicing they would become inebriated. Such an evening would begin with dancing and singing after their barbarous fashion, then the drinking would start and the hubbub would increase until the small hours of the morning when they would be senseless with wine and sleep. Promiscuous immoralities extending even to incest took place on such occasions. They were generally prone to marry among relatives. Polygamy, however, though occasionally practiced was not prevalent among them.

Unlike the Tepehuanes to the south, the Tarahumares were not given to the worship of stone idols, though they adored the sun, the moon, and the stars. They had various practices of magic, and like savages all over the globe they were exceedingly superstitious. If calamity befell them they thought their gods were angry. Was one struck dead by a thunderbolt, or did hail tear and beat down their growing corn, such things they attributed to a neglected deity: they had not of late sufficiently honored the sun and the moon through dancing and singing and drinking.

To the despair of the missionaries, calamities which should have led these Indians to the true God in repentance and prayer only flung them headlong into drunkenness and vice. Those persons struck by lightning were considered to be the born enemies of thunder. Their parents had not sacrificed them at the first thunderstorm after birth. Or, perhaps, the unfortunate one had shown displeasure at one time when a storm was approaching. This particular superstition led to a humorous practice, for although the savage children of Mapimí to the southeast placated the god of plague with dance, baskets of prickly pears, and tails of fox or mountain lion, these Tarahumares at the approach of thunder would begin to shout with joy, to dance, to jump, to laugh, and to make merry: thus thinking to conciliate the god of thunder.

Yet, withal, the Tarahumares of the north were cunning, knowing how to procure their own advantage and speedily learning how to hide their vices or drunken orgies from the missionary. Sometimes they would feign goodness and pretend to be Christians for the advantage it would bring them. Oftentimes those who appeared most docile and friendly were those most to be suspected. No use to try to order or command them, for they would then surely do the opposite. They were open only to kindly persuasion, having to be shown the advantages which such and such a mode of action would bring them or the reasons why it would be good for them to do it.

Finally, like all these Indians of northern Mexico, they were fickle. In the beginning of their evangelization, after gathering to hear or greet the father, they would slink away to their woods and caves and manage to keep good distances between themselves and the missionary. Often, after baptism, they would relapse to their ancient and savage mode of life. Indeed, one Black Robe who was soon to come to the mission, Joseph Neumann, called them a "stony-hearted people" for whom "the result does not repay the hard labor and the valuable seed. The seed of the gospel does not sprout, or if it sprouts, it is spoiled by the thorns of carnal desire."[3]

This, indeed, is quite different from the enthusiasms of Pérez de Ribas and Méndez expressed a few decades earlier from their missions among the Mayos and the Yaquis on the west coast. That such, however, was not always the case, we have seen from the enthusiasm exhibited at Cárichic when Guadalajara came among them and from the invitation extended from far western Tutuaca. Indeed, Neumann closes an earlier letter in the following vein: "They are simple of nature, and unpolished; swarthy of color, but not black; of good height and solidly made; but extremely unwilling to work. They always go armed with bows and arrows, and these are their only weapons. Their arrows are envenomed with a deadly poison, and for this reason they are much feared by other tribes; yet they are naturally peace loving, and never quarrel among themselves."[4]

From all of this it can be readily understood that the new missionary unit of the northwestern Tarahumares was not given birth without travail. Through all the progress, with expansion and baptisms made by Tardá and Guadalajara in the fall and spring of 1675–1676, the fathers had to battle with two kinds of enemies instead of only one. Normally it was the hechicero, medicine man, or wizard. But in Tarahumara, because of the former rebellions, there was the apostate to deal with. As the simple Indian collapses morally before even the most obvious propaganda, accepting as true anything that is told him, these apostates, dissatisfied and treacherous, could be a source of extreme annoyance to the fathers, and they were. Such was the troublemaker who went from pueblo to pueblo saying that with the fathers and baptism would enter sickness and death in Tarahumara. The sowing of this seed from place to place resulted in an ugly and rank crop of weeds and stickers. Though admitted into the pueblos and even invited by their chiefs, such as we have seen at Cárichic, Papigochic, Tutuaca, and Nonoava (thanks in great measure to the splendid work of Don Pablo) individuals showed themselves frightened by the presence of the missionary and reluctant to receive baptism.

To avoid the saving waters some would make weak and senseless excuses. Others would run from the missionary and remain in hiding. Others again, still pagans, were more bold. At the arrival of the padre these people went about the village dissuading the men and women from baptism and exhorting them to beware of the Black Robe. They tried also to dissuade the formerly baptized from leading a Christian life. One would say that he was now old and had lived well enough without baptism. Others simply gave a flat refusal, and there was nothing the missionary could do about it. These people responded "*nagoche,*" which meant "not right now." Some men feigning to think baptism was only for the women would say when the father approached to offer the sacrament: "*Yo soy hombre,*" "I am a man." When baptized tribesmen were pointed out to him he simply repeated the refrain, "*Yo soy hombre.*"

The troublemakers were called by Tardá and Guadalajara *tlatoleros,* for the tlatole was a meeting, often a sort of indignation meeting which preceded a rebellion. For one of these evildoers of Tesorachic the father gave a rather primitive demonstration of one of the dogmas of the Faith. It was one which seemed to have been used among them most frequently because doubtless the primitive could most readily understand it. The missionary on this occasion warned the tlatolero of the terrors of hell and of its dreadful fire. The latter said he would gladly go there. A lighted candle was procured and its flame passed under the finger of the refractory Indian. The missionary made some very obvious comparisons. But the savage was unmoved; rather did his stubbornness increase, for when asked whether he would then go there alone, since his tribesmen were being baptized, he vowed he would go through all Tarahumara persuading the nation not to become Christians that they might go with him to hell. The padre was amazed at such unwonted boldness and arrogance, for usually the savage would put on a meek front in presence of the missionary and would spread his venom secretly in the night. But this particular savage was infuriated and there might have been tragedy, for as he sulked away those near by noticed that he was preparing his bow for shooting. The padre reached safety and the incident was ended.

In spite of such frequent unpleasantnesses, many Tarahumares were being won over through kindness. An argument of one of the father's was however controverted with some success in one of the pueblos. The missionaries, here as elsewhere, were accustomed to narrate to the savage how they themselves had left their homes and their beautiful country and come into this strange and difficult life just in order to save the souls of the natives. But one of the tlatoleros gained a following by telling a different story which for a while was believed. The fathers, said he, came here and did this work just in order to get paid in money by the King of Spain.[5] Such were the annoyances of a moral nature which the first missionaries of the new unit had to endure, and to all of this was added their continued physical discomfort. They complained often of the cold and it was rare that they could have even straw to sleep upon.

That the progress thus far made was nevertheless consoling is seen by a report of April 28 of the Father Visitor, Bernabé Francisco Gutierrez, sent up by the Provincial in the spring of 1676. The Visitor has extraordinary praise for both Tardá and Guadalajara, calling them real apostles, but he gives the palm to the latter, "whom God has reserved for His great glory in these lands." Guadalajara enjoyed in an especial manner, it seems, the gift of winning hearts through tact, understanding, and kindness. "It is impossible," wrote the Visitor, "to describe the love and veneration the Indians have for both the fathers." Gutierrez himself took a hand in the baptisms which were continually going on and after traveling hundreds of miles through Tarahumara he considers this vineyard to be in a state of readiness for the total reception of the gospel. All that is required are workers. Four more are needed in the area, wrote the Visitor to the Provincial, and he recommended the pueblos of Papigochic, Cárichic, Tutuaca, and Nonoava as residences of the new Black Robes when they should come. But they must be Jesuits of the highest caliber, for the labors are heavy and dangerous and unless the laborers be inflamed with zeal from above they will not endure.[6]

This letter of the Visitor Father Bernabé Gutierrez, may well have been the final argument which decided the authorities to act in favor of the new territory now opened up for the Faith. The visits of the caciques to the captain-general at Parral, the representations made by the Governor of Nueva Vizcaya that more fathers be sent to Tarahumara, and now a most favorable report by the Jesuit Visitor to those new missions, all of this was going to bear fruit. In the late summer of 1677 four new Jesuit missionaries for the Tarahumares were on their way north.

Not long, however, before the fresh missionaries arrived trouble from another and entirely new and unexpected quarter threatened annoyance and setback. This was a dispute between Jesuits and Franciscans as to the limits of their respective fields in the evangelization of the savage. We have seen how the Franciscans had preceded the Jesuits into all the more southern districts of this country. At Culiacán, in the mountains of Topia, in Durango, at Atotonilco among the Tepehuanes, the Gray Robe had been in advance of the Black Robe. Indeed, the Franciscans were already active in Mexico in the 'sixties of the preceding century, before ever a Jesuit set foot in New Spain. Their convent of San Francisco in Zacatecas might be called the mother house of these missions whence came priests to residences in Sinaloa, Durango, and Coahuila, just as Mexico City with its convent of San Fernando with its Fernandinos became in the eighteenth century the mother house of the Alta California missions.

Lack of men hampered Franciscan missionary work substantially. Many a mission begun in the sixteenth century before Jesuit arrival, such as those at Culiacán, Topia, Parras, had to be abandoned or neglected.[7] When the Jesuits arrived in the north as missionaries, beginning with Tapia and Martín Pérez on the Sinaloa in 1591 these places could be refilled by Jesuits and the missionary work begun anew. The Franciscans continued to hold their residences in the Valle de Topia, in Durango, at Santa Bárbara, at Atotonilco, and to further their missionary work to the east of the Jesuits.

Amicable relations between the orders were a matter of course in the mission field, nor is there word in the mission annals of any strife between them. Rather, there are recurrent indications of friendliness and coöperation such as at Durango during the time of the Tepehuán revolt and later during the repeated incursions of the Tobosos in the country near Parral. But in 1677, on the eve of the founding of the second unit of missions embracing the northern Tarahumares, there was trouble. It seems, however, to have been caused chiefly or entirely by one man, Fray Alonso de Mesa, and the dispute concerned the pueblo of Yepómera.[8]

The Viceroy, the Marqués de Cerralvo, had given a decision in 1629 that the Tarahumar nation should be the exclusive field of Jesuit missionaries.⁹ It was, moreover, clearly understood in the meeting of 1673 at Parral that the Jesuits were officially to be in charge of the whole nation of the Tarahumares as their field of mission activity. But the friars of the Concho missions had recently entered some of the Tarahumar pueblos to the north in which there lived a few Conchos, and they had likewise visited some purely Tarahumar settlements. Fray Alonso himself had evangelized in the pueblo of Amiquipa where there was a small number of Conchos and in Yepómera where there were fewer still or none. In 1675 Tomás de Guadalajara went up the Río Papigochic to Mátachic to look over the ground in the great trek which we have described, and we have seen that he went as far as Yepómera. When he returned to his mission of Santa Ana he received a letter from Fray Alonso calling his attention to the fact that Yepómera belonged to his jurisdiction. The Jesuit sent the letter to official headquarters in Mexico. The results were satisfactory to the Jesuits. The Franciscan Provincial averred that for lack of men and money Yepómera had been abandoned by the friars, and the secular officials made it clear that, since all the Tarahumares were under Jesuit tutelage and since those of Yepómera were chiefly pagan Tarahumares, the pueblo was to be looked after by the Black Robes. Besides, Fray Alonso was ordered not to work among the Tarahumares.

The following year, 1676, Father Guadalajara was commissioned to begin a Christian mission at Mátachic. According to his own account the Jesuit acted with propriety. On arriving at Mátachic he wrote to Fray Alonso, who was at Amiquipa, thirty miles northeast in Concho territory, saying he did not desire Yepómera, and offering his services. When Fray Alonso replied asking him to send a letter to him at Ochimuri Father Guadalajara thought the misunderstanding was over. But when the Jesuit was away from his mission of Mátachic early in 1677 the Concho Indians invaded the Tarahumar country, not bringing war, but trouble. They brought officials of their own to rule over the new Christian Tarahumar pueblos and said that Father Guadalajara would never return to them. The people of Yepómera and other Tarahumares had never liked the Franciscans, wrote Guadalajara; they made bitter complaints against them, accusing the friars of stealing their goods and produce and of worse misdemeanors. Guadalajara gave no ear to this accusation and defended the friars, but when upon his return he desired to work among the Tarahumares of the lower Papigochic these Conchos endeavored to keep him out of the country. When Guadalajara returned to Mátachic Fray Alonso wrote to him an accusing letter and enclosed an order from his Provincial to work among all Conchos and indeed in all territory on the right bank of the Río Papigochic. The Franciscan went on to accuse the Jesuit of choosing Mátachic for residence because of the comfortable house built there for the missionary.

Word of the quarrel reached headquarters, and the ears of the Franciscan and Jesuit Provincials in the capital. The two superiors put their heads together and an agreement was easily reached, that is, the old and original settlement was confirmed: all Tarahumares were to be under the care of the Jesuits, all Conchos under that of the Franciscans. As to Yepómera, the Tarahumares there were to be under Guadalajara, the Conchos under Fray Alonso. Guadalajara, however, maintained there were no Conchos in Yepómera, but admitted that some of the Conchos did come over into other Tarahumar pueblos to live under the Jesuit fathers. A copy of this document was given to the Viceroy in Mexico City and to the Governor of Nueva Vizcaya in Durango, Don Lope de Sierra y Osorio. But since the Franciscans of the north continued to claim all the right bank of the Río Papigochic, as Figueroa made clear in his letters, the Jesuit Visitor, Bernabé Gutierrez, endeavored to get the pertinent document, namely, the settlement made by the Provincials at the Governor's office in Durango. Alas, the document could not be found so that the quarrel continued. Should the contention of the Durango Franciscans hold good, argued Guadalajara and the Jesuits, then the hallowed spots where Beudin and Basilio shed their blood for the Faith and even the site of the ancient Villa de Aguilar, where the Jesuits had labored since the beginning, would all be given over to the Seraphic Order.

Great scandal and disorder, wrote Guadalajara to his Provincial, was caused by the claim of the Franciscans, and especially by the attitude of Fray Alonso. It was to be feared that the loyal Tarahumares would murder the Franciscan, or that Alonso's loyal supporters would come and murder Guadalajara. Indeed, if this thing was not soon settled the Jesuit feared a general uprising of both nations against God and King. Did the Franciscan Provincial know what things were being carried on here by his sons he would feel his conscience heavily burdened. Guadalajara begged his Provincial to see to it that the trouble cease.[10]

However, neither the Franciscan nor the Jesuit was murdered by their opposing neophytes, and Provincial Altamirano in the capital was able to bring about the proper settlement. The Franciscan Provincial had indeed conceded all the Tarahumares to the Jesuits. The affair was not difficult of settlement in any case since from the beginning this had been the arrangement. We hear no more of the quarrel and Yepómera in the next year was listed as a Jesuit mission post. It was a consolation to Guadalajara that while the trouble was on, his loyal Tarahumares from Papigochic exerted themselves to suppress the discontent caused by Fray Alonso and to reconcile to the Jesuit missionary those who had become estranged.

Yepómera was typical of many of the Indian pueblos when the first missionaries came to the Indians. It was not consolidated into a compact unit similar to a medieval walled town in Europe, or even as we are accustomed to picture a settlement of any kind, with a cluster of houses gathered about a center which would be the market place or center of administration. Instead this pueblo resembled certain of those smaller villages in England which have but one street, the highway, which passes through and which have dwellings on either side of it for longer or shorter distances. Still more did Yepómera resemble the modern mining town of Bingham, near Salt Lake City in Utah, which for a matter of three miles or more has its houses and its shops bordering the paved highway which winds up a canyon to where the copper ore is blasted out.

Such Indian villages had no shops, of course, but only huts, *xacales*, dwellings of poles and branches of trees covered over with straw. They were rarely of adobe. When the pueblo was on a stream these dwellings were built near the rich land along the banks, for on such land was the ranchería and field of corn and beans.

Such was Yepómera when Father Guadalajara began to introduce the Christian Faith among its inhabitants. The settlement followed an arroyo six or eight miles down to where it joined the Río

Papigochic just before the latter ran between two mountains. Guadalajara informs us that the settlement was divided into an upper and lower Yepómera, each section was sometimes given different names. The lower section was called Yepómera la Baja in Spanish or Tlaxomoho in Mexican; the string of dwellings farther up the arroyo was named in Tarahumar Xicurichic, which in Spanish is Rinconada, or corner. Each section already had its church. Further to illustrate this characteristic of Tarahumar settlements, across the river from Mátachic ten rancherías were strung along fifteen miles of the river bank; Cárichic extended for nine miles down the banks of the arroyo.[11]

There was still another and more unusual characteristic of Yepómera, its people were a mixture of the Tarahumar and Jova nations. In the lower section all were Tarahumares, in the upper some Jovas were mingled with the former. The first missionaries were a little puzzled about these Jovas, for they were often referred to as Tepehuanes by the Indians and their language was similar to the Tepehuán tongue; yet in all other respects they seemed to belong to the distinct Jova group, and it later became evident that the Jovas were actually a distinct nation.[12]

Such were the conditions in the northwestern corner of Tarahumara on the eve of Zapata's famous visitation. Tomás de Guadalajara, apart from what Visitor Gutierrez wrote of him, seems generally from the records to have been the most active and the most successful of the Jesuits then working in Tarahumara. His letters were more frequent and more detailed and the virgin territory he covered, some of it in the company of Tardá, was vast, as will appear more plainly when his excursions far into Jova territory become known. He enjoyed the pleasure of success too. His neophytes loved him and he knew it. Father Gutierrez had reported on the charm and kindliness of Guadalajara's personality and the padre himself, writing in simple vein to his Provincial, speaks of the loyal coöperation of the Tarahumares of Papigochic and ends with the significant words, "They show me great affection."[13]

The year following another Visitor was to make the rounds of all the Jesuit mission system of northwestern Mexico. He and Guadalajara were to become great companions and travel together on muleback over many a wild league of the plain and many a rugged spur of the sierra.

Top: *church at Narárachic;* left: *the ruins of San Rafael de Mátachic;* right: *the bells of Yepómera.*

Chapter XVI

ZAPATA VISITS TARAHUMARA

IN THE YEAR 1678 the Provincial, Father Tomás Altamirano, did a magnificent thing for the whole Jesuit mission system of northwestern Mexico; he sent a visitor, named Juan Ortiz[1] Zapata, to make the rounds of all the establishments and to report minutely upon them. The visitation was carried out with the result that the historian today can bequeath to his readers a grand perspective of the whole Jesuit missionary organization in southwestern North America. This view though panoramic is yet minute so that all the details of the comprehensive picture are brought to view as by a telescopic lens in a camera. Each of the ten units of the system is accounted for, and statistics for each are recorded. Of these, three belong to the mountains: the Xixime mission, San Andrés, and Santa Cruz de Topia; four were on the west coast over the divide: San Felipe y Santiago, mother mission of them all, San Ignacio de Yaqui, San Francisco Javier, and San Francisco Borja; three were east of the divide and are the subject of this account: the Tepehuán mission, Tarahumara Antigua (thus did Zapata designate Baja Tarahumara), and the northern Tarahumar mission, called in the record Mission Nueva de San Joaquín y Santa Ana. The Parras partido, as we have seen, was taken over by the Bishop of Durango in the 1640's.

Visitor Zapata began his tour in the south going first to the mountain missions of the Xiximes and to San Andrés among the southern Acaxées. Thence going east to Durango he began the first stage of a great ellipse, passing north through the Tepehuán and the two Tarahumar missions, then westward through the divide of the Río Papigochic into Sonora, and thereafter passing south through the four west coast units just mentioned. The Visitor concluded his journey at the mission of Santa Cruz de Topia having turned east into the mountains again somewhat north of the district among the Xiximes where he had started. It was an immense undertaking requiring many months to complete. A conservative estimate makes the distance covered up and down the valleys and over the mountains 2,250 miles.

---

[1] For notes to chapter xvi see page 250.

The survey of Father Zapata gives us a clear conception of the manner into which the whole system was organized. Each mission was divided into groups or partidos and each partido comprised several pueblos. Each pueblo would today be called a mission. A partido was administered by one or two missionaries, who resided in the chief pueblo, called the *cabecera*, or head. If the other pueblos did not have a resident padre they were regularly visited and therefore were called visitas. The most flourishing missions were those on the west coast, both in numbers of partidos and of neophytes. San Francisco Borja at this date had nine partidos with 10,871 Indians of various tribes of Sonora; San Ignacio de Yaqui numbered nine partidos harboring 19,560 Yaqui Indians. The missions in the mountains to the south were the smallest. The Xixime mission had four partidos with only 1,006 Xixime Indians in all, and the whole San Andrés mission with four partidos cared for only 591 Acaxée Indians. According to this record the grand total of Indians cared for in the whole mission system was 62,599.[3]

But our concern here is with the Tarahumares and the organization of the new Tarahumar mission in the north and the new missionaries who came to labor therein.[4] By the time of Father Zapata's visit the Mission Nueva de San Joaquín y Santa Ana was set up and organized into eight partidos spiritually nursing 5,358 baptized Tarahumar Indians. The most southerly partido of the new unit was Nonoava near the banks of the upper Conchos. To the north, along a line lay in succession San Joaquín y Santa Ana, Cárichic, and San Bernabé. Each was a cabecera or chief pueblo in the partido and was distant one from the other between twenty-five and thirty-five miles. West and northwest of these four, beginning with Sisoguichic, thirty miles southwest of Cárichic, were Temechic, Papigochic, and Mátachic. In the last cabecera Father Guadalajara resided the year before the visitation of Zapata. Each of these cabeceras as well as each of the visitas was given a saintly or angelic name. Guadalajara's pueblo of Mátachic was called San Rafael, and the partido which he cared for was named El Triunfo de los Angeles. The other pueblos of his partido—Temósachic, Yepómera, and Ocomorachic—were called San Miguel, San Gabriel, and San Pablo, respectively. The first three were on almost a direct line running northwest with Río Papigochic and a tributary. Ocomorachic lay to the west over a sierra on another tributary of the river. These four pueblos were between ten and fifteen miles from one another. Here in this northwest corner of the mission system Father Guadalajara cared for 648 Christians divided among his four pueblos, and baptisms took place every day. Even while the visitation was in progress Father Guadalajara on a visit to Ocomorachic (perhaps in the company of the Visitor) baptized forty Indians, which Zapata figures immediately records, so that this partido numbering 106 Christians when the visitation began, had 146 when it ended.

Father José Tardá, many times mentioned in these pages and Guadalajara's devoted companion, was rector of the whole mission group and had particular charge of the partido called San Bernabé. It took its name from its chief pueblo, San Bernabé, which had formerly been called Cusihuiriachic. San Bernabé was the oldest of the Christian pueblos of this new Tarahumar unit, having been founded, as we have seen, by Fathers Gamboa and Tardá in February, 1674. Here Father Tardá, alone in his partido, as were all the others, administered to 912 Christians scattered in eight pueblos. At Cárichic, where Father Guadalajara three years before had enjoyed so great a success, was one of the four new arrivals, Father Diego de Contreras, caring for five pueblos numbering in all 706 Christians. At Papigochic, once so turbulent and revolutionary, now called La Purísima, Nicolás Ferrer was the padre of 417 Christians in four pueblos. Baptisms here too were still going on.

In charge of Temechic in 1678 was another Black Robe who had just arrived in the mission field, Father José de Guevara. This father did not immediately take up his residence at Temechic, but stayed for a time with José Tardá at Cusihuiriachic to the north until his partido and its chief pueblo, Temechic, were better prepared to receive him. In the four pueblos of the partido of Temechic there were only 253 Christians. For instance, Pachera, a few miles north northwest of Temechic was as yet totally pagan, whereas in Píchachic to the west, a settlement spread for several miles along a beautiful and fertile cañada, there were but four Christian families numbering in all eleven persons.

Things were better at Tosaboreachic, now fortunately named San Juan, for in this pueblo which was some twenty miles to the east there resided thirty families numbering ninety-two persons who had received the waters of baptism. At Temechic itself, however, there were 150 Christians, belonging to thirty families. Here were relics of Jácome Basilio who a quarter of a century before had begun the baptisms. He had built a small adobe to serve as a church on those occasions when he visited this pueblo. The roof had collapsed since, but had been recently restored during the course of the renewed missionary activity in this region. Father Guevara was to live here and in a few years all the Tarahumares of his four pueblos were to be Christianized.

At Sisoguichic, many miles south, resided Father Antonio Oreña, new in the mission. In the pueblo only 179 Christians lived, and, though not very well disciplined because they were so recently brought to the Faith, they yet manifested good will and were busily engaged at the time of the visitation in building a church and a residence for the father. To Sisoguichic, called Nombre de María Santísima, there were later joined two other pueblos. One, Cuitego, lay forty miles southwest, a two days' journey over the mountains, on the fringes of the Guazápares, who were cared for from the Sinaloa mission. At Nonoava, likewise in the south, resided Francisco de Arteaga. This partido bore the name of the famous shrine in the mountains of Catalonia, Santa María de Monserrat. It was flourishing at the time of Zapata's visitation, for its two pueblos by this time had a good start in their combined number of 352 Christians.

The most flourishing of the eight partidos was San Joaquín y Santa Ana, administered by the well-tried Francisco de Zeleda. It lay in the very center of Tarahumar territory and radiating off from it at all points of the compass were organized partidos—Satevó east, Cusihuiria-chic north, Cárichic and Sisoguichic west, and Nonoava south. It numbered in this year of 1678 more than 1,300 Christians, and its principal pueblo was Tayeguachic, called San Francisco Borja. Three other pueblos were under Zeleda's care—Yeguachic called Santa Ana, Saguarichic called Nuestra Señora de Guadalupe, and Purúachic named after San Francisco Javier. Twelve hundred and forty natives had been recently baptized in the partido, and an excellent spirit was generally evinced by these neophytes, especially by those of Saguari-chic, in thir elimination of drunken carousals. This pueblo had recently completed one of the finest churches in all Tarahumara.

What of the far northwest in this year of 1678? What of Tutuaca which Tardá and Guadalajara had visited two years before? It, too, was now organized into a partido, but only on paper. Even if it were quite ready for a missionary, none could be spared for permanent residence, even though Tutuaca now had thirty Christian families numbering in all 126 individuals. The partido on paper was given three pueblos, besides Tutuaca: San Juan de Tosanachic, San Juan de Moagina, and Santiago de Yepachic. Tutuaca itself, the cabecera, was called pleasingly Jesús del Monte. Since this partido lacked a resident Black Robe, Tomás de Guadalajara—whose own partido was nearest to this group of pueblos—kept an eye on it. He occasionally made the rounds here, rough country though it was, and he was continually augmenting the number of Christians. He succeeded in baptizing 126 throughout the territory. He hoped soon to have them all in the Faith, but the partido of Tutuaca de Jesús del Monte was shortly to have its own padre.

Tutuaca to the west bordered on and partly included territory occupied by two different nations, the lower Pimas and the Jovas, and it is precisely in this region that the missions east of the Sierra Madre came into contact with those of the west. Indeed, Yepachic of the Tarahumar partido of Tutuaca was little more than twenty miles from the pueblo mission of the Pimas, Maicoba, which belonged to the partido of Yécora of the old and flourishing mission of San Francisco de Borja on the west coast. All residents of Maicoba were Christians. North of Tutuaca lay the Jovas, and while Father Zapata was visiting Tutuaca both he and Guadalajara made an excursion into the Jova country where the Río Papigochic makes some snaky turns and comes out as the Río Yaqui to run into the Gulf of California. Both fathers visited the Christian pueblo of Sahuaripa and they returned through the territory of the Jova nation.

The reason for this extended journey was that the Jovas were already acquainted with Father Guadalajara, for the indefatigable missionary had formerly penetrated as far as Natora on the Papigochic and there had baptized some Jovas. From that time on the Jovas had visited their padre at Mátachic and begged him to organize a permanent mission among them. On returning to their country they had raised crosses, chosen fiscals to represent them spiritually, and set about preparations for the building of churches or chapels. Now, hearing that the Visitor was at Tutuaca, bands of Jovas came in begging for the fathers and a mission.

Thus it was that the two Jesuits, the Visitor Zapata and the missionary Guadalajara, consoled and encouraged these earnest people by journeying to their pueblo of Sahuaripa and returning east through the heart of their country. The western Jovas were already Christians and had their padres of the Xavier mission. Sahuaripa was the head of a partido and thirty miles to the east was Teopari on the Papigochic. But still farther east lay more than half of Jova territory and it was Indians from this region who were begging for padres of their own.

This time Guadalajara was able to satisfy the desires of the eastern Jovas, since they bordered on the territory of his partido of Mátachic. Passing through Natora where formerly he had baptized a few, he invited the Indians there to migrate to a better spot where other Christians lived and to unite with the Jovas of two other pueblos farther up the river. This was done and the new pueblo was called San Simón de Baripoa. Following great curves up the river into Chihuahua the two fathers visited Harosaqui, which they dubbed San Matías, Sirupa, which they called San Andrés, and, on a tributary not far from Yepómera, Nahuarachic, which was Tarahumar. In addition to these pueblos there were Comora and Mayachic. This group made up of Tarahumares and Jovas, formed thus another large partido of the northern Tarahumar mission. In all of these pueblos the unwearying Guadalajara had already baptized some 230 souls belonging to the one or the other group.

Visitor Juan Ortiz Zapata now returned to the western mission, San Francisco Javier, to continue his visitation of the populous Indian nations, the Ópatas, lower Pimas, and the Yaquis, who formed part of the larger Cáhita nation. The Visitor probably began his journey from Tutuaca, thence traveling south and west to Yécora, and from this Pima pueblo he continued his interesting account of the state of the missions in 1678. Guadalajara still in residence at Mátachic girded himself for still greater labors, for, besides his own partido and that of Tutuaca, he must now care for the pueblos among the Jovas.

But what of the southern Tarahumar pueblos and partidos, those which since 1639 had been organized into the mission unit of Baja

Tarahumara and which were now in 1678 called as a group the mission of Tarahumara Antigua? Visitor Zapata had passed through each of these partidos, and concerning them he has left us an enlightening report.[5] It was this mission which had carried on so bravely during the repeated uprisings of Tarahumares and Tobosos during the 1640's and which, early in the following decade, had witnessed the struggles with the northern Tarahumares when Fathers Beudin and Basilio were slain at Papigochic. During the twenty years which had elapsed since the death of Basilio in 1652, while the north was for the time neglected, this southern Tarahumar country had been making steady progress and stabilizing itself into the populous pueblos the beginnings of which were described in earlier chapters. In 1678 Visitor Zapata found the pueblos and the partidos of this mission in excellent condition.

Tizonazo, called San José, was not officially designated as belonging to the Tarahumar missions, but was the most northern pueblo of the Tepehuán group. It was now the head of a partido comprising only one other pueblo, that of Santa Cruz. The number of neophytes for the two pueblos came to only 199 individuals, a number almost as low as that for some of the Xixime pueblos. Tizonazo had supported numerous Salineros as well as Tepehuanes and some Tarahumares. But the revolts had ruined it, for the Salineros had joined the Toboso rebels. All its inhabitants had fled, and the Governor of Nueva Vizcaya was driven to transplanting an entirely new population from Sinaloa and Sonora. Its visita, Santa Cruz, was Tepehuán.[6]

We find the mission of Baja Tarahumara or Antigua consisting of five partidos which had a population of baptized Indians numbering close to 4,000. San Miguel de las Bocas, south of Parral, was a partido all to itself, having in residence there Father Pedro de Escalante. It held 386 Christian Indians. North from Las Bocas was San Pablo Ballesa, sixty miles west of Parral on a north-flowing branch of the Conchos, marking Fonte's original settlement of Tarahumares in 1608. This place, the old veteran Gerónimo de Figueroa, now dead, had built up into a splendid mission and had erected there the finest church in the country. Father Martín de Prado resided here in 1678 and visited two other pueblos, San Juan and San Mateo, on the banks of the same arroyo. San Juan was a settlement of Tepehuanes, San Mateo of Tarahumares.

The Tepehuanes of San Juan were at the time of the visitation engaged in building a church which would rival the one at San Pablo. Prado's Indian family amounted to 633, some Tepehuanes, some Tarahumares. Bordering east of San Pablo was the partido of San Gerónimo de Huejotitlán where Father Gabriel de Villar, rector of the whole mission, resided, and looked after the two other pueblos where Tepehuanes predominated. The total number of neophytes in the partido was 754. From San Felipe on the Conchos Father Francisco de Valdés cared for 1,010 Tarahumares mixed with a few Tepehuanes. At Satevó Julio Sarmiento ministered to a pure Tarahumar family of 1,134.

Throughout these southern pueblos the missionaries looked after certain families of Spaniards who, with their servants and farm hands, lived on ranches called estancias, near the missions. Such families, mentioned as a rule by the Visitor, added slightly to the number of souls administered to by the Jesuits in the land of the Tarahumar.

In this year 1678, so important historically for our knowledge of the condition of the Jesuit missions, the southern and older Tarahumar unit, called now La Natividad, cared for 3,917 neophytes; the northern group of partidos just organized already numbered 5,358, which brought the total to 9,275. In all of these missions, both east and west of the Sierra Madre and north and south into the mountains, the grand total in 1678 was 62,599 Christians.

Chapter XVII

NEUMANN BEGINS A CAREER

I N 1678, the year of Father Juan Zapata's famous visitation to all the establishments, many other missionaries setting out from their native lands—Bohemia, Germany, and Italy—sailed from Genoa for Spain and the port of Cádiz, thence to embark for various areas of the mission field. Among them was Father Joseph Neumann, if not the most famous, perhaps the greatest, certainly the most important Black Robe in all the Tarahumar missions.

In the year 1677 two energetic procurators from two Jesuit provinces, that of New Spain and that of the Philippines, were sent to Rome to transact business pertaining to their respective provinces. The task of seeking missionaries for the New World was always part of this business. On their way to Rome they stopped in Seville to confer with the Council of the Indies. They both presented a strong plea for their respective missions begging leave to recruit man power. The Mexican procurator represented that a vast new field, Upper Tarahumara, was now open to the fathers, and the Philippine procurator described the new lands in the Mariana Islands, far off the coast of the Philippines, one of which, whose modern name is Guam, was given prominence in 1898; another, Saipan, in 1944. New mission fields meant new provinces in Spain's colonial empire, and the Council of the Indies was generous in its permissions, authorizing the Philippine procurator to carry forty missionaries back with him, and the Mexican procurator to carry twenty. One-third of these could be foreigners, or non-Spaniards. The difference in numbers is easily explained. Mexico could draw from the creole population for missionary recruits, but this additional supply was not available to the Jesuits in the Philippines.

Arrived in Rome the procurators announced the glad tidings to the General, John Paul Oliva, who was only too happy to comply with the wishes of the two provinces of the New World, since, as was always the case, numerous names of volunteers for the missions were in his files. General Oliva in selecting twenty non-Spaniards for the

[1] For notes to chapter xvii see pages 250-251.

long mission journey chose twelve from Germany and eight from Italy, all of them priests. Among those from Germany was Father Joseph Neumann.[1]

By the early part of June, 1678, nineteen Jesuits were gathered at Genoa, the rendezvous for embarkation to Cádiz. Joseph Neumann was among them, and also Father Juan María Ratkay, a Hungarian nobleman, who had been page to the Emperor Leopold. Neumann was born in Brussels of a German father and early taken to Vienna. When he became a Jesuit he entered the Bohemian Province of the Order. He was fifteen years a Jesuit when he sailed for America. Ratkay was destined to go all the way to Tarahumara with Neumann. There was another in the group destined to become the most famous of them all, the illustrious Eusebio Francisco Kino. Judging from their names which one of their number, Father Adam Gerstl, gives in a letter to his father, eleven were Germans and the rest Italians, except Brother Simón Poruhradiski, who was a Bohemian, and another whose name is missing.[2]

Neumann left Prague on April 11. He set sail from Genoa with the group on June 12, and after storms and an alarm from pirates of the Barbary coast, and after having been flung back from the gates of Gibraltar three times by contrary winds, the party arrived in Spain— alas, too late to take ship that year for the New World. The fleet had left two days before! They saw it in the distance putting out to sea.[3] Since it would be two years before a fleet would sail again, there was nothing for it but to wait.[4]

The enforced leisure was partly utilized by the missionaries in making and buying a great collection of articles useful for the missions: tools, toys for the savage, pious objects, and various knickknacks. As a later Jesuit wrote: "The missionaries who travel from Germany to America provide themselves generously with Roman indulgenced medals, copper-plate prints large and small, agnus dei, relics and small crosses, all of which are greatly valued in this country."[5] Since in the missions the fathers had to be jacks-of-all-trades, they took time by the forelock during their enforced stay in Spain and became experts in various crafts before they sailed for Mexico. Ratkay, for instance, learned "to blow bottles, carve wood, solder tin, sew clothes and furs, make trinkets, and perform a hundred and one other tasks."[6]

The two years crept slowly by and in 1680 the fleet was again ready
to weigh anchor. The twenty-three Jesuits with all their belongings
finally boarded the good ship *Nazareno*. Eighteen were assigned to
the Philippines; five to Mexico, including Kino, Neumann, and Ratkay. But disaster awaited them all. On the way out of the harbor the
captain of the *Nazareno* ran on a sandbank and then into a rock which
tore the vessel's keel so that she began to leak. The fathers were res-
cued by a skiff, but all their belongings were lost. Through begging
and the good offices of the new Viceroy, Don Antonio de la Cerda,
sailing with his wife to take office in Mexico, eleven of the Jesuits
were reluctantly taken on other ships. Among these were Ratkay and
Neumann; Kino was among the unlucky twelve who were left behind
to wait still another year!

Ratkay was particularly fortunate. The good ship *San Diego* which
took him on board in his shipwrecked plight had a distinguished per-
sonage among its passengers, the new Bishop of Manila, of the Order
of St. Dominic. The captain too was a gentleman. Ratkay and his
companion, De Angelis, were invited to share the table of the Bishop,
and the captain lodged them in his own quarters. "We were much
surprised to get so many good things for our meals," wrote the Jesuit.
"For breakfast we had the wing or a leg of a chicken, a piece of beef
or pork, and candy or preserves. For dinner the meal consisted of lapary
cabbage, mutton, olla (or meat stew), rice, a piece of tart, and finally
cheese and olives. On fast days they served the same number of dishes
of smoked or salted seafish. There was also no lack of lemonades and
wines."[7] Breakfast was at nine, dinner at two.

After a near wreck because of a hurricane the fleet arrived at Vera
Cruz September 25, and the eleven Jesuits disembarked to spend the
night in the Jesuit house at Vera Cruz. Soon they were on their way
over the well-worn trail, first blazed by Cortés, up from the *tierra
caliente,* called the graveyard of Europeans, past the glittering cone of
snow-capped Orizaba and into beautiful Puebla, guarded on the west
by its towering peaks, Popocatepetl and Iztaccihuatl, clothed through
all the year in a glistening garment of snow. The travelers marveled
at the splendors even of the city of Puebla and when they threaded
the pass and descended into the delightful Anáhuac, Valley of Waters,
and witnessed the grandeurs of the capital of New Spain their astonish-

ment knew no bounds. They were warmly received by their brethren, both in Puebla and in Mexico City. The Provincial had come to Puebla from the capital to greet them. He met the group near the town with coaches and drove them to the college where forty of their fellow Black Robes were assembled at the gate to bid them welcome.

Early in October they were in Puebla, soon after in Mexico City, and by the middle of November Neumann and Ratkay set out upon the rough and rocky trail for the distant northern mission. Ratkay in a long letter of November 16 to a Jesuit friend in Europe, Father Nicolaus Avancinus, says that he and Neumann were leaving next day for the northern missions.[8] Actually they left two days later, November 18, as one of Neumann's letters informs us.

The twenty-three Black Robe missionaries who departed for the New World in 1680 and the following year were soon scattered to the far quarters of two hemispheres. Eight were sent to South America. Of those who touched at Mexico, most continued on across the wide Pacific. Five went to the Marianas, two to the Philippines, and one, Father Gerstl, to China. Three of the five who went to the Marianas—Borabgo, Strobach, and De Angelis—were slain by the natives. Neumann and Ratkay went to Tarahumara.

There were places open for new missionaries in Sinaloa, Sonora, Topia, and Tarahumara. The Provincial, Bernardo Pardo, graciously allowed the newcomers to choose what mission post they desired. Instinctively with the Loyolan spirit, these two men chose what they knew was the most difficult mission, that of the northern Tarahumares. Because of the isolation and the cold and difficult climate this mission was considered a particularly hard post, but Neumann was possessed of a vigorous constitution.[9]

Thither they slowly trudged on muleback out of Mexico City on November 18, bearing a note from the Provincial to the Tarahumar Superior in which he said that these two Jesuits could do the work of twelve men. They had muleteers, servants, and a guide. Their cavalcade consisted of fifteen or twenty horses and mules, carrying provisions for all the journey, all the earthly belongings of the fathers (greatly reduced since the shipwreck at Cádiz), all articles necessary for the celebration of Mass and the divine service, and, finally, gadgets, trinkets, medals, images, beads and colored cloth, with needles, nails, thread, string, and rope; also wine for Mass, chocolate for diversion, and medicine for necessity.[10]

It took the missionaries twenty days to reach Zacatecas, the old mining town, 325 miles away. The dryness of the country struck Neumann. "Our route," he wrote, "lay for the most part through uninhabited deserts. Of springs and streams we found scarcely any. Often we were exposed to the burning sun, for the land is barren and treeless. At night we frequently had to sleep under the cold sky. There are no inns whatever, and in this long stretch of one hundred leagues Indian villages are very few, as is apparent from the fact that in the course of three weeks we saw and passed through barely fifteen."[11] A few days later the travelers reached Durango where they tarried a week visiting with their five brethren who made up the college there. The Bishop of Nueva Vizcaya, the Franciscan Bartolomé de Escañuela, was most friendly and invited them to dinner. On the day before their departure the same prelate honored them by a visit to the college to bid them godspeed.

There was a reason for the stopover in Durango. There had been trouble in the Tepehuán country and bands of hostile Indians roved the hills. The two fathers therefore waited for other travelers to take the road north, thus, like caravans of the desert, finding safety in numbers. Riding out of town December 27, the party trod the broad dry plain of Durango north, entered a pass west through a sierra and descended into the delightful uplands watered by the Río de Ramos. Situated on the banks of this stream was Papasquiaro where now for more than eighty years the Jesuits had administered their chief Tepehuán mission. A few days here and the missionaries were on their way again. After leaving Santa Catalina they traversed difficult mountainous country until they came to Zape. From there on it was smoother going, and they were accompanied by four soldiers for more than a hundred miles to the end of Tepehuán territory. Neumann considered himself fortunate to have escaped all danger, for he reported that two days later five Spaniards were murdered while traveling the same highway.[12]

At Parral Fathers Neumann and Ratkay met the Governor who had within recent years transferred his seat to this mining center of the far north. The travelers continued on to the northwest to meet the Father Visitor, who was staying in San Ignacio Coyachic. They remained at this place through February, 1681, learning the language. At long last, early in March, the Visitor sent Neumann to his mission which was to be Sisoguichic, and Ratkay to his mission of Cárichic.[13] Father Juan María Ratkay died at Cárichic after two years, but the vigorous Joseph Neumann began at Sisoguichic a splendid career of half a century.

Sisoguichic at the time that Neumann arrived had been three years without a resident missionary. At Cárichic Ratkay replaced Father Rolandegui who had been recalled to the capital. The shortage of men in Tarahumara at the time of Neumann's arrival was due to the weakness of certain individuals. When four years earlier six new missionaries entered Tarahumara they filled the various posts in which Visitor Zapata saw them in 1678. Of the eight fathers then laboring, four were Spaniards born in Spain, the other four were creoles, born in Mexico. Now it often happened that the creoles were not possessed of the same vigorous spirit as the Europeans and sometimes lacked their robust constitution. Indeed, this was very particularly noted in this century in Peru, where the creole was characterized in an official report by the Visitor to the General Claudius Aquaviva, as soft and indolent. This Visitor, Father Páez, expelled ten or twelve subjects from the Order in Peru during his visitation, 1599 to 1602, and Aquaviva ruled that creoles were not to be admitted in that province until they had reached the age of twenty. Special provision was to be made, if possible, for their training during their pre-Jesuit youth.[14]

Neumann hints at the same weakness among the Mexicans, for he says that of the eight who had preceded him into Upper Tarahumara, the four creoles weakened and had to be replaced. One, "taking too great care of his health," which was indeed bad, died; the other three, growing despondent because of the difficulties of the situation and the slight response from their charges, asked to be removed to the more populous and easier missions of Sonora. This left Tarahumara with only four workers, which was the situation when our two newcomers arrived in Cárachic and Sisoguichic respectively.[15]

Father Joseph Neumann, vigorous, strong of mind and resolute, with the stolidity characteristic of his race, settled himself down to his life work among the Tarahumares at Sisoguichic, the most isolated of all the pueblos. In the midst of the Tarahumar nation Neumann was to grow old, and after half a century of labor and privation of every kind his work was ended by death. After a year at Sisoguichic he wrote to the Province of Bohemia one of his most informative letters, copies of which we are fortunate to possess.[16]

Neumann's route to his pueblo lay through Cárichic. The padre there, Bernardo Rolandegui, soon to depart for the capital, accompanied Neumann to Sisoguichic. Rolandegui had sent messengers ahead to announce the arrival. The two missionaries started west over hills, skidded down precipitous banks to the riverbed of the upper Conchos, crossed brush-choked and wooded canyons, until, emerging into more open country, they were heartened by a surprise: the Indian governor of the valley of Sisoguichic with four of his braves awaited their father in order to accompany him to their land.

It was altogether a picturesque performance, these five copper-skinned Tarahumares with bands about their heads, clothed only in loin cloth and jacket, guiding the two Black Robes through the wooded mountains of western Chihuahua. As they trudged along Father Rolandegui explained to the natives why their new missionary was coming among them, through baptism to make them subjects of the King of Heaven, and through education and gentle manners to make them good subjects of the King of Spain. The Redmen seemed pleased. They expressed joy and promised to gather in all the heathen of their valley to be washed by the sacramental waters. They asked many questions about Father Joseph Neumann, which Rolandegui, possessing a more facile grasp of their language, was happy to answer. They encouraged Neumann, holding out hopes of happy success.[17]

Darkness overtook the party when their journey was but half done. That night they slept under the dark sky. Wooded ridges rose on either side of the narrow glen where they camped, and perhaps the sound of a running stream was conducive to pleasant sensations and to sleep. The following afternoon at two o'clock two padres and the five Tarahumares arrived at the spot in the valley of Sisoguichic where Neumann's predecessor had lived three years before. It was in a narrow vale closed in by wooded hills. Here was the little church, hard by it the father's hut. It was March 7, 1681, the Feast of St. Thomas Aquinas.

A happy welcome had been prepared by the Indians for the coming of the Black Robe. Over the path leading to this spot they had erected two arches made of the boughs of trees, concrete expression of their desire to honor their missionary. They first entered the church and there Neumann in the silent chambers of his own heart expressed to God his gratitude. It had taken him almost four months to come from Mexico City. Well nigh three years had passed from the time he had set out from Prague for the mission fields of the New World. Now at last he stood in his own mission.

The hut was inspected. This required a second of time—it was so small and poor. A meal was then served by the Indians. Since it was Lent and the cacique knew the fathers would eat neither flesh nor fowl, some eggs, cooked beans, and tortillas helped to drive away their hunger.

Tarahumares from the vicinity had been slowly gathering about. After the meal Father Rolandegui had them collected in the church and gave instructions for their future behavior. The new father would live with them and care for their spiritual welfare provided they would agree to fulfill certain conditions. The new church which they had begun was to be finished as soon as possible, because the father disliked to say Mass in a hovel. They were likewise to finish the larger and better house they had begun for him near the new church. They must send their children daily to the father to be instructed in the Christian religion and ultimately to be baptized. They must lead to him other heathen for the same purpose. Finally, what other services might be necessary at a given time, they must perform at the behest of their Black Robe. The Tarahumares of Sisoguichic agreed to fulfill the father's wishes.

Thus the Basque Rolandegui introduced Neumann the German to his Tarahumares. The former then departed to return to his mission. Many of his flock were ill at Cárichic and the padre was anxious to return to them. Rolandegui departed the following day; Neumann was left in extreme isolation among the heathen.

These simple children fell to work with a will. The church was finished within three weeks and the father's house in another three. To Neumann's great delight, the church was completed just in time for Easter and so it was christened, so to speak, by its first Mass on Easter

Sunday. Then Neumann applied his sound psychology and intelligence of human nature. He organized a feast for his neophytes on this his first Easter day in the wilds. Rolandegui with thoughtful generosity had weeks before seen to it that thirty head of cattle were driven up into the valley for the sustenance of the padre. Neumann ordered two of the beasts slain and their flesh distributed generously among his Indians. After such a gesture the padre's prestige ran high throughout all the valley and over into the other vales and glens of the sierra.

Neumann described in a letter the activities of these earliest days of his missionary career: "I devoted myself to the instruction of the children. Twice daily I gathered them into the church. In the morning after Mass I repeated with them the *Pater Noster,* the *Ave Maria,* the *Credo,* the precepts of the Decalogue, the sacraments of the Church, and the rudiments of Christian doctrine. I had brought these with me in a translation into the Tarahumar tongue, and I repeated them from the written text. In the evening I reviewed the lesson and also asked the children questions from the catechism, At the same time I gave instruction to those among them who were still pagan, acquainting them with the principal mysteries of the Faith and preparing them to receive baptism. The rest of the day was spent in visiting the sick and hearing confessions—although, to be sure, I heard but few—or in assisting the builders and directing their operations. For in these countries the fathers themselves are the only architects, and the Indians are the only masons."[18]

Neumann's new dwelling had three rooms. The largest was his dining- and living-room, another his bedroom, the third was used as a storeroom. Neumann himself made the partitions and made and fitted the doors with his own hands. "I myself have also been carpenter and cabinetmaker," he wrote. He was his own "cook and steward, tailor and launderer, sacristan and nurse for the sick—in a word, everything—for the Indians have no knowledge or understanding of any of these offices." The missionaries were not allowed to have a female servant or cook, but regulations drawn up for the missionary fathers did permit an Indian woman to come once a week to the father's cabin and bake for him his week's supply of tortillas. This practice was followed by Neumann who found it impossible to procure competent male help. A little kitchen stood a few yards off from the rest of the house.

As was usual, however, in these missions, the Indians sent to Neumann two small boys to live with him and to be his servants. He fed them and clothed them and took care to treat them with the utmost gentleness, else they would run away to their homes and parents. Neumann was unable to procure a third boy. But the two aided him in the morning when he said Mass and served at his meals. To them he gave special instruction and he reflects that often in the past when such boys grew up they became the father's consolation and valued assistants. When he was away these boys took charge of the mission, led in prayer and catechism, and in general helped in the Christian training of the others. Such boys were called *temastianes,* and were familiar figures in all the Jesuit missions. Neumann, then from the first, raised and trained two little *temastianes.*

Such was the beginning of labors in Sisoguichic, chief pueblo or cabecera of his partido, which was officially listed and named as Nombre de María Santísima, as we learn from the record of Zapata's visitation made three years before.[19] At that time there were at Sisoguichic but seventy-four Christian families making in all 179 persons. Twelve miles northwest was the only other pueblo of this partido, Echoguita, named by the previous missionary Asunción. Only nine had been baptized here by that time, and early in 1681 the nine were probably scattered, for though these settlements were called pueblos, the dwellings of these ragged people were, like many others at this period, not yet clustered into a village, but strung along the banks of an arroyo.

At Sisoguichic Neumann's charges were scattered for eight or ten miles along the stream, tributary of the upper Conchos. Sisoguichic lay almost a hundred and fifty miles from Parral; its nearest neighbor was Cárichic thirty miles away as the crow flies, but well nigh doubled in distance by the ridges which had to be skirted and the streams followed. Here Neumann lived remote from all fellowship and for months at a time he was unable even to make his confession.

In another valley thirty miles away a few families were living on a stream and this place was called Panálachic; southeast fifteen miles was still another vale belonging to his territory where lay a settlement called Coácichic. In this place was one Christian, in the former none at all. To the south was the famous gorge of the Río Urique, which dizzied the head of Salvatierra as he gazed down its ribs of rock. On the west was the missionary partido just newly organized of the Témores, the Varohíos, and the Guazápares, belonging to the Sinaloa west coast unit. There at the time of Neumann's arrival were working Fathers Nicolás de Prado, Fernando Pecoro, and Juan María Salvatierra, later to become the illustrious founder of the California missions.[20] In the western districts of Neumann's partido the mountains rose higher and the valleys were cut deeper. Here, as Neumann informs us, were numerous pagans inhabiting two valleys. Such difficult country, including the headwaters of the Conchos and the Papigochic, was for fifteen years to be the theater of Neumann's apostolic labors. Before his maiden year had run its course the vigorous missioner was to visit these sequestered vales.

At Sisoguichic, as the first weeks of his residence slipped by, Neumann was preparing a number of adults for baptism. Even before that first Easter he had baptized four women, and five after the feast. He notices with satisfaction that on Sundays those baptized by his predecessor came, sometimes for miles, from their hovels up or down the river, to attend Mass. They loyally summoned him when one of their number grew ill, and again, if the sickness grew serious, that he might administer the last sacraments. Once when a man died suddenly without having confessed the Indians refused to bury him in the consecrated ground even though Neumann pressed them to do so. The padre prudently yielded to their somewhat exaggerated ideas. Soon he was making excursions to his visita of Echoguita twelve miles distant where a handful had been baptized, and to Coácichic over in another valley, and to far-distant Panálachic in the south. In one of these narrow vales he had baptized before the year was over a large number of his people.[21]

Such were the maiden activities of one of the most vigorous spirits that ever labored in Tarahumara. Indeed, Joseph Neumann can be called Tarahumara's most important apostle. He several times served as superior of the whole mission of San Joaquín y Santa Ana and was once named its official visitor. During the many years of his labor he had passed through many hairbreadth escapes, suffered the anxieties and dangers of several serious revolts, witnessed the massacre of two Jesuits, and finally, even with his vigorous frame, worn out with labors and with years, he died at a ripe old age shortly after the first quarter of the 1700's, having spent almost half a century in the wilds of Alta Tarahumara.

Chapter XVIII

A KALEIDOSCOPIC TWELVEMONTH

THE ARRIVAL of six new men into Alta Tarahumara in 1677, of Neumann and Ratkay in 1681 and later of others, signified the permanency of the missions in northern Mexico. Nevertheless, it has already become evident that the Tarahumares were not the easiest people to deal with. They had not the frankness and generosity of certain of the west coast primitives, and even the steady and vigorous Neumann admitted that to labor among them required infinite patience and endurance. Many a weaker or more impetuous spirit among the missionaries became discouraged. Indications of this we have already seen. In his history of the Tarahumar mission Neumann reminds us that "these Indians are by nature and disposition a sly and crafty folk, from whom sincerity is not to be expected. They are accomplished hypocrites, and as a rule the ones who seem the most virtuous should be considered the most wicked of all. They say one thing to their people when in the presence of the missionaries and later in secret they say another directly the contrary."[1] When the missionaries chose as Indian governors of the pueblos those whom they thought were trustworthy and honest, they were frequently deceived. Therefore our Black Robe writes: "The missionaries were deceived by these men too, for they were addicted to the same vices. . . . Superficially the Governors conformed to the wishes of the fathers, and their lives had the appearance of probity, but all the while they were secretly seeking the favor of their people by tolerating and cloaking their offenses."[2]

Many a Black Robe, therefore, became discouraged. It was not always or perhaps even chiefly the difficulties and hardness of the life. The Jesuit missionary was proverbially able to endure such conditions; but the lack of response from the people, the slight numbers they were at first able to baptize, the sense of time lost and effort wasted—this (we can understand it well) could bring discouragement to the souls of even the strong. And so the ancient historian of the mission avers: "In fact, I cannot deny that with these stony-hearted people the result does

[1] For notes to chapter xviii see page 252.

not repay the hard labor and the valuable seed. The seed of the gospel does not sprout, or if it does spring up it is spoiled by the thorns of carnal desire."[3] "For this reason," says the missionary, "we find little eagerness among our new converts who prepare for baptism. Indeed, some only pretend to believe, showing no inclination for spiritual things, such as prayers, divine services, and Christian doctrine. They show no aversion to sin, no anxiety about their eternal happiness, no eagerness to persuade their relatives to be baptized. They show rather a lazy indifference to everything good, unlimited sensual desire, an irresistible habit of getting drunk, and stubborn silence in regard to hidden pagans, and so we cannot find them and bring them into the fold of Christ."[4]

The modern reader can easily understand the psychological reaction upon the missionary, who in Europe had dreamed, perhaps, of converting like another Xavier his thousands and thousands of primitive natives. The fame of the missions on the coast had gone abroad in books and in letters; the story of the tens of thousands of generous Mayos and loyal Yaquis and Pimas had inflamed the heart of many a young Jesuit in the seminaries and colleges of Europe. And, since generalizations are easy and since as the wish is so often father to the thought, young and ardent spirits foresaw the same abundant harvest in all the mission fields of the Americas. They forgot that as it is on the earth's surface, so it is with human hearts: deep and rich soil is replaced as we move along by hard and rocky surface. "Consequently," writes Father Neumann in 1686 to his Jesuit friend Stowasser of the Province of Bohemia, "many missionaries who were anxious to come to the Indies, expecting to convert many heathen, begin to imagine that they are wasting their time and labor, because all their efforts have come to naught. Others complain that they have been deceived in their profession, and hence painfully regret their holy undertaking because they do not achieve their goal here. And so they anxiously beg their superiors for other missions, where they could be of greater use. Among the fourteen priests," Neumann continues, "who are in these missions there are not more than two who have not asked the Father Visitor for a change, so that they may be able to devote their hard efforts and their best years to the saving of more souls among the heathen."[5]

When our missionary historian wrote these sentences he had already been more than five years among the Tarahumares and he was speaking therefore from ripened knowledge. But, though others may have become discouraged, his own spirit never drooped, because it seems he was a realist of the finest type, one, namely, who seeing the weakness and shoddiness of certain manifestations of human nature, yet quietly and strongly applies to it the philosophy of the strong but gentle Nazarene. For Neumann had written: ". . . It is not sublime theology or subtlety of knowledge in any of the other sciences that is needed in the work of instilling Christian doctrine into these people. There is need only of the gentleness of the lamb in directing them; of invincible patience in bearing with them; and, finally, of Christian humility, which enables you to become all things to all men, to disdain no one, to perform without shrinking the meanest task, and, if the barbarians scorn you, to endure their contempt to the end."[6]

Perhaps the twentieth-century North American can understand the psychology of the seventeenth-century Tarahumar. These people had not asked for the Spaniard who was, from their point of view, an intruder. The Christian ethic which the missionary tried to impose was and is difficult for human nature to live up to. Moreover, the padres endeavored to gather the Indians into more compact pueblos so that they could be more easily instructed. This worked a hardship on many, it was a restriction of the wild freedom of their former life, and actually (though the Indians did not realize the fact) it facilitated the spread of dread diseases. The discipline and confinement of pueblo life sometimes became irksome and rebels against it were sometimes punished with the lash. It was often true, however, as the record abundantly shows, that once the Spaniard came and the Indian could not get rid of him, the primitive made the best of the situation and accepted the Spaniard with his Christianity, especially when the latter was represented by the kindliness and charm which the missionary often possessed. The native more readily accepted Christianity when it was connected with certain temporal advantages, such as gifts of meat and other food, trinkets and other gewgaws. Such considerations help to explain the undoubted fact that groups of Indians often asked the fathers to come among them and to propagate the religion of their conquerors. To say nothing of the spiritual and supernatural, the Indians often appreciated the psychological, social, and economic advantages which life in a Christian pueblo afforded them. Christian civilization put a stop to their decimating civil wars, the cannibalism practiced by certain groups, and their furious intertribal feuds and raids. It taught them to expand their crops, to care for herds of animals, and it led to the possession of security and inner peace.

Many things happened in the mission field of Upper Tarahumara during the twelve months from February to February, 1681 to 1682. There were storms and treacheries, alarms and revolts, floods and snows.

In the first place, trouble started among the Guazápares just beyond the western border of the Tarahumar mission. Into this rugged region Julio Pascual had penetrated in 1626 and there both he and his companion Manuel Martínez had been slain by the Guazápares and Varohíos. This spelled the ruin of the mission throughout all the Chínipas country. Decades passed until, through a felicitous chain of events, a new entrada was made in April, 1676, by the arrival in the precipitous barrancas of the two Italian Jesuits, Nicolás de Prado and Fernando Pecoro. During the visitation of Zapata in 1678 three partidos for each of the three tribes of the region, the Chínipas, the Varohíos, and the Guazápares, were organized and added to the already large mission unit of San Ignacio de Yaqui. In 1680 the illustrious Juan María Salvatierra arrived to take over one of the partidos.[7]

Unfortunately, the following year a conspiracy was hatched by an apostate neophyte of the Guazápar tribe. It was the old story. The natives resented the presence of the missionary who took away their plurality of wives and forced them into compact pueblos where he could watch them and keep them from their carousals. The leader of the malcontents acquired a certain following. The rebels vowed to rouse the whole country, slay the three missionaries, and go back to their caves, their wives, and their drinking bouts. The fathers learned of what was going on and sent word to the Governor of Sinaloa. This official averted the danger by quick and energetic action. He surprised the rebels by the sudden appearance of soldiers sent among them. Meanwhile the fathers in the Guazápar country sent word to Sisoguichic warning Neumann of what was taking place, for had the rebellion broken out Neumann's mission would have been the first among the Tarahumares to be affected. The new missionary thus warned watched closely.

Although Neumann was thus on the alert his own Indian governor of Sisoguichic and the Indian fiscal became near rebels. They had heard of the trouble in the higher sierra and they went over to confer with these people with whom they had enjoyed a long friendship. The purpose of this particular visit was not clear. But for the occasion the Christian Guazápares prepared to stage one of their all-night carousals. The padre, probably Salvatierra, learned of the projected affair and broke it up. Next morning he assembled all the people of his pueblo, and ordered his Indian officials, the governor, fiscal, and perhaps temastián, to have the culprits, those who had planned the celebration, flogged and so it was done. Now, the two visiting Tarahumares also felt the lash upon their backs. Since they had been guests, they resented the punishment as a particular indignity and returned to Sisoguichic in haste and high temper, but said not one word to Neumann. But the padre was informed by the Guazápar missionaries about everything that had taken place. The padre learned, moreover, that his Indian governor was spreading discontent by slandering the missionaries of the mountains. He therefore called his neophyte and rebuked him, threatening, did he not mend his ways, to have him removed from his office by the Spanish Governor at Parral.[8]

All these incidents took place during the early summer of 1681. Later that summer the whole mission, under the leadership of Tomás Guadalajara at Mátachic, rector of the unit, was preparing for a typical Jesuit celebration. The final vows of the Order were to be taken by some of the new arrivals, Neumann among them. The date fixed was August 15, Feast of the Assumption. Neumann on this occasion was to pronounce his final vows as spiritual coadjutor of the Society of Jesus. As a spiritual preparation for such an event, which would bind the padre definitely to the Order, certain spiritual activities were prescribed by the Jesuit Constitutions, such as the eight days' retreat, instructing children in the catechism, and begging from door to door throughout the town.

Now, the first requirement, the retreat, was easily complied with immediately before the vows were pronounced; the second, Neumann was fulfilling every day at his mission. The third seemed impractical if not impossible in the circumstances. The padre was in the wilds nearly one hundred and fifty miles away from the nearest town, Parral.

He could not go through the ridiculous gesture of begging from his Indians. It would seem, and so Neumann thought, that here was just reason for dispensation from the third and nonessential point of spiritual discipline. Such a dispensation could have been easily granted by the Provincial, Bernardo Pardo, or he could have delegated the Visitor to concede it according to his judgment of the circumstances. However, the superiors held to the letter of the law, with the result that Joseph Neumann had to leave his mission, trudge the hundred and fifty miles to Parral, beg in the streets for three days, and then return to Sisoguichic. "I was absent from my mission for a whole month," he wrote somewhat querulously, "and traversed more than one hundred and fifty leagues, solely on account of my begging."⁹ He covered about five hundred miles before he got back home again. He set forth at the end of June with at least two Indian guides, but he kept the purpose of his visit secret so that any unquiet spirit among his people might not learn of his enforced absence from the pueblo.

He put to practical purpose his visit to Parral. He called upon the Governor and procured letters patent which would permit the Governor of Sinaloa to enter his mission with soldiers in the event of any trouble, even though Sisoguichic was under the jurisdiction of Parral. The Governor of Parral could not protect the padre, for besides the distance, there was a dearth of soldiers in this isolated capital of Nueva Vizcaya. Neumann also procured written official instructions for the good behavior and proper organization of the Indians of his partido. Thus armed and his penance of begging performed, he retraced his steps to his mission.

But the return was not to be easy. The Black Robe was overtaken by continuous rains and by flood. After going north to San Felipe on the Conchos and then west along its southern bank, he found he could not ford the tributaries. It was probably the Río San Juan, flowing north into the Conchos, which blocked his passage. For several days he awaited the subsidence of the flood, but since the waters increased, he made his way back to San Felipe and decided to cross the Conchos at that place where the stream runs broadly and smoothly. If he could cross at San Felipe he would thus eliminate the fording of two other streams by going west along the north bank of the Conchos. The Indians of San Felipe made Neumann and his companions a raft large enough to support them and their saddles. The raft was launched after Mass on the Feast of St. James, the good Indians of San Felipe surrounded it and by swimming propelled it slowly to the north bank of the Conchos. The horses and mules swam the stream. In this same way Anza a century later crossed the Colorado into California with the help of his faithful Yumas.

Neumann got back to Sisoguichic at two in the morning, July 31, 1681. Sometime after daybreak he summoned the Indian governor and all his people and officially acquainted them with the commands of the Governor at Parral: they were to form a pueblo around the church, were to adhere strictly to the Christian doctrine, were to eschew drunkenness, concubinage, disobedience, and all seditious talk. The Indian judges were to punish severely offenses against the commands of the governor, lest they be chastized by the Spaniards. All of this program of reform was aimed chiefly at the Indian governor who had caused the trouble. He felt his guilt and promised to fulfill all that was contained in the instructions.

But the padre had to leave immediately for Mátachic there to take his last vows on August 15. He must make another journey of forty-five miles, this time directly north over a divide from the headwaters of the Conchos to the middle Papigochic; from the divide where the streams flow sluggishly into the Gulf of Mexico to the country where the streams rapidly spill their waters into the Gulf of California.

Father Neumann arrived at San Rafael Mátachic, August 6, where six of his brethren were to assemble. He began immediately his eight days' retreat of spiritual exercises in preparation for his vows and thus was ready for the ecclesiastical festal day of the fifteenth.

Neumann was the first to arrive so that he and Guadalajara were alone for five days. After this period various distractions affected Neumann's retreat. Two days before the feast came the Visitor with two other missionaries, one of them the Belgian Juan Baustido Copart from Papigochic. Father Guadalajara's loyal Indians had erected four arbors of boughs and flowers over the path to honor the distinguished guests as they rode into the mission, and when news of their proximity was announced a band of Indian horsemen rode out to accompany them into the pueblo. Guadalajara did the honors as they rode into the village. Next day these six made up the complete number of the mission of Alta Tarahumara, with the exception of Ratkay who remained purposely at his mission, since it was central and he could be on hand for any emergency in the organized pueblos. Five Spanish laymen graced the occasion, including Captain García, old friend of Father Guadalajara, who with his sons came a three days' journey to honor and enjoy the occasion. Bands of Tarahumares with their Indian governors came in likewise and were at Mátachic on the eve of the feast.

Guadalajara now used his intelligence and ordered three beeves killed and a feast for all the natives. He wanted his people to be happy and content. It was a famine year; the Indians had been living chiefly on fish. They would devour the meat both on the vigil and on the feast itself. There was music too for this vigil. Guadalajara at Mátachic had trained a skillful choir of Indian boys and the Visitor had brought with him three or four musicians. Thus vespers were chanted that evening and on the morrow, and the choir graced the ceremony of the Mass and the pronouncement of the final vows.

The feast day was indeed a joyous occasion. The Indian governor of Mátachic invited the fathers to witness an exhibition of horsemanship by his men. Fifty Indians mounted on excellent horses deployed on the broad level which lay north of the mission. These savages on horseback made evolutions and formed figures to the delight of the witnesses. This show went on all the afternoon and ended toward evening in a sham battle. Nor was this all. The Indians celebrated throughout the night: they sang, they hooted, they jumped, and they thought they danced. Little sleep for the padres that night, and, the following morning at least, the Indians were happier that they had not taken intoxicating liquor. But tired or not, four of the fathers had to depart for their respective missions. Neumann went back to Sisoguichic.

Not long after this happy event a cloud appeared upon the horizon and grew to black and ugly proportions. Father Tomás de Guadalajara noticed the first signs of disaffection among his own Indians, heretofore so personally loyal and so well behaved. The padre noted that his neophytes ceased to obey his commands, and they discontinued coming for their usual instructions in the catechism. Other acts of courtesy or service they likewise began to omit. Further signs were more disheartening and disquieting. They carried on carousals with great effrontery near the mission, openly, so they would be noticed; they bore their corn away, and hid it in remote places; they began manufacturing great numbers of darts and arrows. This was a profound alteration, and their padre was filled with the gravest apprehensions. Scraps of information were reported to him by loyal Indians: such as the intent to murder the father and provoke rebellion so that the primitives might flee the mission and go back to their ancient pagan freedom. Finally an Indian woman came to Father Guadalajara and in trepidation bade him flee for his life, for within three days the fires of revolt would spread over the mission.

This was enough. Guadalajara fled. He sped to Papigochic and warned Father Copart, begging him to flee likewise to the south. Copart had seen no signs among his own primitives and demurred, but when, soon after, a young Spaniard rushed in with worse reports telling of Indian plans for the murder also of Copart, to accomplish whose death three different bands had been assigned, he too fled in the wake of Guadalajara. He caught up with the latter at San Francisco de Borja. Ordering Father Celada, the padre of San Francisco, to send warning to all the fathers in the Upper Tarahumar mission and to direct them to speed eastward to San Francisco, Guadalajara made his way posthaste to Parral, to engage the protective arm of the Governor and his soldiers. But before leaving, he gave the alarm to an old Indian who was looked upon as chief of all the Tarahumares, and pressed him to go north and endeavor to stay the flood before it should gather further force. But the old man protested. No single word had he received, no sign of any trouble among his people had he seen. There must be some mistake, he objected. Guadalajara nevertheless fled from San Francisco by night, giving Celada authority to act as vice-rector in his absence.

The messenger of disaster arrived at Sisoguichic two hours before dawn. Neumann was still asleep. The Indian messenger beat upon the door crying out that he held a letter for the padre. Wakened, Neumann bustled excitedly out of bed, struck a light, pulled back the bolt of the door, and admitted the Indian. He took the letter and read it. The strong and steady Neumann was not greatly alarmed at this announcement of Indian rebellion. Nevertheless he prepared to obey the summons and go obediently to San Francisco. Since his Indian governor was absent, Neumann called up his Indian lieutenant and the captain of the people, two Indians of whom he was very fond. He bade them accompany him to San Francisco on urgent business. They obeyed at once and soon the three were on their way, rounding the shoulders of wooded hills and threading deep and steep-banked arroyos on their way to Cárichic and thence to San Francisco. At Pesiquechic, in the partido of Father Ratkay, Neumann learned that the father had left for the east two days before. Here the three spent the night. Next morning they pressed on to Cárichic where Neumann summoning all the pueblo said Mass for the people, for it was Sunday, and then continued on to San Francisco.

Here all was alarm. The missionaries had sent messengers to Papigochic and to Mátachic, commanding the governors and captains of the respective pueblos to come to San Francisco. If these Indian officers did not obey it would confirm the fathers' worst suspicions; if they did, it would be a favorable sign. During the three days of waiting for the arrival of the Indian officers the fathers carefully questioned the chiefs who had come in already with other fathers. All of them swore they had not the slightest inkling of any rebellion or trouble whatsoever. After three days the governors of the northwestern pueblos did come in, from Mátachic and Papigochic. This was a great relief. What they said was doubly reassuring. They agreed with their tribesmen from the other missions that there was no preparation for rebellion. Especially emphatic was the governor of Papigochic who solemnly protested that in his mission there reigned unbroken peace. Even the governor of Mátachic made similar statements. The fathers carefully interrogated the latter, questioning him about the suspicious circumstances which Guadalajara had noticed and all the other indications of rebellion. "But," reported Neumann, "he defended himself so skillfully and was so successful in explaining everything by the malevolence of certain foreigners, that he practically cleared both himself and the people of his mission of every charge, and left us wondering whether there was even a slight danger of the kind that the Father-rector [Guadalajara] had imagined."[10]

The missionaries who were assembled at San Francisco de Borja wrote to this effect to Guadalajara who was staying at San Gerónimo, the mission nearest to Parral. Copart volunteered to put his head into the lion's mouth and go to Mátachic to see for himself. In a few days his letters came to San Francisco reporting that all was well, that things were quiet there where the seat of the rebellion was supposed to be. There was rejoicing at San Francisco and the fathers, writing this news to their superior, prepared to return to their respective missions.

But Tomás Guadalajara was not convinced. He urged the greatest caution upon the fathers, and gave it as his opinion that the rebels, knowing they had been discovered, were merely simulating obedience and peacefulness. Neumann investigated for himself and wrote letters to the rector of the Guazápar mission, Nicolás de Prado. The latter replied immediately and his answer held the key to the whole trouble. He sent it by swift messengers but these, falling in with the ringleader of all the disturbance, delayed its delivery two weeks.

The story in the delayed letter was the following: Carosia, pagan cacique of a pagan Guazápar pueblo called Cacerici, had hatched a rebellion. He tried to stir up a general revolt against the missionaries not only among his fellow tribesmen, the Guazápares, but likewise among their neighbors on the north and east, the Tarahumares. He had collected a group of seventy men, well armed with poisoned arrows, and had gone to the Christian pueblos of the high mountains. These pueblos, however, remained loyal, all except Santa Ana of the Varohíos, where Pecoro had worked, but from which he had departed sometime before. Then the would-be rebel began to corrupt those about Mátachic with the results that caused Father Guadalajara to fear a general uprising. When Carosia heard that the fathers of Alta Tarahumara had fled their missions he tried to bring matters to a head.

Thus Prado wrote from his mountains of the Guazápares. Rebel Carosia seems to have been in touch only with those about Mátachic and without any real success. For whether their former deep loyalty to Guadalajara did in the end prevail, or whether these Tarahumares had been finally intimidated by the knowledge of the fathers' suspicion does not appear in the record. However, Neumann himself discovered, apart from Prado's information, that Carosia's rebel band of seventy did actually pass through Sisoguichic on their way to the other Tarahumar pueblos and had solicited Neumann's Indians. None, however, was corrupted. Thus there floated away the lowering clouds which for a time seemed to threaten with a general storm the new mission of Alta Tarahumara.

But that same year, 1681, just prior to the alarm caused by the would-be rebellion, another disturbing situation arose. This time it was an ecclesiastical and jurisdictional matter. The Bishop of Nueva Vizcaya, residing in Durango, was again causing worry to the Black Robe missionaries. Bartolomé de Escañuela was the bishop who had been so friendly to Neumann and Ratkay when they passed through Durango the year before. He was a Franciscan and, it appears, at bottom unfriendly to the Jesuits. He succeeded in procuring from the Council of the Indies a royal decree that all missionaries in his diocese (which would include also the missions on the coast) be subject entirely to his jurisdiction. This meant that no missionary could enter the country without his approval, nor leave it. He would install the padres as he installed his parish priests. He could order a man from the missions did he so desire. This would mean that the Bishop, not the Jesuit superior, would control the men. His desires, so Joseph Neumann informs us, were to install his own diocesan clergy in some of the more prosperous missions of Sinaloa and Sonora. The Bishop was, moreover, sending an official Visitor, Francisco de los Ríos, ex-Jesuit of the Philippines, to visit the Tarahumar missions. Such an arrangement was, of course, against ecclesiastical law, running counter to the canonical privileges of the regular clergy. If there were no other means to avoid the disorder the Jesuit superiors would have to recall their subjects from the missions of the diocese of Durango.

In this emergency the Governor of Nueva Vizcaya took a firm stand. The Governor felt that there was enough trouble in the northern sections of New Spain without adding more fuel to inflame Indian discontent. Just the preceding year, 1680, in New Mexico, the Cacique Popé of San Juan mission had rebelled, killed four hundred Spaniards, and destroyed twenty-one missions, created and cared for since the beginning of the century by Franciscans who had entered with Oñate. All the great far-northern section of Santa Fe was in ruins and the surviving Spaniards had been forced to flee the country and retire to safety to El Paso on the lower Río Grande. This was no time surely for innovations. Therefore, the Governor of Nueva Vizcaya "gave his solemn word, that if the Bishop should urge the execution of the royal decree and should ask assistance to carry it out, then in no regard would he, the Governor, comply with the request."[11]

But this jurisdictional storm also passed. The ancient rights of the missionaries prevailed in the threatened conflict. The Bishop's friend, Francisco de los Ríos, whom he had made vicar and *visitador-general* of the missions, was commanded to leave the kingdom and go into exile. The Bishop of Durango, moreover, was rebuked by the archiepiscopal government of Mexico City, which reminded him that continual quest and love of strife was unbecoming to the episcopal character. Indeed, Viceroy Tomás Antonio de la Cerda y Aragón, he who had sailed from Cádiz in the same fleet with Neumann and Ratkay, was especially devoted to the Jesuits. At this juncture, he ordered the number of Tarahumar missionaries to be increased and set aside new funds from the royal treasury for their support.[12]

The stormy twelvemonth ended severely for the Black Robes, at least for Neumann in his isolation at Sisoguichic. In the beginning of February, 1682, the heaviest snow in the memory of old-timers blanketed the hills and mountains of Upper Tarahumara. Everybody was snowed in—animals on the range, sheep on the hillsides, Indians in their caves, Neumann in his little hut. Neumann was imprisoned in his cabin for days and his neophytes were practically buried in their huts. "I could not go out of my house for many days," he wrote, "although I nearly perished with the cold. I had no wood on hand with which to make a fire, and for several days not one of the Indians came to my rescue. Moreover, I suffered greatly from lack of other supplies, for no funds have come to us this year from the royal treasury in Mexico. I was forced to live in cold and want, hunger and thirst, with the result that I fell ill. I had a very acute pain in my spine, and another in my side; the latter interfered with my breathing and well nigh suffocated me. For some time I was unable to leave my bed, and there I lay with no one to help me, and without a confessor to attend me. . . . It would not have been easy for a man to reach me even within three days, and even though he had used all possible speed. Therefore, I put my trust in God alone, and bade myself be patient; and presently, as the cold relaxed a little, I grew better."[13]

Joseph Neumann came out of the ordeal unharmed, but not so the missions and the country. Nearly all the sheep belonging to his Indians died of hunger and cold. Cattle, horses, and beasts of burden perished, and in the spring they were uncovered by the melting snows.

But in spite of all the disturbances of the twelvemonth from February to February of 1681–1682, the missions progressed. Baptisms continued to be administered, and settlements deeply enfolded in the mountains continued to be visited. Neumann himself, in his isolation far from other missions, was being "cobbler, tailor, mason, carpenter, cook, nurse, and physician for the sick." He was intent on building up Echoguita, the other pueblo of his partido. Only nine Indians had been baptized there by Neumanns' predecessor, but in January, before the heavy snows, the padre baptized twenty adults and had a large cross made from the trunk of a tree erected on the spot of the holy rite. He promised to visit these neophytes once a month and gradually to baptize them all. They were willing and on their part promised to build a church. Not a week went by but baptisms were performed. Neumann, like the other fathers, had become attached to his Indians, and he lauds their generosity. He was very fond of his lieutenant-governor and captain-general, those whom he had bade accompany him in his flight to San Francisco de Borja, and he speaks of their goodness of heart. All of which warns the modern reader against generalizations too hastily gathered from some of this missionary's descriptions of the spiritual difficulty of the mission and the spiritual stupidity of the people.

In February of 1682, Father Bernardo Rolandegui, whom Ratkay had succeeded at Cárichic, wrote a glowing report of the progress of Alta Tarahumara as a result of an official visitation he had just completed. He urges the sending of additional missionaries for this harvest, white in its ripe maturity, and now being so rapidly gathered in.[14]

Thus it was by the labors of each of the seven padres that the new unit of Alta Tarahumara, called San Joaquín y Santa Ana, increased and prospered. Within three years the new men promised by the Viceroy went into the field. Seven were added to the seven already there. Of these, three were Bohemians and three were Italians.[15] The baptized, from the five thousand odd Christians in the mission at Zapata's visitation in 1678, rose to the impressive figure of fourteen thousand. Other trials, however, were soon to come. A new revolt broke out; two more Jesuits fell; but their blood, according to the old belief, did but enrich the spiritual soil.

Chapter XIX

STORM, TREASON, AND REVOLT

THE REMAINING years of the decade were progressive and compara-
tively serene. A slight stir of trouble was caused by two Indians of
the Guazápar country, the least peaceful district of all the Jesuit missions. Two young neophytes, servants and cantors of Father Nicolás
de Prado, who resided in the pueblo of Chínipas, leaving their homes
and their wives, fled the country. They took refuge among the Tarahumares, where they remained hidden for a while. An urge for a more
open and freer life had been upon them. They were discovered and
taken back to Chínipas. They then began to agitate for the rising of
the whole of Father Prado's pueblo of Chínipas. The matter was
delated to Prado the very day upon which an indignation meeting, or
tlatole, was to be held. The same two malcontents again proved guilty.
They were arrested and sent to the Governor of Sinaloa where they
confessed their crime and were hanged. From the confessions it appeared there was discontent among the Tarahumares and a secret
desire for freedom. But for the present nothing untoward happened.[1]

Joseph Neumann was saddened at this time and the mission was
diminished by the loss of the Hungarian nobleman Juan María Ratkay.
He had succeeded Rolandegui in Cárichic, and after laboring there
for two years finally succumbed to a slow malady in December, 1683.
He was succeeded by the ardent Sicilian Francisco María Pícolo who,
after building splendidly in Cárichic, went far to the west, crossed the
Gulf, and aided Salvatierra in Lower California. By 1685 Tomás Guadalajara was made superior of the Jesuit residence and church in Parral,
and it was he who was able in that year to accomplish the long-desired
wish to found a college there. The Jesuit church, so long desired, had
existed since 1669 when Governor Antonio de Oca y Sarmiento
financed its construction and had it dedicated, December 2, in high
festivity. A college was desired and needed, but awaited a founder.
This it obtained in 1685 in the person of Don Luis de Simois who,
out of esteem and affection for the superior, Father Guadalajara, by
deed of November 9, made over some buildings and the sum of

[1] For notes to chapter xix see page 252.

eighteen thousand pesos. The existence of the college was now assured, and when the founder died his bones were interred within its walls.[2]

Neumann during this period enjoyed the high satisfaction of baptizing the rebel Carosia, fomentor of the would-be revolt of 1681. Carosia had been a leader highly esteemed among the pagans of the Guazápar mountains for his machinations against the Spaniards and his success in eluding the enemy. Now, late in 1685, for what cause we know not, his tribesmen turned against him and he was forced to flee. He came into the district of Neumann's partido of Sisoguichic, a fugitive from his own people. Neumann learned of his proximity and was suspicious of it. The chief was accused, moreover, of certain robberies recently perpetrated in the Guazápar mountains. Neumann ferreted out the case and discovered that Carosia, for once, was innocent of this recent wrongdoing. The Governor of Sinaloa sent a captain with a band of fifty soldiers in pursuit of the supposed culprit, and the troop penetrated even into Sisoguichic from over the mountains and distant Sinaloa. The father upheld the innocence of the fugitive chief and rebuked the captain for having, without orders, entered another jurisdiction, that of Nueva Vizcaya, especially in pursuit of one who was proved innocent. The captain retraced his steps without his prey, who had been thus protected by the padre.

Such justice made a deep impression upon the former terror of the Guazápares, and he asked Neumann for instruction and baptism. When, therefore, he had sworn to give up forever his robber's life and after he had received what Neumann judged to be sufficient instruction, Chief Carosia with his wife and three daughters received at Neumann's hands the sacrament of baptism. The chief was named Dionysius, his wife Eleanora, his eldest daughter Marguerita. Carosia's younger brother and three other relatives were at the same time made Christians. "It took much effort," wrote Neumann, "and great patience to tame this savage lion and make of him a gentle lamb."[3] The fathers, as well as the Christians of the Guazápar mission, were delighted at this striking conversion of one who had been for so long a time a terror in their mountains. Carosia on a goodwill tour visited the Guazápares and his Christian fellow tribesmen. Fathers and Indians alike received him with joy and welcome, and the former gave him gifts to clinch his loyalty.[4]

If the other six fathers in the mission and those who came during the later 1680's had as much trouble as Neumann in suppressing drunkenness, that tenacious vice of the Tarahumares, they were burdened with heavy labor and worry indeed. Toward the end of 1685, just about the time that Carosia fled to Sisoguichic, Joseph Neumann was invited by Father Francisco Pícolo to spend New Year's Day in his mission and celebrate with him the Feast of the Holy Name of Jesus. Neumann left Sisoguichic December 30. But after two hours on the road the horse of his Indian boy ran away toward home. Neumann pursued the beast all the way back to Sisoguichic. What was his surprise to find the village empty. He suspected what had happened, that his neophytes, having learned some days previously of his intended visit to the mountains, had made strong liquor and intended to enjoy a celebration as soon as the padre was gone. Neumann galloped over into a little glen where his Indians had been accustomed to hold these carousals. He had sensed correctly. There his children were all gathered. Not drinking yet, but dancing and yelling preparatory to the feast. Like a wrathful Moses discovering the golden calf, Neumann galloped his horse in among the roisterers and upset their fourteen jugs of liquor. The Indians taken completely by surprise dispersed in every direction, except a few old people who, bewildered, sat where they were with the spilled beverage forming a puddle in their midst.

The following day Neumann was off again. After a three-day visit he returned to his mission to find his people all at home and very quiet and respectful. But the padre sniffed intrigue in the atmosphere. His suspicions ripened and were again correct, for his neophytes had planned another party for a certain night. To keep the padre away they sent a woman to him supposed to be troubled in her conscience; then another who told of the anger of his children at their former disappointment and that should he break up their sport again they would kill him. Father Ratkay, she said, had died of poison at Cárichic, through the anger of his Indians. Neumann's Indian boy had told him at supper that a drinking bout had been scheduled for late that night. He determined, disregarding all threats and danger, to break it up again. The padre disguised himself as one of their own, wrapped himself in a striped blanket and put a band around his head. Darkness did the rest. He and his boy went unrecognized to the glen together with the others of the pueblo on their way to the party. Everybody was lively and spirited in anticipation of the fun; the women carried large containers of wine on their heads.

Arrived at the place Neumann, unrecognized, squatted on the ground as one of the crowd. He waited until all had arrived, until the fire was lit and the revelry about to begin. Then he flung away his disguise and broke into a torrent of words against them for their deceitful, wicked behavior. He again upset all the vessels, while all except four of the chief men of the pueblo ran away. Either in awe of the padre's determination, or suffering from a conscience-stricken spirit, these four harbored no thoughts of violence against Neumann, instead they asked forgiveness for their weakness and disobedience and promised amendment for an enduring future. With that the five walked back to the village. Neumann could now rest and retire to sleep, for he had been worn out with his journey back from the mountains and had not up to this time been able to relax even for a moment.[5]

The year before the happening just related gold was discovered in or near Sisoguichic in northern Tarahumara. In 1684 silver mines were found at Coyachic just a few miles northeast of Cusihuiriachic or Mission San Bernabé. Three years later another and richer mine was discovered in the sierra which, close to San Bernabé itself, rises to a pointed and picturesque peak called Monte Cusihuiriachic. This peak, a landmark for miles around, can be descried in the blue distance from almost as far as Cárichic.

Each of these discoveries was followed by the inevitable gold rush. Just as the miners rushed into Parral in 1631 when its riches were first discovered, so now to the immense discomfiture of the missionaries they rushed into the heart of this mission country in north central Tarahumara and into the immediate vicinity of the two missions, San Bernabé Cusihuiriachic and San Ignacio Coyachic. Throngs of people came, extensive diggings were begun, houses were built, and smelters erected. Merchants followed in the wake of the miners and after the merchants came ranchers to make their homes in lands that had formerly been too far removed from white habitation to be safe.

Age-old abuses now sprouted like ugly weeds in the heart of Tarahumara. The rough miner gave an evil example to the neophyte. The

Indian was irritated at seeing great sections of his land taken because of the wood they yielded or the grazing facilities they afforded; and, worst of all, there began again the forced labor of the poor Indian —used by the Spaniards in mines, in the construction of homes, and in personal service.

All of this abuse was against the laws, as we have seen, and it was in vain that the missionaries would point it out to the Spaniards, unless there was at hand the strong secular arm to enforce the provisions of the law. Such guardians of the law had been Hurdaide years before in Sinaloa, and Juan Antonio de Sarriá at the mid-century; but such was not the Governor of Nueva Vizcaya at the end of the 1620's, the period with which we are now concerned.

"Don Juan Isidro de Pardiñas Villar de Francos, Knight of the Order of Santiago and Governor and Captain-General of the Kingdom of Nueva Vizcaya for His Majesty" was a mark upon the frontier of the decadence of Spain. He had bought his office for a sum of money proffered to the king; and when because of his weakness, arrogance, and mistakes he had made a failure of his administration he bought an immunity from punishment and a continuance in office by the handsome gift of thirty thousand crowns offered to and accepted by the Viceroy, Gaspar de la Cerda, Conde de Galve. Again the frontier would have to pay for inefficiency and corruption. The great rebellion of 1690 burst forth. Two Jesuits were killed and the northwestern missions were for the time ruined.

The conspiracy which led to the uprising was hatched during the year of 1689, the year in which two Bohemian fathers entered northwest Tarahumara—Wilhelm Illink, sent to Cahurichic, and George Hostinsky, missionary of Tomochic. The Tarahumares were joined by the Concho nation, whose land and pueblos began only about twenty-five miles north of Coyachic. The Conchos, avid and impatient, could not wait for the time agreed upon. They made depredations upon the Spaniards late in 1689, were caught and were punished.

But on April 1, 1690, which was the Tuesday after Easter, they burst in fury upon Yepómera, the residence of Father Juan Ortiz Foronda, who for some time had been living on this isolated edge of northwestern Tarahumara.[8] The rebels slew Foronda and two other Spaniards who were living with him and proceeded to commit the atrocities which usually accompany such an uprising: they destroyed the furnishings of the altar and the father's household goods, they burned his house and his church; they drove away the herds of cattle belonging to the mission. In all of these rascalities the Conchos were joined by the Tarahumares of Yepómera itself. Then the hurricane of destruction passed on up the Río Papigochic to rush in fury against the mission at Temósachic, and then on to Nahuarachic and Sirupa. These all belonged to the newly organized partido of Yepómera. The last two pueblos were in Jova territory and the Jovas also rose. Conchos, Jovas, and northwestern Tarahumares were now on the warpath.[7]

At Tutuaca was Father Manuel Sánchez. So soon as he noticed the sullen change among his Indians which is the dark cloud presaging storm, he sped to Sonora to petition the Governor for protection against eventualities. The Governor ordered his lieutenant, Manuel Clavero, to accompany the father back to his mission, but on the way they were ambushed and slain. Fathers Illink and Hostinsky were forced to flee from their respective pueblos of Cahurichic and Tomochic. These two pueblos together with Cocomarachic, all of them west toward the mountains from Papigochic, were devastated and destroyed.

When the Spaniards of the mines, formerly incredulous, now heard of the death or flight of the missionaries and of the destruction of the missions, they rushed to arms without waiting for the services of Governor Pardiñas at Parral. Abandoning their mines, they resolved to make war upon the rebels and to protect the lives of the remaining fathers. The Governor acted too. He sent Captain Juan Fernando de Retana with fifty soldiers to Papigochic with orders to remain there until he should be able to take the field with a larger force.

While on the march, however, the troop of Retana was suddenly attacked. This temerity on the part of the Indians was effected by the assurances of their leader, a known deceiver, who had convinced this simple folk that through magic he had corrupted and rendered useless the gunpowder of the Spaniards. The rebels need not, then, fear the Spanish muskets. Should one fall by sword or lance he would arise within three days, sane and sound. It was by this same kind of hoax that Quautlatas in 1616 had screwed up the courage of the Tepehuanes at the time of the great revolt. Now in April of 1690 Captain Retana and his troops had time to form and await the onslaught. The rebel leader was conspicuous, wearing the biretta of the murdered Foronda. When the hostiles were within spear's throw the Spaniards fired. The leader fell with others. Some were wounded, and when the rebels nevertheless pressed on the attack the Spaniards drew their swords and made at them. The Indians now broke and fled. It was an easy victory.

In the meantime Governor Pardiñas came up with an army of two hundred soldiers and a host of Indian allies. But the rebels had dispersed to the well-nigh inaccessible fastnesses of the rugged mountains to the southwest, nor could they be dislodged without a long extended campaign. This the Governor was not willing to embark upon. He marched unmolested to Yepómera with two Jesuits in order to give decent burial to the three who had fallen there—Foronda and the two other Spaniards. By this time the corpses had lain without burial more than three months and were quite undistinguishable. The three were therefore buried together near the altar of the destroyed church.

Governor Pardiñas remained here at Yepómera for some time, sending his scouts of loyal Indians into the wild mountains which lay to the south to seize and bring in for punishment what rebels they could. The result was not encouraging. The Governor spent much time in investigating, through witnesses and enquiries, the causes of the revolt. He was told, truly or falsely, that the conspiracy had existed for four years and that eleven nations had joined it, including the Tobosos to the east and the Apaches in the northeast. The Governor sent the rebels a general pardon and even released some he had taken as prisoners. Going to the extreme of weakness, he gave these people gifts to bring to those hiding in the mountains as pledge of his forgiveness. The rebels with fair words promised all peace. But they did not trust Pardiñas, nor did they intend to keep their plighted word.

Leaving Yepómera the Governor with his troops now made his way southeast to Cárichic where the Visitor of the missions and four other fathers were staying. He then began political intrigues against the missionaries. Evil report had gone to the Viceroy about his inefficacy, and, placating this high official with the bribe above mentioned, Pardiñas just escaped dismissal from office. Suspecting the missionaries of having accused him, he now turned his pen against them and wrote calumnious accusations to the capital. One of his accusing letters was given by an official to a missionary, his friend, who handed it on to the Visitor. The Governor was caught red-handed.

The Jesuits now acted in self-defense and dispatched Neumann by the circuitous route of the west coast missions, to go to the capital and confer with the Viceroy in person. Neumann remained in the capital six weeks, enjoying entire success with the Viceroy, who heretofore had been puzzled by the conflicting reports coming in from the north. When Governor Pardiñas learned that the Jesuit missionaries had stolen a march on him and that he was discovered in the capital, he performed an about-face concerning the padres, and praised them henceforth in the highest terms to his superior.

Neumann returned from his long journey well satisfied with his mission and well filled with consolation for his fellow missionaries. The Viceroy acted in a manner to forestall any treachery on the part of the Governor of Nueva Vizcaya. A letter of instructions to him was carried by Neumann, who was told to show it to the Father Provincial before delivery to the Governor for whom it was intended. Neumann was to meet the Provincial on the way north. The Governor could therefore no longer deceive. The instructions provided adequate protection for the missions and the fathers. Twelve soldiers were to be assigned to the missionaries on return to their pueblos, until such time as all danger was over and the destroyed churches and mission residences rebuilt. Besides, a presidio of thirty soldiers was to be stationed in Tarahumara to hold the country against any such recurrence of the calamities which had just befallen the mission.

But the Governor of Nueva Vizcaya made excuses to his superior, the Viceroy. He could not spare the men. In his mind the highways leading to the mines of Parral were of paramount importance and the commerce farther south must be protected against the incursions of the Tobosos again on the warpath. The Governor insisted that the soldiers were for the protection of the Spanish merchants, the miners, and their workmen. In short, Governor Pardiñas did not fulfill the orders of his superior for the adequate protection of the padres and the missions. However, it seemed wise to the Black Robes to disregard the fact, and to go back to the missions under conditions which were, to say the least, dangerous. Neumann had brought back with him many supplies for the churches and the altars, and this was a solace.

Shortly after Neumann's return, the Visitor authorized the padres to go back to their posts, for they were anxious to begin the work of reconstruction. They did go back to all but the two most isolated pueblos, Cahurichic and Tutuaca. The former never again had a resident missionary; the area was practically abandoned; Tutuaca remained without a padre for two years. The Indian governor here, though a Christian, was known a vicious man, notorious for polygamy and murder. So long as he was the head of the pueblo it would be dangerous for a padre to return.

Thus ended the revolt of 1690. Two other Jesuits, considered martyrs, increased the spiritual luster of the province and stirred the spiritual ardor of young Jesuits in the seminaries of Europe. The blood of Sánchez and Foronda was now commingled with the dust. But in the eyes of the seventeenth-century Spaniard their spirits, blent in another world with those of Beudin and Basilio, would continue from Heaven to fertilize the spiritual soil of hearts for the production of more abundant harvests in the land of the Tarahumar.

Chapter XX

THE UPRISING OF 1697

I<small>T WAS</small> unfortunate for the prosperity and contentedness of the Upper Tarahumar mission that the country of the turbulent Tobosos lay so close to it. This nation gave no end of trouble to the Franciscan missionaries among the Conchos and to the Spanish settlers, the miners and ranchmen of eastern Nueva Vizcaya. It was, too, an unfortunate thing that the Jesuit missions among what the fathers called the Laguneros, with the principal seat at Parras in the Laguna country, had been secularized in 1646 by Bishop Evía y Valdés of Durango. It was out of this country and out of country contiguous to it that the Tobosos came. With their padres withdrawn, the Lagunero Indians, among whom were some of the Tobosos, lapsed into their primitive barbarism, so that Christian influences were farther removed from the whole Toboso nation. Had the Jesuit missions been allowed to develop and to spread north and west from the lagoons, this wild and murderous people could gradually have been incorporated into the mission system and tamed to a quiet and civilized existence. With the removal of the Black Robes the country of what is now southern Coahuila declined and the result was disastrous for Nueva Vizcaya of which it was then a part. Out of these great level stretches left without missionaries came the Tobosos, who agitated the Conchos, who in turn disturbed the Tarahumares. Thus it was that in the late 1640's, Tobosos, Cabesas, Salineros rebelled and then the Conchos rose. It meant trouble at that time for the missions of Baja Tarahumara.

Neumann comments rather caustically in one of his letters: "Because a certain Bishop urged the move, the Society withdrew from three missions in the province of Parras, among the Toboso Indians, and a parish priest was placed in charge. The Indians promptly revolted and are living a roving life to this day, supporting themselves by robbing the Spaniards. For twenty-five years now the Spaniards have been unable to pacify or suppress them."[1]

Thus it was that subsequently the Tobosos were the constant pest of the country around Parral, making unsafe the highways leading to

---

[1] For notes to chapter xx see page 253.

the mines and hampering the development of commerce in the whole of eastern Nueva Vizcaya. When Fathers Neumann and Ratkay were traveling north from Durango in 1680 they had not dared to travel unaccompanied. Wild bands were roving over the country robbing the rancher and murdering the wayfarer. Neumann's group saw the tracks of these marauders.

Neumann is speaking of such rebels when he writes: "They live like wild beasts. They go completely naked, with their faces horribly painted, so that they look more like devils than men. Their only weapons are bows and poisoned arrows. . . . They esteem the flesh of horses and mules as a delicacy; they also eat human flesh and drink the blood. They have no fixed place of residence, but change their abode almost daily in order to avoid detection. They sometimes run as many as thirty leagues within twenty-four hours, for in their ability to climb mountains and in their speed they resemble goats and deer. They infest the roads and attack travelers, terrifying the horses and mules with their yells."[2]

Now, these may have been untamed bands of Tarahumares which Neumann described, and the notice of their fleetness of foot leads us to suspect as much, for these Indians were famous runners then and are still noted for that physical quality. But they may just as well have been Tobosos, for they were the Iroquois of eastern Nueva Vizcaya. A report of 1693 avers that this road which Neumann traveled was unsafe because "squads of Tobosos continually spy upon it."[3] For instance, in April, 1693, Indian bandits put to death a respected merchant, Andrés de Jáuregin, and six others of his party on the way to the mines of Santa Rosa at Cusihuiriachic. They tied Jáuregin to a tree, skinned him alive, and perpetrated other horrible atrocities.[4]

The official Spanish records issuing from Durango and Parral during the second half of the seventeenth century are full of complaints against these marauders. Captains and generals tell of their inroads; governors report uprisings and plunderings, with the consequent depopulation of the country. "What does it matter, Sir," wrote Don Joseph Francisco Marín to the Viceroy in 1693, "that nature has deposited in the entrails of this land such a sum of riches if the value of those already discovered cannot be realized on account of its being depopulated, as is the case, and despoiled of almost everything."[5]

Since what used to be the main road north by way of Papasquiaro, Santa Catalina, and Zape was rendered unsafe by the hostiles, another and shorter route became more frequented because of the three presidios of El Pasaje, El Gallo, and Cerro Gordo stationed along its route. This lay seventy-five miles east of the older road. From Durango, where there were fifteen soldiers, this highway led ninety miles north to El Pasaje, protected by a presidio of fifty soldiers and a captain. El Gallo lay seventy miles farther north and harbored fifty; and Cerro Gordo, sixty miles beyond, had twenty-three. Fifty soldiers were resident at Parral itself, but all these defense measures were evidently not enough to protect the country from hostile raids.[6] All through the 1690's disastrous attacks and inroads continued, and the reports are loud in their complaints.[7] These troubles rendered unstable the northeastern frontier of Nueva Vizcaya, and they made the Conchos and Tarahumares restless and more or less easily inclined toward rebellion.

It is true that by the middle of the 1690's the upper Tarahumares were fairly well settled in Christian life and Spanish civilization. They enjoyed the presence of the Black Robes in their most important pueblos and they had built churches of which they were proud. A report of 1693 speaks of the Tepehuanes and Tarahumares as "highly Hispanicized," averring that they "have some degree of culture, and greatly apply themselves to the raising of cattle and the cultivation of their lands."[8]

But there was one point among others in which the Tarahumares differed from their more docile countrymen on the west coast: they were exceedingly attached to their scattered existence, and pressure needed to be exerted to bring them to live together more closely in pueblos. Once there they often chafed under the discipline of the settlements and the constraints of Christian life. This matter the letters of Neumann indicate time and time again. Not that other tribes in the beginning did not show the same propensity to flee the pueblos and be off to the hills. However, the Tarahumares seem to have been particularly attached to their sequestered hideouts, their lairs, and their caves.

Neumann was made rector of the whole Upper Tarahumar unit after the revolt of 1690 and consequently found himself in 1693 the general superior of eight partidos, comprising about thirty mission pueblos, including his own of Sisoguichic. And he had his trials, for this year of 1693 a plague of smallpox and measles broke out among the upper Tarahumares and carried off the flower and hope of his nation, the young people who would develop a deep-rooted Christianity. When the stricken were recovering from the smallpox, they were attacked by the measles and with a kind of violet-colored rash, resembling ulcers. Upon this followed dysentery accompanied by a bloody flux. Neumann says this latter lasted five or six days and scarcely anybody attacked survived it. The padre adds: "This pestilence destroyed a great number of children and many pregnant women; indeed, hardly any of the latter escaped. In short, it took the young, the flower of our reductions; whereas old people and a small number of the mature men and women were untouched." Forty in Sisoguichic took sick within four days and most of them died.

The strain on the missionaries during such a visitation was exceedingly severe. There was need to visit the sick night and day, administer the last sacraments to the dying, and finally to bury the dead. "It may be considered as miraculous that no one of us perished from exhaustion," writes Neumann, "and that only one in our Society was attacked by the plague."[9] Europeans seemed immune to the worst ravages of diseases which decimated the Indians.

Nevertheless progress continued. Neumann built a new church this year in his visita of Echoguita. The padre was proud of his church, for he says it had many carvings in stone. It was dedicated on the Feast of the Assumption, 1693, with the presence, besides Neumann, of Father Wenceslaus Eymer from Tomochic and Father Jean Verdier from Papigochic. For his mission church at Sisoguichic Neumann had a benefactor who gave him funds. The church received five chasubles, silk altar frontals of many colors, cloths of flowered damask, and parchments worked with gold and silver. On feast days the mission could spread itself in silk banners, umbrellas, and baldequins.[10] Two hundred souls were this year added to Neumann's flock.

Unfortunately, another plague broke out in 1695 carrying off again many of the young. "I myself am an eyewitness," wrote Neumann in his history of this mission, "that in one instance in a family of thirteen members the mother and all the children died, whereas the husband remained immune."[11]

Hechiceros began to be more active and their feats of magic, if we are to accept the weird demonology reported by the missionaries, worked in sundry and horrible fashion. An old man among the wizards was regarded as their high priest. The simple people of these wilds bent the knee before him and kissed his feet. He threatened dire punishment of those who did not follow him. He granted them unwonted license, for they might have several wives, said he. This hechicero led in their oldtime dances and once he was seen conducting these festivities from the air. These men enjoyed a familiar spirit with whom they held carnal intercourse. These spirits at other times took horrible shapes of large flies, bears, wolves, and mountain lions. The sound of the church bells, said the wizards, provoked the plague, therefore it was necessary to flee the pueblos and live as formerly along the streams and in the mountains and the caves.

Gradually the poisonous spirit of revolt seeped deeper and deeper through the population of the various pueblos. The Indian governor of Papigochic was among the many infected by the moral plague. Finally the neophytes were only awaiting an opportunity to rebel, burn the mission churches and houses, and flee off to the wilds. All of this information was collected by Father Joseph Neumann now appointed official Visitor, to take official accounting of each pueblo, in place of the Father Provincial, who was too far away in the capital.

All of this evil spirit among the Indians was confirmed, according to what the fathers told the Visitor, by signs and portents. In April, 1696, Tarahumara was shaken by an earthquake; in October a comet appeared in the sky; first only the tail was visible, then the head appeared and for three weeks it terrified all beholders. Fires darted to and fro in the hills near Papigochic. On Good Friday, though no man was near, the bells of the mission church pealed in slow and doleful tones. The flowing waters of the river were seen to build themselves suddenly up into a cone twelve feet high and then collapse with a mighty roar. At Cocomorachic in May, 1696, at three in the afternoon, a giant so tall that the surrounding trees reached only to his breast, was seen on the hills by the padre. The big fellow stooped down as if gathering stones, then suddenly vanished. And to cap all this climax of terror, in April of that same year the sun went into eclipse. All of this Neumann heard during his visitation of 1697.

At the mission of San Francisco de Borja, Visitor Neumann heard from its missionary, Francisco Celada, what to a modern would be considered the only sane portent of coming trouble. Celada showed Neumann a letter he held from the missionary of San Tomás, nine miles from Papigochic, carrying definite word of a conspiracy among the Tarahumares. An Indian boy at San Tomás was greatly attached to the missionary. Now the boy's mother hearing of the intended revolt and fearing for the safety of her son so close to the father, bade him flee since soon the Indians would be up in arms and they would kill the fathers and burn all the churches. The boy carried the alarm to the padre, and the padre wrote to Celada. Such was the disconcerting news which Neumann heard in making his visitation of San Francisco de Borja in the south.

The opportunity was given the secret rebels by the absence of the chief military force of Parral, led by Captain Juan Fernández de Retana. Retana had been sent by the then Governor, Don Gabriel del Castillo, out of the province against the usually troublesome Tobosos to the east. With the soldiers far away the rebellion came to a head. But the missionaries had already acted. Upon the alarming report from San Tomás, Neumann sent a message in all haste to the Governor in Parral, urging him to recall Retana from the Tobosos that he might turn his arms against the Tarahumares, now again on the point of rebellion. The Governor, demurring at first, allowed himself finally to be persuaded and Retana was ordered out of Toboso country into Tarahumara. Captain Retana went up the Conchos, and over the divide into the Papigochic country, where he followed the river down to the pueblo. He questioned the Indian governor who slyly deceived him, for the Captain generally noticed no sign of rebellion.

Captain Retana was led to consider that the fathers had been duped by the word of a boy. Proceeding farther northwest to Yepómera, seat of the former outbreak, Retana met there Father Johann Baptist Haller, recently arrived, innocent, and unsuspecting of Indian wiles. This padre, therefore, persuaded the Captain to proceed to Cocomorachic, to Father Pietro Protho, a Sicilian, for here was more dangerous territory, it being closer to the rugged sierras.

What Father Protho had to tell the Captain dissipated all his previous illusions concerning the existence of peace and quiet. The missionary pointed out to the Captain that corn had for some time been taken by his Indians to the mountains, that large numbers of poisoned arrows had been made, that many of his neophytes had left the villages and were assembled on a high cliff, resembling a fortress, overlooking the valley of Sirupa.

Captain Retana, persuaded now that trouble was afoot, took measures. He sent Indians he could trust to the Tarahumares on the cliff with a message from the Captain summoning them in obedience to come to see him in Cocomorachic. These envoys were met with insults and revilings and a shower of arrows. When they returned to report this treatment to the Captain the latter knew the revolt was on. Retana prepared to capture the occupants of the stronghold whether by storming or by starvation. He sent some Indian allies ahead to surround the place and prevent escape. They were attacked and driven back with loss. But when the rebels heard that this Basque captain was approaching in force, they stole away silently in the night, through a secret crevice in the rock, leaving their bleating sheep behind as a ruse for their continued presence. The rebel birds had flown, and they were now roving over the mountains to stir the country and do what other mischief they might fancy.

Retana sent for help from the Governor of Sonora in the west and ordered his Indian allies out scouting for the rebels. These were so far successful that they brought into camp nearly sixty captives. When the reinforcements arrived Retana had the captured rebels one and all executed, in order to strike terror into the hearts of the others. Those killed included two of the sorcerers, who had expected their chains to be broken by greater than human force, but who were caught and killed on the spot. In March, 1697, thirty of the culprits were shot. Then their heads were cut off, impaled on spears and displayed to the public view at Cocomarachic and along the road to Yepómera. Thus were they left to be a warning how all rebels would perish and to serve as the food for crows. The remaining captives were taken to Mátachic where the same punishment was inflicted on all except a few for whom the missionaries successfully pleaded, since they were less guilty than the others.[12]

The Spaniards now suffered from overconfidence, especially the Governor at Parral. Del Castillo considered that the hostiles, suffi-

ciently cowed by these summary executions, would understand the evil
of their ways and return to peace. It was wishful thinking. He had
given orders that Captain Retana return east against the Tobosos, and
the army was about to depart when another alarm was sounded. An
excited report came in that Tarahumares in large numbers, joined now
by Jovas and even Pimas from the west, were preparing an ambush
for the Spanish troops in a narrow defile through which the route out
of Tarahumara lay. That the report was not false was soon proved, for
at Tomochic while the padre was absent there was sacking and burning by a rebel band. The fathers' dwelling and church were, according
to the classic method, sacked and burned, and all the cattle of the
mission were killed. The maize the rebels divided among themselves.
That night at Tomochic the Indians celebrated with feasting and dancing, with yells and general bedlam. The following day they proceeded
to Meseachic, residence of Father Georg Hostinsky. But the padre had
been warned in time. He had gathered up the sacred vessels and
hastened to join the Spanish troops at Papigochic, where Retana had
more than a hundred men.

The Spanish leaders had miscalculated: the rebel spirit had in no
way been suppressed. And the most discouraging indication was that
the inhabitants of Tomochic joined the rebels without demur. So it was
generally in other pueblos when the rebel band reached them. Some,
looking to the possibilities of the future, feigned reluctance to join.
Only a few remained loyal and these fled to the padres in the protected
mission of Papigochic where Retana was staying with his army. The inhabitants of Alescachic felt themselves threatened and they sent messages to Captain Retana at Papigochic. Suspecting this to be a false request, since Alescachic had not been noted for the loyalty of its people,
and thinking the rebels hoped thus to divide the Spanish force, Retana
sent up one hundred and fifty Indians from Papigochic to give to the
village the requested help. But these hundred and fifty had no sooner
arrived on the scene than they became rebels themselves and so Alescachic revolted. Its church was burned and the whole pueblo was made
a smoking ruin. On the same day Cocomorachic rose, taking advantage
of the absence of its missionary, the Sicilian, Father Protho, who was
now superior of the whole mission unit, just as Neumann was its official Visitor. He was about to return to his pueblo of Cocomorachic

when his servant brought the news that all was lost: his house and church burned, the village a deserted ruin.

It was evident that the uprising was general and no one could be trusted. Therefore Protho sent swift messages to the padre at Yepómera ordering him to collect what valuables he could and flee to Papigochic. The Black Robes of both Yepómera and Mátachic fled that very night for Papigochic where, in the presence of the Spanish troops, they would be safe.

If no resistance were offered them the rebels would continue going from pueblo to pueblo pouring out the vials of their fury upon all things connected with the Church, burning, plundering, and destroying. The Spaniards in Papigochic were in a quandary. They suspected and with reason that many of the Indians in the pueblo were secret traitors, awaiting only the marching off of the soldiers to do for Papigochic what their tribesmen were doing for the other missions. Indeed, it was later learned that many supposedly loyal were keeping in secret touch with the rebels. Today, we would call them fifth-column men. More than this, Indians came to Papigochic feigning loyalty and flight from the rebels, seeking admission into the pueblo. Once admitted, they plotted with the secret rebels and then fled in the night to bring news to those in the field. Impossible then to go forth to meet and defeat the rebels in the northwest on the fringe of the mountains. Papigochic would then itself become a smoking ruins. It was equally dangerous to divide the force. The rebels were too numerous, more than a thousand now, so that the army needed to be held together. There was nothing for it but to remain in Papigochic and await the arrival of another army. Thirty men were dispatched to meet Father Haller who was fleeing from Yepómera and conduct him safely to the protected pueblo. There were now six missionaries at Papigochic.

So the revolt continued unabated. Mátachic and Yepómera fell and the rebels went over the border of their own territory into the land of the Concho Indians and desolated the missions of the Franciscans, who in their turn were forced to flee. Then they began ravaging south beyond Papigochic and entered the territory of Neumann's partido of Sisoguichic and Echoguita. Here, as we have narrated, was a new church dedicated in recent years with the attendance of fourteen of the fathers. Neumann was proud of his work; but it was doomed.

Neumann had not been notified. It was thought his isolated partido was safe. He was on the spot when he heard of the approaching rebels. His own Indians up to this point had proved loyal. A messenger from the mountain tribes coming to corrupt them was given a beating and sent back home with the word that the men of Sisoguichic would never rebel, rather would they defend their mission with their lives. But on June 11 at midnight one of Neumann's neophytes came in with the report that rebels were preparing to attack Echoguita. The padre sent his own scouts out to explore the roads and he asked Captain Retana for a guard of thirty men. Neumann's Indians reported back that they had seen no sign of danger, and Captain Retana turned back because he too had seen no sign of trouble in this country. He feared for Papigochic with part of the army absent. In the meantime Neumann had gone to Echoguita to look to its defense, but thinking danger over he returned to Sisoguichic and sent his men into the fields to gather in the harvest, for the time was ripe. But on June 21 the rebels suddenly appeared in Echoguita, arrested the Indian governor, pulled down the large cross, and put it and the church to the flames.

Neumann himself describes the swiftness of their havoc: "They then surrounded the group of buildings, battered upon the doors of the church, and with wild and furious yells rushed in. They climbed upon the altars, tore from their places the images of the Mother of God and of the saints, rent them asunder, and cast the pieces into the river which flowed close by. They smashed the altars and the baptismal font, which was of carved stone; pillaged the sacristy: tore to ribbons six chasubles and all the other vestments, and scattered the fragments; beat the chalice against a rock and broke it into three pieces; and laid sacrilegious hands upon everything else, destroying and ruining all."[13] Then came the usual holocaust of fire: church, house, and every standing object of wood was burnt to cinders. The Indian governor whom the rebels had arrested was threatened with death did he not discover the hideout of the people of Echoguita. He, feigning compliance, escaped and fled.

The rebels now pressed on to Sisoguichic. Night overtook them half way. They stopped to gorge themselves with the food they had stolen from Echoguita and to sleep the night. That evening scouts rushed in giving the terrifying news: the rebels were on the march toward Sisoguichic. The women fled, driving before them the flocks and taking their children. The men fled too all except a handful who would not desert their padre, for he refused to seek safety in flight. Neumann packed the sacred vessels in bundles and bade his men hide them in near-by caves. His Indian governor came up with a horse ready and saddled for the road. He begged the padre to flee for his life, and promised to see to it that the rest of the sacred vessels were removed and placed in hiding. Neumann accepted this arrangement and late on the night of June 21 he rode out of his mission on the horse the Indian governor had furnished, and from a height when he stopped to look back upon his mission "he saw many fires moving to and fro. They were the flames of pine torches, and by their light the loyal Indians were carrying away the furnishings of the church and the dwelling house."[14] The padre made straight for Cárichic where he urged the Christians there to hasten to the protection of Sisoguichic. They acted immediately but arrived, alas, too late. What they saw was the smoking remnants of the church, the house, the huts, and even the crops. All the inhabitants had fled.

Now the neophytes of Neumann at Sisoguichic displayed an unwonted resourcefulness. They knew the rebels were short of food and they made the following proposal. Let the rebels remain at Sisoguichic until its people could go and gather in the flocks to be butchered and feasted upon and then they themselves would join the rebels and thus augment their numbers. The rebels accepted.

These good Tarahumares then quickly communicated their ruse to Captain Retana who acted at once. Risking absence from Papigochic, he stealthily placed numbers of his men on the hills about Sisoguichic until the rebels were surrounded. When they realized what had taken place the rebellious Indians were filled with terror. Some fled singly through the wilds and escaped. Others seized their weapons and ascended a hill crowned with large stones which served as a fortification. Here Spanish troops were awaiting them and a battle ensued. Neumann describes it: "Here they were beset on all sides by the Spaniards and the Indian allies. They looked around them and saw no means of escape. Then in desperation they flung themselves upon the soldiers, striking with such violence as to pierce the Spanish shields, though these were made of two thicknesses of ox hide. Nor did they cease from fighting until every one of them on that hill was dead of his wounds. Not a man among them was taken alive, or suffered himself to be captured. Of our own soldiers, one was stabbed in the throat and died. Fifteen others were wounded with poisoned arrows. Remedies were applied without delay and they escaped death and recovered....." Four friendly Indians were slain. "The heads of thirty-three of the rebels were struck from their bodies, set upon spears, and exposed on a hill near the ruins of the church of Sisoguichic.... Other men would find in them an example and a warning."[15]

This action and victory at the end of June, 1697, was a turning point in the whole rebellion, although it dragged on through all that year and part of the next. In the meantime it was learned that the Indians did not really want to kill the padres, but only to destroy the missions and drive out the Spaniards. Peace was ultimately brought about the following spring.

In the north, however, warfare continued. A large body of rebels were perched on the great ledge of Sopezi near Tomochic overlooking the river of that name. It was impossible to dislodge them by a direct attack upon the precipitous heights of this aerie; nor could they be starved out, for it backed up into mountains as precipitous as the ledge and over these needle-pointed rocks some food could be brought in. The Spaniards lay waste the country round about so that no bands of rebels could live upon the land. When a hostile group attacked Guazimba, a Franciscan mission to the north in Concho country, Retana went in pursuit, overtook and soundly defeated them, killing the leader and fifteen others, dispersing the rest far and wide. Then the summer rains set in and there was much suffering for all. The Spaniards offered peace, but the proposal was rejected.

The backwash of the revolt penetrated the mountains of the Guazápar country. Two villages on the fringes of this territory revolted, and when attacked by the Spaniards the inhabitants fled into the mountains. The Guazápares for once had been loyal and they enjoyed abundant food from bumper crops. The rebels entered either to corrupt the Guazápares or to take their food by force. Both the missionaries and the Indians called upon Captain Aldago of the presidio at San Felipe in Sinaloa to come to their assistance. This he did with the result that the rebels suffered defeat in two pitched battles. Father Ordaz independently of the Captain, then went himself with three domestics into the enemy's camp to try to persuade them to peace. The only result was that two of his domestics were killed in his presence, a third bolted for safety, and when the father was kneeling to receive his stroke of death, the blow was stayed by the influence of an old man who had him sent back unharmed to his pueblo.

It was now November of the year 1697. The Spaniards under Retana dared to sally forth from Papigochic, and marching three days west and north through country of extreme roughness came up with a band of the hostiles near Cahusolichic. Braving an attack across a deep canyon they were routed with the loss of twenty-five men. The rebel governor of Tomochic was among the dead.

The rebels had suffered much and toward January when famine was upon them they again stubbornly refused the proffered peace. Another expedition was therefore made, the men breaking camp at Papigochic on January 26, 1698. Now the route lay northwest toward Cocomorachic. In the mountains of Tosónachic two rebel chiefs were brought in by the Indian allies, caciques of the places just named. Still another band of auxiliaries had captured the cacique of Yepómera. This was encouraging, for every chief slain or captured meant the weakening of the revolt. Sometimes but one leader would be responsible for the prolongation of hostilities.

Famine was stalking with deadly tread among the rebels, which explains why the captive chiefs when offered their lives provided they would persuade their people to peace, were willing to accept. Others learning of the offer came in good numbers to throw themselves upon the mercy of the Spaniards.[16] The whole long and ruinous affair seemed about to end. However, there was yet one more difficulty to overcome. Retana learned that the revolt would have ended long ago were it not for the constant urgings to continue rebellion on the part of two brothers of Yepómera, both of them caciques, and both of them apostates from the Christian religion. Retana put a price upon their heads and promised fifty crowns to the man who would take them dead or alive. A Pima Indian of Mátachic took up the gage. He led a band to ruined Yepómera, found the culprits, and attacked them out of hand. They were taken but not alive. The Pima received his fifty crowns and he became the wealthiest Indian in all that country.

Trouble continued in the Guazápar region, however. The Bohemian Jesuit, Father Wilhelm Illink, had been sent there and when the final and victorious battle was being fought at Guadalupe just north of Chínipas he distinguished himself by standing in the forefront of flying arrows and speeding bullets, crucifix in hand, exhorting Captain Andrés Resabello of Sinaloa and his troops to the stand which spelled defeat for the opposing rebels. All were killed or fled except one called Santiago, who later became a Christian and ultimately Indian governor of the pueblo of Chínipas.

The revolt dragged on in Sonora where the rebels had destroyed the missions of Maicoba and Ónaba. Captain Retana was summoned by Father Daniel Janusky, onetime missionary in Tarahumara. The Pima rebels were threatening his mission of Teopari. In this Sonoran district they had become so hard-pressed by hunger and Retana's pursuit that when Father Natal Lombardo after repeated attempts again offered peace they accepted. Retana had spent a month in Sonora, and in June, 1698, returned victorious to now quiet but partly ruined Tarahumara.

Chapter XXI

PRECARIOUS APPEASEMENT

In the summer of 1698, just as the Tarahumara troubles seemed at last to be definitely quieted, a new governor came to Parral to replace Don Gabriel del Castillo. As had been the case with Isidro de Pardiñas, the office had again been bought with money, not by the new governor himself, but by his father, a man of great wealth, who spent a hundred thousand crowns to acquire for himself a title of nobility, and for his son the governorship of Nueva Vizcaya. His name was Don Juan Bautista de Larrea.

Since it had always been Spain's policy to change her viceroys and governors in her American colonies periodically, lest prolonged enjoyment of power tend to an independent and absolute spirit, Governor del Castillo, "a mature man of sound and sober judgment," had to make way for the upstart whose father had trafficked in titles and honors. Neither the Spanish frontiersmen of Nueva Vizcaya nor the fathers were pleased. This was quite evidently not the time to make a replacement, when the whole province had just been shaken by a serious revolt and when peace was only now beginning to be restored to the frontier state. But the main seat of government was very far away, and the routine of bureaucracy does not always take account of the circumstances of time and place. There was nothing for it but to make the best of the change.

Governor del Castillo summoned the captains of the four presidios of the province, namely of Santa Catalina, El Pasaje, El Gallo, and Cerro Gordo, that they might give an account of their stewardship to the incoming official and explain to him the expenses they had incurred and the problems they had to meet. Among these captains was Retana, just returned from Pima land in Sonora and holding his soldiers in Papigochic. The new Governor must soon have realized that his father had bought him chiefly a thing of sorrow and worry. Governor de Larrea saw that the difficulties were great and that the complaints of the Spanish inhabitants of the land were loud. A disastrous rebellion in Tarahumara was hardly ended, and because soldiers had

---

[1] For notes to chapter xxi see pages 253-254.

been needed there the turbulent Tobosos had taken occasion to molest the highways and to harry traffic to and from Parral. Captain Retana represented to the Governor that permanency would not be given to the present precarious peace among the Tarahumares until fourteen of the leaders still at large were sent out of the country. The names of these fourteen were given by Retana to the Governor.

The Visitor of the missions, our old friend Father Joseph Neumann, came to Parral to pay his respects to the new official. He had a double purpose in the visit, besides the gesture of courtesy. He wanted to represent to Governor Larrea the continued necessity for the residence of soldiers in Tarahumara, and to dispel certain false reports which had got about concerning the Jesuit missionaries. A grapevine of gossip had spread it abroad that the missionaries were chiefly responsible for the revolt. Neumann refuted the charge and pointed out to the Governor that not all the rebels had been brought back to the pueblos, and so long as they were at large a secure tranquility was not to be expected. The Governor saw the justice of this representation and decided to leave one company of soldiers in Tarahumara.[1]

Governor de Larrea, in spite of prejudicial appearances, showed energy and he developed a new policy which worked: he transplanted disaffected or suspected natives of disloyal districts into populous centers of loyal Indians. Thus mixed with the rest they would be harmless. The Governor resolved to visit Tarahumara to see for himself. He started out in the fall of 1698 and reached Papigochic in October, where Captain Retana and Father Visitor Neumann met him. Thence the group accompanied by a force of one hundred Spanish soldiers and one hundred and fifty Indian allies began a long round of visitations to the various districts of Tarahumara and its mission pueblos. They started northwest down the Río Papigochic. To San Tomás, to Mátachic, to Yepómera they went viewing the ravages of the rebellion, the ruins of the churches, the diminution of the population. From Yepómera scouts preceded the Governor into the Sirupa valleys to search out fugitives and report on the present loyalty of the Hoba tribe. Some would-be rebels, Pima, Hoba, and Tarahumar, were gathered in and sent to Naniguipa, there to be merged into a group of Tarahumares long peaceful. Nevertheless, a giant leader of rebellion, Puzilegi, a Concho, was executed together with an accomplice.

From the Yepómera country the party swung south into the wildest corner of the province and visited the pueblos of Cocomorachic, Alescachic, Tutuaca, and Yepachic, this last situated on the very western edge of Tarahumara. Indian governors gathered their peoples together to salute their new civic superior and pledge their loyalty. The governor of Tosánachic had collected a hundred families to greet the Governor. Turning east again the party returned by a more southerly route through Parazeachic, Cahurichic, and Guebachic. There were not many families in these places, but they were chiefly guilty of fomenting the recent rebellion and others as well. They were therefore ordered to migrate to Papigochic and there to live in peace with their fellow tribesmen. Neumann comments on this: "But in reality, they deserved severe punishment, for it was from these lurking places, as if from the Trojan horse, that the instigators of the revolt had issued forth to burn churches, houses, and villages."[2]

The Governor emerged from the mountains by way of Sisoguichic and Cárichic and went north to visit the mines of Santa Rosa at Cusihuiriachic. Meanwhile Retana was concluding his search through the mountains and was able to bring in a number of fugitives. These Indians were dispersed throughout the pueblos of Papigochic, San Tomás, and Paquirachic, and others along the Río Papigochic.

These developments bring our story to the beginning of 1699 when it was evident that peace had come to stay. Father Haller went back to Yepómera, and Father Protho to San Tomás. Wenceslaus Eymer remained at Papigochic, but charged himself with the care of the neophytes in Tutuaca and Yepachic which meant frequent and rough mountain travel. Father Diego Lilin, a Sardinian, had just come to the mission and took charge of Mátachic with Cocomorachic for a visita. Tomochic and Cahurichic were definitely abandoned. And when a summary of the whole revolt of 1697 was taken, it seemed to Neumann, who unquestionably was the best informed of all the missionaries, that not even one half of the whole Tarahumara had risen and there were twenty-four pueblos untouched and intact.[3]

The partido of Cárichic, for example, numbered three thousand persons. The pueblo had a beautiful church with a double row of columns built by Father Pícolo, long resident missionary there ever since Ratkay's death. He had built his church with the financial assistance of many friends and there was nothing like it to be seen in any mission in all the vast country of Mexico, avers Neumann. This beautiful fabric still in the mid-twentieth century adorned the country of the upper Conchos. Its double row of pillars, bulging and tinted, were such as to do honor to any mission church. It was still a center of mission work. Within its ancient walls young Tarahumares were still instructed in the Faith by nuns, while a Black Robe blessed the highland vale with daily Mass.

Just prior to the trouble of 1697 Pícolo had gone off to the newly organized missions of Lower California. Eymer succeeded Neumann as Visitor in 1699, and the latter took up his residence at Cárichic with its three thousand inhabitants of the partido.

Neumann now set himself to rebuild what had been destroyed, for though residing at Cárichic and having charge of that partido, he did not relinquish the spiritual administration of Sisoguichic. At Sisoguichic, at Echoguita, and at one of the visitas of Cárichic he began to rebuild the churches. In three years the three were completed. He had them beautifully decorated, and "provided them so abundantly with sacred vessels that when passing priests chanced to visit them, they discovered nothing lacking, no matter what the service to be performed."[4] Neumann provided the church at Cárichic with a quantity of vessels curiously wrought in silver, and for the chanting of Litanies of Loreto and for the music for the solemn Mass of festal occasions, he procured an organ and instruments of various kinds which his neophytes learned to play with skill. Neumann's celebration of Corpus Christi, with the procession marching to four altars placed in the line of procession, with its decorations, its music and its gaiety, attracted throngs of Indians from far and wide and many Spaniards came to see so novel a sight in lands so remote from the centers of civilized life.

The peace, however, proved precarious. What started new unrest, according to a padre on the spot, was the imprudence of one of the missionaries. We have seen all through this story what a child the Indian was, easily led, suspicious, fickle. "These Indians," wrote the veteran Black Robe, Joseph Neumann, ". . . not infrequently forsake the worship of the true God, and go into mountains to render vain and superstitious homage to devils." The trouble arose at Temechic, a cabecera which now included three other pueblos in its partido. The padre, whose name was charitably omitted from the record, reproved his neophytes too sharply. The rebuke turned the inhabitants of the four villages, especially of Pozera, against him, and they plotted not actual rebellion, but some destruction and flight to the mountains. They awaited an opportunity to put their design into execution and found it in an absence of the father from the partido while he was visiting Cuisihuiriachic. Seizing this opportunity the people of Pozera rose, came in a body to Temechic, and endeavored to set fire to the church. There was still sufficient loyalty at Temechic to prevent the destruction. Those of Pozera retired frustrated in their purpose.[5]

Anything might have happened under such circumstances. Rumor sped on wings of wind and soon it was all over the province that an attempt to destroy the church at Temechic had taken place. A woman seeing fires at night fled to Tahirachic, where Neumann was giving the final touches to a new church he had built, reporting that the church at Temechic had already gone up in flames. This report spread apace. Scouts discovered and reported the truth, only that an attempt had been made, but that the Indians there hated their padre. Captain Retana marched into the country with his troops, and Neumann wrote to the missionary of Temechic not to return to his pueblo, but to leave immediately for Mexico.

It was now the month of November. When word that the military were again on the march reached the Indians of Pozera, they, conscious of their guilt, fled the plains and sought refuge in the sequestered folds of the rugged Guebachic sierra. Retana's entrada was this time a mistake. It only increased the disturbance and led to the flight to the sierra, which the veteran Neumann with his tact and knowledge of the Indian mind would probably have been able to avert. Here was now a nucleus of trouble and discontent, these fugitives in the gorges, and, acting like a magnetic field, they drew from day to day additional renegades.

Did they intend actual rebellion with attack and destruction, or was their intent only to escape the discipline of the pueblos and the restraints of the Christian life? It was uncertain. Retana sought advice from his superiors and was ordered to remain in Papigochic until he might discover through spies the real mind of the runaways. Word was finally brought to him that here was no rebellion, only flight. Relieved at not having to march against the snows and perils of the winter cold, he abided in Papigochic.

With the more propitious season of spring Governor de Larrea himself appeared at Papigochic with additional troops. Thinking by his presence to strike terror into the fugitives, who had now fortified themselves on some lofty crags of the sierra, he summoned them to return to their homes, else he would force them from their lairs. The bluster had no effect. To salvage honor, there was nothing for it but to march into the fastness and dig out the rebels by force.

Retana was given the commission, the Governor remaining at Papigochic. The fugitives were discovered hiding beyond a narrow defile, but perched high on a ledge and beyond the range of bullets. To starve them out was the only thing to do. They were surrounded and their exits closed. Retana sat down to wait. But about noon on June 24, while the soldiers were lunching, a fracas and war whoop burst upon them which made the Spaniards leap to their feet and scurry for their arms. And well they might. The enemy was upon them. Descending by a secret passage from their lofty perch, they killed the sentinel in their path and rushed upon Retana's men, who were now formed to await the onset. The rebels seeing the formation turned and fled back up the precipitous ridge, rolling behind them murderous stones to prevent pursuit by the soldiers.

June was now spent and the rainy season was upon them. No time now for military operations. Retana returned to Papigochic, and the Governor, seeing his presence was futile, went back to Parral. Here and in the immediate east this official was faced with the usual problem, the thorn which had been constantly in the side of the government, the unruly Tobosos. Troops entering Tarahumara were but a signal for the Tobosos to become again more daring. More dangerous than ever became the highways; traffic to and from the mines was seriously hampered. So many complaints were lodged with the Viceroy against the Governor that he was summoned to the capital to answer the charges. He went armed with letters of exculpation which the Jesuits, his friends, had given him. Thus shielded he was saved, and returned to his post with feelings of gratitude toward the fathers.

The opening years of the eighteenth century were difficult for Spain. The War of the Spanish Succession was being waged in Europe. Spain was linked in alliance with France, whose prince of the blood, Philip, grandson of Louis XIV, had been designated by Spain's dying king as his successor. To the French king a grandson on the throne of Spain meant that the Pyrenees were no longer: Spain and France would be one and their power irresistible. Europe rushed to arms to check such unbalance of power. The War of the Spanish Succession ensued. England with her Marlborough, Germany with her Prince Eugene of Savoy, linked with Holland, took the field. In 1704 the smashing blow of Blenheim was sustained by France and Spain, and in that same year Spain lost her pride and her protection, rock-bastioned Gibraltar, which was taken by the British, and she lost moreover her fair Isle of Minorca, taken likewise by the men from the north.

Never before had Spain needed so desperately to husband all her resources and gird herself with single eye to combat. Never before throughout Spain's long decline were the sinews of war so desperately in demand. To the New World, therefore, was issued an order "to all governors, captains, judges, and officials of the provinces" that they give the Indians of the Americas no cause for rebellion, since moneys which might be expended for repression were henceforth to be sent to Spain.° And so it happened that in faraway Tarahumara, on the edge of the civilized world, the poor little bedraggled group of fugitives who had fled from Pozera, were left alone in their mountain fastness among their rocks and their crags, because a Frenchman had been designated King of Spain.

These developments mothered a new, and as it turned out, a more successful method of procedure, at least so far as the Tarahumares were concerned. When hereafter Tarahumares, individually or in groups, deserted their Christian pueblos and made off to the mountains no action was to be taken against them as heretofore. They were not considered as rebels simply because they went back to their wild haunts because the routine life of the Christian pueblo was irksome to them. And, when they were not looked upon or treated as rebels they did not act as such.

The group which had fled from the pueblo of Pozera in the partido of Temechic gradually quieted down when they no longer saw defiling in among their precipitous gorges the armored and arquebused troops of Captain Retana; thus they observed that the government of

Spain was taking no further action against them. Friendly and loyal Christians whom the missionaries sent among them to discover of what spirit they were reported favorably. It became recognized that the fathers might well visit them, to baptize their infants and nourish among them a continuance of Christianity which they had imbibed in the pueblos of the lower country. There came about, therefore, a new development of the method of these missions. Those who had fled to the hills were no longer forced, or even urged, to come down into the valleys and be "reduced" into a pueblo.

So it developed with the people of Pozera and those who had joined them. It was discovered that they were plotting neither rebellion nor destruction. On the contrary, they showed themselves friendly and respectful to those padres who were able to visit them. As the chronicler and eyewitness recounts: "They are quite and peaceable, and our brethren visit them frequently and in perfect safety, baptizing the children and feeding the others with the food of the divine word. At the principal feasts of the year the fathers summon them to the missions, to the end that they may learn Christian gentleness, may rid themselves of their vices and heathen customs, and may thus in every respect lead a better life."[7]

These fugitives, and at one time would-be rebels, went even further in their coöperation. They built houses for the lodging of their padre whenever he would be able to come to them. Gradually they went so far in their good spirit as to build churches in the wild. This fine piece of work was done with no extrinsic urging. "Therefore they show plainly," comments Neumann, "what their feeling is toward us, and reveal their desire to preserve the peace which has been granted to them."[8] As Bolton has remarked: "Henceforth they [the Tarahumares] remained peaceful, and the Jesuits went forward with their apostolic labors among them."[9] And we can agree with the biographer of Kino when he writes: "The transplantation policy as applied to these people had been a mistake from the beginning."[10]

There was still another development in the treatment of the Indians. Captain Juan Retana, by this time promoted to general, seems to have had some of the qualities of his great predecessor on the coast, Diego Martínez de Hurdaide, and he played an important role in the new trend. This consisted in the art of teaching the Indian governors of the various Tarahumar pueblos how they might themselves discipline their own people, without having to call upon padre or captain. From the point of view of the Spanish authority it was the only wise thing to do, provided only the Indian governors were capable of assuming the responsibiilty. Having a troublesome or immoral redskin flogged by order of the captain of Spanish soldiery at the delation of the missionary was not a thing to sit so well even with these simple children. This procedure had led to unrest before, as when Nacabeba, murderer of Tapia, was flogged in 1594 for disobedience. And when among the Tepehuanes in 1616 Quautlatas was flogged for his wizardry, the act only made him still more intent upon rebellion. Surely it was wise that the role of the padre as disciplinarian be made as little odious as possible.

So it was that between Captain Retana and the fathers the Indian governors seriously took upon themselves the maintenance of discipline in their respective pueblos and of punishing it in the breach. The Indian governors learned to perform their duty and task of punishing criminals and chastizing culprits as they deserved. Such a case ran its course in the partido San Francisco de Borja while the veteran Celada was still its missionary. A criminal Indian at Soquerichic had been condemned to death by Retana. Celada interceded with the Captain so that the sentence was commuted to life imprisonment and forced labor in a smelting works not far from San Francisco. The kind-hearted Black Robe seeing the poor fellow wasting away with labor and slight nourishment, procured his deliverance to freedom. The rascal requited this kindness by bringing about the death, assertedly by arts of wizardry and magic, of a beautiful girl who, as a good Christian, had repelled his advances. The girl died in Cárichic. Neumann, who was still there at the time, wrote to Celada telling of the malpractice of this ingrate hechicero and murderer. Celada informed the Indian governor of San Francisco of what had been done. The latter consulted with his tribesmen. They decided the culprit ought to die and that same night they saw to the fulfillment of the sentence. Under cover of darkness the Indian governor and his men crept secretly to Soquerichic, seized the criminal in his sleep, and hanged him forthwith.

A notorious wizard of one of the pueblos was accustomed, so the good padre reports, to take successively the shapes of bears, tigers, and mountain lions. He was summarily dealt with by the governor of his own pueblo and other tribesmen. Since this method of handling such problems was a new thing, the Tarahumares, ignorant of the details, judged that the padre had ordered the execution. This report spread not only in Tarahumara, but sped to Mexico City and thence across the seas where the General, Father Thirso Gonzales, picked it up in the official reports. Was it true, the General inquired, that a missionary ordered one of his neophytes hanged. If so it was an egregious imprudence and the father must be punished. But General Gonzales finally received the true story: that the trial and execution of the wizard had taken place without the knowledge of the Jesuit missionary.[11]

The new system had its dangers. For although the witch craze was dying out in Europe it was still vigorous in America, as witness Cotton Mather and the incidents in New England. Jesuit missionaries did not, as we have seen, rise superior to their age in rejecting these superstitions. Like their neophytes, they were staunch believers in the constant interference of the preternatural, even though in this kind of faith their neophytes far surpassed them. It was dangerous, therefore, to put into the hands of the Tarahumar Indian governor the ferreting out and the punishment of an alleged witch. Nevertheless it was permitted and when the Indians at Papigochic brought a female witch to Captain Retana for punishment he bade them judge her themselves. This they did with the application of the European law: faggots were piled high and the flames consumed her body. Thus did the witch hunt also pursue its ghastly course in eighteenth-century Tarahumara.

But it was a relief to the missionaries, a weight off their shoulders, that owing to the tact and strength of Captain Retana the Indians themselves took over successfully the responsibility for the punishment of their own criminals. As the method worked out the fathers were confirmed in their judgment of its practicability. "We are no longer uncertain," wrote one of them, "whether the Indians who are appointed to administer justice in the villages are empowered to put criminals to death."[12] The fathers no longer feared being charged with passing the sentence. Instead, coöperating with Captain Retana, they lent sufficient authority to the Indian governors that the decisions of the latter were respected by their tribesmen.

Such were the circumstances under which the alarms and rebellions, with their crop of arson, destruction, and murder, were after more than fifty years finally eliminated in Alta Tarahumara. The tide turned at the end of the century. Tolerance and a friendly spirit toward the fugitives in the mountains and the instruction of the Indian governors in the responsibilities of administering justice themselves had influenced a lasting peace.[13]

The official visitation in 1715 and 1717 of Bishop Pedro Tapiz of Durango, twelfth of the line, confirms the peaceful and prosperous condition of the missions in the first quarter of the eighteenth century. The visitation included the Franciscan missions, but the Bishop saw eleven of the Jesuit Tarahumar establishments. That His Excellency was pleased, even delighted, is evident from the official report.[14] He found the Indians in good condition, both materially and spiritually, and the mission churches clean and well kept, and the divine offices carried out with propriety. The report praises the successful zeal of the Jesuits which could overcome, through paternal affection, the inveterate vice of drunkenness among these people together with other barbarities of their former pagan state. He noted that the Indians were well clothed and well fed, for they sowed corn, wheat, and legumes, and from the sale and barter of such products were able to procure a reasonably high grade of clothing for their present condition.

But his greatest pleasure and surprise was that the Indian boys and youths of his diocese had been taught to write, to read Spanish, to sing, and to play on musical instruments. The Bishop was at the mission of San Francisco Satevó on the Feast of St. Ignatius Loyola. He graciously lent dignity to the pontifical Mass which was celebrated that morning and wondered at the skill of the neophytes who assisted at the ceremonies and entoned the chants and other songs. The orchestra and choir, on this occasion, did itself proud. There were flageolets, bassoons, violins, harps, and an organ. The choir and orchestra were led by the *maestro de capilla,* or choirmaster, himself a Tarahumar. On this occasion the Jesuit Rector of Alta Tarahumara was present, and there was a sermon by the Black Robe from Coyachic. The Bishop reflected that he might just as well as not have been in his cathedral in Durango. Well indeed might His Excellency have been delighted at what he saw, and the writer of the official report says that Bishop Pedro Tapiz was, and concludes: "Without any doubt these missions are to the Bishops [of Durango] their joy, their jewel, and their consolation."[15]

Thus it was that Father Joseph Neumann himself, firm pillar of this mission since his advent in 1681 and witness of its repeated troubles, tranquilly lived out the last twenty years of his mission life.

In 1724 Neumann completed his famous history and composed its dedication from Cárichic on April 15th of that year. He was seventy-six years of age at the time and had only two years to go before reaching the golden anniversary of his priesthood. He was the first of the Bohemian Province to go to the wilds of Alta Tarahumara, but many followed him: Gilg, Amarel, Verdier, Eymer, Illink, and Janusky. The last-named father had died just three weeks before Neumann finished and dedicated his work. Hostinsky was with Neumann the only survivor at the quarter century of a valiant band of Jesuits of different nationalities who had been spiritually nurtured within the Bohemian Province of the Society of Jesus.[16]

Joseph Neumann, the most valiant and able of them all, lived to see his golden jubilee as a priest, for death did not call him until May 1, 1732, having permitted him to live more than fifty years amid the stern hardships of the Tarahumar missions.[17] Of the fifty-one years he labored in this thorny field (1681–1732) the first twenty were spent in Sisoguichic in the extreme southwest of Alta Tarahumara, the remaining thirty-one at Cárichic thirty miles away. Cárichic was a fitting place for Father Joseph Neumann to lay his bones to rest. Here his traveling companion from Europe, Juan María Ratkay, had labored and had died; here the saintly Pícolo had built the finest church in all the land. Had Neumann with prophetic eye been able to pierce the veil of the immediate future, his would have been a spirit of contentment and of peace, for others would follow him peacefully at Cárichic, and the missions would continue to spread northwest to cover much of the ground of northern Mexico.

Chapter XXII

TARAHUMARA'S NORTHERN HOME

IN THE history of the New World there was now repeated an experience which had often taken place and which had happened before in the mission land of Tarahumara: mines were discovered farther north. There was another gold rush and the frontier was extended. In Mexican frontier history it was one gold rush after another which brought the frontier to Zacatecas, to Sombrerete, to San Juan del Río, to Durango, to Santa Bárbara, to Parral, to Cusihuiriachic or Santa Rosa, and now finally to the spot we know today as the city of Chihuahua. At the very end of the 1600's there was a gold rush thither: northward leaped the frontier, northward went the padres, and new missions were founded.

But this rush was not for gold, for the mines which the Spaniards now discovered were of silver. All during the first decade of the eighteenth century there was a continuous stream of miners to the north. True, the tempo was not quite the pace of the vigorous and excited rush to Alta California, but it was for all that a steady stream, so that a settlement established on the banks of a stream, grew into a town, and then into a city which eventually became the capital of a state in the Republic of Mexico. The settlement was formally organized into a town in 1709 called El Real de San Francisco de Cuellar. In 1716 the town was promoted through the official exertions of Don Juan Felipe de Orozco y Molina to the status of a city and called Villa de San Felipe of the mine or real de Chihuahua.[1]

Already in Neumann's day, that is before 1725, the silver mines and the houses of the inhabitants extended for nearly a mile, so that, as this Black Robe says, "it seemed rather a city than a town by reason of the throng of merchants and artisans who, if they managed their business properly, in a short time acquired great wealth. For the amount of silver taken out of these new mines daily was incredible. Thus this latest Spanish settlement became the most populous of all while the other mines which were either exhausted or less productive were abandoned."[2]

[1] For notes to chapter xxii see page 254.

It had been the Jesuit tradition to seek the more populous centers and there, if possible, establish an institution for the education of the young. Now that a northern settlement had been established and had grown great, the Jesuits in the early 1700's thought of a college for Chihuahua just as they had thought of one for Parral in the early 1600's, and for Durango before that.

The chief promoter of a college in Chihuahua was the wealthy General Don Manuel de San Juan y Santa Cruz, who was Governor of Nueva Vizcaya from 1714 to 1720. This excellent type of Spanish gentleman pressed his suit with the Viceroy, and his permission was obtained. Going the full length of generosity and religious zeal Governor San Juan y Santa Cruz proceeded at once to endow the prospective college with two estates and made over for the erection of the church and buildings the sum of sixty thousand pesos. A site was chosen, ground was broken January 14, 1718, the year of the founding of New Orleans, and on February 2 amidst formal ceremony and festive rejoicing the cornerstone of the college was laid. The college was named after Our Lady of Loreto, and Father Francisco Navarrete was appointed its rector.[3]

The Jesuits looked far ahead in the establishment of this college for boys, for they had in mind the interests of the missions. The idea was to attract youths to these halls who would be taught Tarahumar and other Indian languages of the northern part of the province. The lads would then become novices of the Society and finally come back from Mexico City well prepared to take up and carry on the missionary work. Old veterans from the mission field were to retire to the college and become professors of the barbarous languages.

The city of Chihuahua became famous in the land and, indeed, in all of Mexico not so much for the number of Jesuit recruits it was able to train for the missions, as for the residence there of an ingenious and learned brother, expert in the art of medicine. He was from the Province of Bohemia and his name was Johann Steinheffer. Brother Steinheffer was sent to this northern outpost of Jesuit education for the purpose of turning to practical use his knowledge and skill, for up to his arrival there was no one to attend, alleviate, or cure the ills from which the old and retired missionaries suffered. This brother became a valued aid not only to the college of Chihuahua, but to all the far-spread northern mission fields of Sinaloa, Sonora, and Tarahumara. Not only did he apply useful and efficacious remedies to the diseases of both sexes, young and old, but he wrote a book on the subject which spread his fame and that of the northern Jesuits. Under its title, *A Medical Anthology,* it was published in Mexico City and received the approbation of the faculty of medicine in the University of Mexico.[4] "It was particularly helpful," writes Neumann, "in treating diseases in the home, . . . for it prescribed reliable remedies for maladies of every kind." Brother Johann Steinheffer, native of Iglau in Moravia, died in Sonora April 2, 1716, at the age of fifty-two, bequeathing as a legacy not only the light of his science, but the aroma of his religious virtues.[5]

Four years later Tarahumara lost one of its most distinguished missionaries and one who can be considered the founder of Alta Tarahumara. Father Tomás de Guadalajara, a creole, after his residence in Parral and the founding of the college there in 1685, went back to the missions and enjoyed a long career of labor in behalf of his Tarahumares. He had written a grammar, dictionary, and general treatise on the Tarahumar, Guazápar, and cognate languages, and died at Huejotitlán on January 6, 1720. His mortal remains were reverently laid in the courtyard before the church, and today at that ancient spot his tombstone, the inscription worn with time, marks the sod where his bones have mouldered into dust.[6]

While all this northward advance was taking place, the missions were enjoying an enduring peace. A ripple now and again slightly disturbed the placid surface of its life, but the mission of Alta Tarahumara had never in its history enjoyed so protracted a period of prosperity. True, a spot of trouble began to form at Tutuaca on the old turbulent western fringe of Tarahumara. It was a Pima chief called Manuel who began the trouble. He had long been a moral rebel, living in open polygamy and was, moreover, suspected of various murders. People said it was he who had waylaid and slain certain Spaniards on their way from Sonora to Tarahumara. The Pima was deposed, therefore, from his office, and another Indian governor placed over Tutuaca. Manuel was furious. He fled to the mountains, took some henchmen with him, and from his sequestered hideaway began the old-practiced method of stirring up discontent and revolt among the mountain tribes. His intrigues extended to seven of the Christian pueblos. Rumors of an impending revolt spread and came to the ears of the Spanish authorities, to Governor Giovanni Guiseppe Mozzoni.

Then it was that Father Georg Hostinsky stepped into the breach. He spoke Tarahumara well, the nation admired and trusted him. He more than anyone else could find out the truth. He went into the hills in search of Manuel and conferred with many of the tribes. He discovered the worst was true. Hostinsky presently showed himself possessed of keen diplomatic ability. Realizing that to arrest and punish ringleader Manuel would take time, cost money, and be dangerous into the bargain, he decided to win the rebel over. His persuasions were successful. Manuel promised amendment and future friendship and virtue. On the strength of such fine words he was reinstated as Indian governor of Tutuaca.

But it was all a deceit. The rebel did not summon his followers down from the mountains as he had promised, and he continued to spread evil word concerning the fathers and Spaniards. He was incorrigible and must be taken. Hostinsky cleverly arranged this. Faithful neophytes of Tutuaca caught the rebel while off his guard, bound him, and brought him to the Governor at Parral. Here the recalcitrant Pima was imprisoned for years and when released was forbidden to return to his Tutuacan country. A resident missionary was able now to live in Tutuaca. A padre was sent, but the rigors of the climate forced him to leave after a year and the charge fell back upon Hostinsky, who was taking the place of four missionaries.[7]

During the last years covered by Joseph Neumann's narrative, that is up to 1724, Tarahumara and the contiguous country continued to flourish. Father Manuel Ordaz advancing from the Tulares east through the mountains established a mission among the Sarichiquis and the Satebonos. Another Black Robe, Martín Benavides, braved the perilous paths along the dizzy precipices of the Río Urique to reach the isolated Parrachis.[8] Later Father Jacob Doye, working among the Tarahumares in Selocaquichic, was sent by the Visitor to found a permanent mission among them. This became a visita of the Belgian Black Robe Doye.[9]

Chihuahua, besides being the seat of a newly founded Jesuit college and a retiring house for careworn missionaries, acted also as a northern center whence missionaries could go forth to different parts of Tarahumara, into the Concho country, and among the Chinarras, the latter being a small tribe living not far from the new city. Indeed, just a mile or so south of the city was the Indian pueblo and mission called San Francisco Gerónimo. It numbered but thirty-eight families and was a babel of tongues, for here were Tobosos, Conchos, Humas, and Chinarras. When their padre, Antonio de Arias, was called south to be missionary in the newly opened Nayarit country, fathers from the college at Chihuahua attended this pueblo. Thus it was that at the end of 1725 the official visitor of the missions, Father Juan de Guendulain, representing his Provincial, set out from Chihuahua to make his rounds. Like his predecessor, Juan Ortiz Zapata, Guendulain, good man, wrote a detailed report of the route he followed and of the condition of each mission which he visited.[10]

This report is as informing as is that of Lizasoain written thirty-six years later. It is encouraging, too; it witnesses to progress and shows that the brave pioneers on the mission, Fonte, Figuerroa, Martínez, Basilio, Tardá, Guadalajara, had not labored and given their blood in vain. The report testifies to the fact that the state of the mission at this period, just forty-two years before its ruin by the general expulsion of all the Jesuits, was in a vitalized and flourishing condition. Guendulain visited the principal cabeceras of the mission of Alta Tarahumara and many of the lesser pueblos of the different partidos. Cusihuiriachic, San Bernabé, Yepómera, Mátachic, San Tomás, Papigochic, Cárichic, and many others were reported on. It is quite evident that the Visitor was not only pleased, but pleasantly surprised to find in such places as Yepómera and Cárichic such large and excellent churches, which were so pleasingly ornamented and well appointed in all things useful and necessary for the divine service.

The Visitor saw that at Yepómera the church "was fine, large and beautiful with its roof supported with beams curiously wrought, sculptured, and painted. The retable of the main altar was formed by a large and good painting which covered the whole space, and each of the side altars was adorned with paintings in their turn." And so it stood in the mid-twentieth century dominating the little village and looking down the arroyo which winds south to the Papigochic.

Thus Yepómera, formerly the seat of so much trouble and rebellion, was at this time most prosperous. It owned 4,000 head of cattle, 92 mules, 147 horses, besides mares, burros, and smaller animals. Its farm, called Babicori, yielded grain and maize, and this was more than enough to support the not very large population of 137 families, which included 211 boys. Twenty-three of the inhabitants were single.

Papigochic possessed 1,200 head of cattle; Cárichic 400. But the church at Cárichic, built by Pícolo and adorned and completed by Neumann, awakened the highest admiration of the Visitor. It had three naves, and the pillars made of pine were so large and fine that "at first sight they seemed to be made of stone. They were sculptured and painted, and tapestries hang from the sides from the sanctuary clear back to the entrance." The main altar was adorned with twelve large candlesticks of wrought silver, and a throne for the bishop, a handsome lectern, and chairs set off the sanctuary. Many kinds of ornaments of gold and silk had been given to Father Neumann by his friends, some of whom were Jews.[11]

The old mission church stands today upon its gentle eminence perfectly intact. It has a pleasing façade, surmounted by an opening from which hang three bells. The whole is crowned by a cross. Here, indeed, was something to delight the Visitor's heart. No wonder the church at Cárichic is called the best in all this land, for as the visitor today gazes upon its venerable walls and admires the artistic setting of the interior, with its pillars "that seemed to be of stone," he can understand the enthusiastic admiration of Visitor Guendulain long ago.

The walls of these ancient churches are for the most part still standing. Besides Yepómera and Cárichic, the traveler today can admire the mission churches of Mátachic, San Tomás, Píchachic, Sisoguichic, Nonoava, and many others. The old mission church at Papigochic, however, has entirely disappeared. Though time has wrought some ruin upon their ancient shells, they still give old and mute testimony of the labors of the Black Robes who built them long ago.

In most of the pueblos at Guendulain's visitation of 1725 there were churches, and even at this time building in certain places was still going on. After much travel, the Visitor threaded the pass of the Río Papigochic and, reaching Sonora, journeyed onward along the banks of the stream now called the Yaqui to arrive, finally, at Cócorin, where he sat down to write his glowing report to his Provincial superior. It is dated December 22, 1725.[12]

During Father Guendulain's visitation of the Tarahumar pueblos he used a set of explicit instructions drawn up for him by the former Provincial in Mexico City, Joseph de Arjó. He was given the full authority of the Provincial, except that he was not to expel a member from the Society or admit a new one, nor sign contracts affecting the financial status of the colleges. The Visitor was given notices of defects and points of weakness in the administration or personnel of the missions and he was instructed to set a hand to their correction. Preaching was neglected by some of the missionaries to an extent that after years of Christian influences, the Indians were still ignorant of the Faith. Some of the fathers were too harsh in their dealings with the natives; some even disdained fastidiously to enter Indian dwellings to administer the last sacraments, compelling the sick to come to the church for the final rites. And some of the missionaries, through softness and lack of discipline, urging the excuse of excessive heat or cold, celebrated Mass only on Sundays. Some imprudently and uncharitably were given to gossip with seculars which often turned out to the offense of persons and a decline in the prestige of the padre. The missionaries were not to act as overnight hosts to their Spanish friends.

Visitor Guendulain was to see that churches were built in each mission pueblo, he was to instruct the fathers to say Mass periodically in their visitas, at least once a month, and to tarry there a few days to make themselves acquainted with this portion of their flock. Very importantly, the missionaries were to learn the language of the Indians of their pueblo. Some fathers had been for years in the missions and yet could not preach to their neophytes. Severe penalties were laid down by the Provincial for such ignorance. Young missionaries were not to be admitted to the Profession or to their last vows until they had demonstrated before their superiors that they could preach satisfactorily in the Indian tongue of their pueblo. Indeed, they were to be ordered to preach in public in the missions and before a committee of their brethren who were to pass on their proficiency. Even the older padres were to be made to learn the language. Let the Visitor proceed with gentleness and charity, but the thing must be done, even to the point of removing a missionary from his pueblo until he learned its language.

If a change of missionary was to be made from one pueblo to another, the departing Black Robe must leave in writing full instructions for the procedure of his successor, must have his accounts satisfactorily drawn up, and leave behind the useful grammars, dictionaries, and confessor's manuals in the language of that pueblo. Thus the new missionary would not be hampered and embarrassed from the start.

Last but not least, Visitor Guendulain was to insist that the annual reports from each pueblo, the famous anuas, be carefully written and periodically handed in to headquarters with the proper specifications as to the number of Christians in a given pueblo, of married and of single persons, of baptisms, of marriages, of the devotions practiced, of the temporal state of the mission, and of extraordinary or miraculous events.

Superiors too were to use proper kindness, prudence, and care in the handling of their subjects. Thus, the abuse of too frequent changes would be avoided, and especially would it bring to an end the hardship of sending a missionary of long years' residence in a pueblo of a certain language to a pueblo where a different tongue was spoken. And, finally, these instructions were to be communicated to all the missionaries of Tarahumara.[13]

All in all, Provincial José de Arjó was an efficient man and effectively did he turn his talents to the betterment of the Tarahumar through Visitor Guendulain. It was such an official visitation, deepening the inner spirit, and such regulations, strengthening external discipline, which helped to render the last decades of the mission sufficiently peaceful and prosperous, though troubles and difficulties continued to exist.

Chapter XXIII

THE LAST GREAT APOSTLE

Among the Jesuits who made a name in the last years of the Tara-humar mission was the German Father Herman Glandorff. If the sprouting of legend is any indication of the importance of the man, or of his power, or of the affection in which he was held, then certainly Francis Herman Glandorff was in truth a famous missionary achieving the highest success of any of his confrères in the whole of Tarahumara.[1]

Riding west over good roads from the city of Chihuahua in northern Mexico the traveler skims the edge of spacious valleys, winds along over barren hills, and emerges at last onto a plain across whose level wastes, in the crystal clear atmosphere, the eye is carried to far blue mountain ranges which mark the rim of the horizon. Beyond, closed in to the north and to the south by black and bold sierras is the Valle de Papigochic watered by its delightful river and famed in the mission history of northern Mexico. Here Jesuit missionaries fell, Cornelio Beudin in 1650 and Jácome Basilio in 1652. The modern Ciudad Guerrero marks the proximity of the hallowed spot. A few miles farther downstream Fathers Juan Ortiz Foronda and Manuel Sánchez fell in 1690.

The father of the northern mission group, Alta Tarahumara, was Tomás de Guadalajara, who by 1675 had the country fairly well organized. Shortly thereafter the partido of Tomochic was created. South and west from the Valle de Papigochic, over a blue sierra, its rugged sides clothed with pine, sits the pueblo of Tomochic, in the middle of a sweet and lovely valley watered by its stream. Here in this isolated spot Glandorff lived for decades, here as Jesuit missionary he achieved fame of holiness, and, among the Indians, legendary repute for prowess in the wilds, for endurance, and fleetness of foot.

Glandorff's name is still a legend in the country. At Cárichic today they point out the site of the dwelling in which the missionary resided, and in Upper Tarahumara there is a ragged canyon called Cañón de La Banderilla where one sees the cave (*la cueva del Padre*

---

[1] For notes to chapter xxiii see pages 255-256.

Glandorff) where the Black Robe is supposed to have lived.[2] At the end of the nineteenth century the Mexican Jesuits were gathering documents and testimonials in order to inaugurate officially a process for his canonization. In 1897 the Mexican Provincial, Father José Alzola, wrote to the Franciscans of Zacatecas, who possessed the body, requesting that the remains be returned to the Mexican Jesuits.[3]

Glandorff was a native of Osnabrück in Germany. Born in 1687, he entered the Jesuit Order at Trèves in 1708 and a few years later applied for the missions. The world might have missed in the missionary a historian of note, for his immediate superiors had destined him for the Bollandists. General Michael Tamburini, however, allowed him, like Kino, to follow the invitations of his ardent spirit, and to go as a missionary to the New World. Glandorff was still a scholastic when he came to the Americas in 1717 or the year following, so that he did his theological work in the famous Colegio de San Pedro y San Pablo in Mexico City. Immediately after his tertianship he went to the missions arriving in Tarahumara late in 1721.[4] He had the good fortune to be sent to Cárichic where Joseph Neumann, now a very old man, was superior.

By 1730 the young missionary was laboring in Tomochic,[5] where he acquired in his years of residence in the mission a great name and reputation as holy man and miracle worker. Tomochic is forty miles southwest of Papigochic and beyond a blue sierra in an isolated valley which took its name from the pueblo. Here Glandorff lived and prayed and attended to his Indians and worked his miracles. He died at Tomochic in 1763, the year when France ceded to England all of Canada and the east Mississippi Valley.

The Tarahumares were hardy walkers and runners and were fleet of foot, scrambling up the banks of ravines and scampering over mountain ledges like wild mountain goats. These same qualities the natives admired in others. Even today they sustain the old reputation. It is a common sight in Mexico to see the Indian trudge along the road passing thus slowly from one village or town to another. But one often sees a pair of stalwart, half-naked Tarahumares break into a run according to the ancient habits of their race. Glandorff, for the speed with which he traversed long stretches of country and for the indefatigable quality of his endurance, gained a name and reputation among Indians and missionaries alike, and this name grew and developed into enduring and even humorous legend. Glandorff's very moccasins were supposed to contain the quality of speed, and once when his fatigued Indian companion collapsed the man was resuscitated and rendered tireless by the wearing of the padre's shoes.[6] The speed of his going and coming was reported as being altogether miraculous, for he could get to a sick call on foot even before his Indians on horse.

Two Franciscans are said to have put the truth of all of this to the test. One of these, Fray Miguel Domínguez, swore to the following: He saw Glandorff leave on foot for a sick call at eight o'clock one morning and return at noon. The two Franciscans wishing to inquire into the distance, indicated to Glandorff that they too desired to visit the place. The good padre lent them horses for the journey. Thus mounted these Franciscans traveled the whole of one day, arriving only after dark at the place to which Glandorff had gone and returned in half a day. Miracle was blended in the popular and ecclesiastical mind with all of this legend. The Black Robe's superior, Bartholomé Braun, from whose pen we have a glowing account, mentions a whole throng of miracles: nothing stopped Glandorff, neither rain or snow, through which he could travel with dry head and dry feet. He would labor through the turbulent waters of flooding rivers without concern and emerge dry on the opposite bank! Once when he was performing the last rites at the burial of an Indian woman she spoke from her bier. And, to crown all this pyramid of wonders, the holy man prophesied his own death.[7]

Father Glandorff's letters added to his fame, for they were copied, handed about, and found their way ultimately to Europe. Father Antonio Benz, a Bavarian of Munich, had heard of Glandorff. Benz was one of those missionaries, delightful to historians, who wrote many letters. All the way from Germany en route to his Sonoran mission he sent missives back to parents and friends. To him at the port of Santa María in Spain, awaiting ship to carry him to Mexico, fame of Glandorff had been carried. In a letter from Spain to a priest friend in Germany, dated October 4, 1749, Benz recounts one of the stories which Glandorff had himself written from his mission and Benz says he had it from a letter from Mexico.[8] We have news, he says, from Taroma, meaning Tarahumara, and from Father Glandorg, meaning of course

Glandorff. Benz, who would soon be in Sonora west over the mountains from Glandorff, gives Glandorff's narrative of the woman Anastasia who, when she died and was being buried, spoke up from her casket and uttered words which described her present condition. Benz quoted her words, which he says were heard by those standing by: "Oh how beautiful is the house of God which we shall enter soon after death." Glandorff himself, however, in a letter to a fellow Jesuit in Germany, January 18, 1752,[9] gives a longer version of this speech from the dead: "Oh how beautiful are the tabernacles of God placed far beyond the stars. I could never have believed it. Soon you will see it with your own eyes."

Benz gave Glandorff the highest praise, calls him a real apostle and says he is regarded as a saint. "He never drinks wine, he never rides, but without fatigue he covers often in one day thirty and more leagues. He had once to visit the mountains on horseback, but he was so ill he had to be taken down from the horse. He began to walk, his strength returned, and soon he went faster than those riding."[10] One morning after a first Mass, writes Benz, Glandorff started out on foot to another pueblo twelve miles distant to say a second Mass. A horse was offered him which he refused. His neophytes took the horse and went thither themselves. They found Glandorff issuing from the church having completed his second Mass.[11] Miracle or no miracle, for one can ride a horse very slowly, this incident of very doubtful veracity given by Benz shows how early sprouted the legend of speed and endurance in connection with the name of Glandorff. The missionary himself, speaking of his privations in the missions avers that "for the first eighteen years I did not taste bread." And he goes on to tell of another miracle, another stirring of speech after death when three of his neophytes, Basil, Ignatius, and Francis, moved at his approach, opened their eyes, and invoked the name of Jesus.[12] Thus was the fame of Father Francis Herman Glandorff spread abroad through his own letters (a common occurrence with missionaries) and those of his confrères.

If the missionary was, as alleged, befriended by Heaven in the form of wonders and miracles, he was also harried by the demons of Hell. This is so if we accept his account in his letter of 1752 to Father Hesselmeier. For years spirits tormented him. "The church bell would ring during the night and even in the day, in the vestibule would be heard a noise as of people jumping, the whole house would roar, doors and windows would fly open. Only my living room was free from these horrors. Perhaps they [the demons] were endeavoring to eject me from this land in which they have long enjoyed rights of prescription." Glandorff, finally, was led to follow the counsels of a sage older missionary, Constantine Gallerati, who later died in the repute of sanctity. Gallerati had been similarly tormented. He decided to face the demons with the exorcisms of the Church, immemorial prayers composed for the expulsion of evil spirits, commanding them in the name of the Almighty Master of creation to recede. Gallerati tried this; he read to the demons the curses and anathemas of the Church commanding them to return to Hell where they belonged, and, as he later told Glandorff, from that moment he was never tormented again. Glandorff acted upon this advice and like his confrère was thereafter rid of the nuisance. "They seemed to have obeyed," wrote Glandorff, "for they never bothered me again."[13]

But in spite of any personal difficulty or illness Glandorff saw the mission of Tomochic thrive and advance under his tutelage and protection. He reports in 1730 on the progress of his partido. Where before there were but seventeen Christians now there were one hundrd and forty. In another settlement the Christian families grew from sixty to two hundred and fifty. The increase had been gathered in from the caves and the ravines. He had early built five churches, one in each of five pueblos which he named (they are oft-repeated names) Santa María Immaculata, San Miguel, San José, San Luis de Gonzaga and Santa María Dei Para Aranzassassana! Glandorff at this period attended altogether 1,575 Christian Indians and had married 661. He had been able to reclaim almost one hundred from servitude. A few incorrigibles living immoral lives Glandorff expelled from the pueblo. But Spaniards got hold of these men and their women and forced them to work in a silver mine near by. Sadly enough, but, as all the mission records run, inevitably, a plague carried off from his two pueblos 800 infants and 664 adults.[14]

We have in Father Braun's biographical note an early notice of the Apaches, who for some time had plagued the northeastern border. One of Glandorff's neophytes confessed he had been among these marauders and had seen among them many Tarahumares living in paganism like beasts. These renegade Tarahumares acted the traitor's part when they would actually be guides for the Apaches into their own territory. Glandorff was alarmed. He wrote of the danger to his superiors and to the Viceroy. When after the passing of years and the continuance of the abuse the devoted missionary saw that no action would be taken, sorrow over the continuance of the disturbance hastened his death.

There was another cause of grief, however, to the heart of the old missionary, and this we gather clearly from his letters to his superiors.[15] This was the misunderstanding and sometimes friction which existed in the mission during the interval between the creole Jesuits of Spanish blood and the foreigners, Germans and Italians, who had come from Europe. This particular internal difficulty was not limited to this period, for the undesirable condition is repeatedly mentioned by the Fathers General in their correspondence with the Provincials of New Spain.[16] The trouble comes out clearly in the correspondence of Glandorff.

These letters do not make edifying reading. It becomes evident from them that all the missionaries were not saints and that even Glandorff himself, for all his reputation and possible heroic qualities, was not immune from some of the shortcomings of human nature. He complains of the fact that he and some of his European confrères are being the subjects of complaints made by some of the native-born Mexican Jesuits to the Jesuit superiors. "Against me, likewise, from what I hear, they have stirred up cruel war."[17]

He strongly resented, moveover, the removal by the Visitor, Carlos de Rojas, from the office of rector the Italian Cristóbal de Lauria. Glandorff wrote to the Provincial September 15, 1749, for a rectification of this injustice to Lauria and averred that seculars both in Sonora and Tarahumara, who were admirers of Lauria, murmured and were scandalized, suspecting some grave fault on the part of the demoted padre. Lauria, moreover, Glandorff complains, after being deposed from his office of Rector of Alta Tarahumara was sent to the ruined mission of Guasarapa among Indians whose language he did not know.

And Glandorff manifests his irritation: "If the fathers of this country wish to devour the fathers from overseas, why do they ask for them at Rome. If they say that Father General obliges them to this, then they will allow us to complain bitterly to Father General that he has sent us as lambs among wolves."[18] Glandorff looks for redress from the fatherly charity and justice of the Provincial, Andrés Xavier García. The story, however, as gathered from these letters is not consistent, for Glandorff also complains of Cosío, who was a Lombard, and defends Andonaegui, who was a creole Mexican. This seeming inconsistency, however, may demonstrate the missionary's basic virtue and sense of justice.

There was another trial which weighed still more heavily upon the spirit of Francis Glandorff. It was mistreatment of the Indians, and not this time only by secular Spaniards and officers of administration or of the army, but by one or another of the missionaries themselves. At the instance of Father Domingo de Cosío, says Glandorff in a letter of 1747 to Visitor Lorenzo Gera, Captain Mendía was sent to Tomochic bringing trouble and suffering to the neophytes. Mendía from Papigochic went to Tomochic with soldiers and other Spaniards to remove from the partido of Glandorff his own neophytes and herd them into the partido of Papigochic. Glandorff, of course, strenuously objected and strengthened his opposition by presenting Captain Mendía with official documents from the court of Madrid. From these same papers, moreover (they were undoubtedly cédulas of the king), he urged arguments whereby the Indians of Papigochic should be more humanely treated. The Captain made a copy of these papers and then wrote to the Governor of Nueva Vizcaya concerning the whole affair. These letters never reached the Governor for they were intercepted and Glandorff suspected Fathers Palma and Cosío.[19] Here was trouble indeed for the padre and for his Indians, coming from his own colleagues.

But the vexations went further. In a later letter to Father Luís Téllez Girón, our missionary complains bitterly about the actions some of his confrères performed to the hurt of the poor neophytes. The rector of Alta Tarahumara, Blas de la Palma, sold to Father Domingo de Cosío the estate called Estancia de Tezcatzi, near Papigochic, where the Indians used to sow their corn and raise some other crops. Cosío, indulging in a centuries-old abuse of farming country, turned this district into pasture and grazing land for his flocks and herds, taking it from its usefulness to the Indians. The same thing happened at Tonachic, at Bachelach, and other places where in like manner the Indians were deprived of their plantation fields and meadows. The fate of "sweet Auburn, loveliest village of the plain," was, it seems, being duplicated in olden Tarahumara.

The neophytes were saddened or even infurated. "What superior," indignantly exclaims Glandorff, "has thus given permission to sell the lands of the missions." One does not know how the Indians can endure so much, he says, for their vexations continue. The indignant padre recalls the incident of Francis Xavier having rebuked a missionary in India for not paying a native his just hire. "What would he [Xavier] say if he saw what was going on here?" "Alas," cries out the disappointed missionary, "life has become a bitterness to me and my natural forces prepare themselves for death. God's will be done."[20] These then were some of the trials of Francis Herman Glandorff and the internal troubles of the mission of Tarahumara.

Well might the aging missionary be sad, for in this same decade of the 1740's the Indians had suffered from other injustices and, consequently, there was trouble with some of them. Glandorff's irritation and sorrow were the result of years of disappointment. Already in 1744 the Governor of Nueva Vizcaya at Chihuahua had indited a long memorial to the Viceroy on the abuse of the Indian by the Spaniards, rancher and mineowner alike. The cédulas of His Majesty which contain all the remedies were not obeyed. Whereas, represented the Governor, the royal cédulas allow the Spaniards to take four per cent of the Indians away from their pueblos, the Spaniards actually carry off a much larger percentage because of their need of laborers. Thus the crops of the poor Indians are not sown, hunger descends upon the pueblos, and the natives flee to the wilds. That very year the people of Tomochic had thus fled as well as some from other pueblos. General Antonio Casuya had to march out to bring them home. He succeeded with all except the men of Tomochic.

Not only do the Spaniards, reports the Governor, far exceed the number of workers allowed them by the king, but they apply none of the remedies ordered by His Majesty for the humane treatment of the poor workers. The regulations are that they be not made to travel to their place of labor more than five leagues a day, that they be given food on the journey, and that they be properly paid for their labors. These regulations are not kept, complains the Governor, and if food is given them on their way to the mines it is taken out of their pay; and when they are actually paid it is in kind, with articles and stuffs the Indians do not want and cannot use, and often the poor people are forced to go all the way to Chihuahua to get the pittance they have earned.

The Governor after this exposition offers the Viceroy twelve points of reform which if applied will remedy the abuse and bring greater peace to the country.[21] There is little new in these recommendations. They had been contained in various royal cédulas as the Governor himself avers, and their application had been requested again and again by the missionaries. The twelve points made by the Governor were, briefly, that the Indians live in pueblos, have lands of their own, have a school in each pueblo, that they may not roam from one pueblo to another, and may not be taken for labor outside the seasons specified in the cédulas. Since the four per cent mentioned in the cédulas is not sufficient to supply all the labor for the ranches, mines, and charcoal burners, let one-third of a pueblo be taken for a shift of one month and then another third. With each group thus released let an old Indian go as captain and have charge; let the Governor supervise the numbers that are needed; on the way to work the commands of the king are to be followed, those who remain at home must labor at the crops. The eleventh point contains a strong indictment against the greed and cruelty of the captains of presidios and alcaldes mayores of the towns who flout every law of God and king in order to profit by the labor and the hunger and nakedness of the poor Indian. And finally, concludes the Governor of Nueva Vizcaya, that such regulations be obeyed by all the ranchers, miners, captains and alcaldes, and all other subjects of the king let the Governor of Nueva Vizcaya have full authority, clearly delegated by the Viceroy, to impose and enforce them.

The Governor concludes with some reflections of great wisdom. He tells the Viceroy that only in this way can the Indians be brought to a lasting peace and that only thus can these outlying provinces be said to be conquered. Otherwise there will be, as in the past, constant uprisings and revolts. Furthermore, the pagan Indians of the mountains keep a constant eye upon the condition of their tribesmen who are Christians and living in pueblos. When these pagans witness the good treatment of the Indians and their consequent happiness, when they see that the weak, the sick, and the women are favored and protected, they will of their own accord come down from the sierra, ask for baptism, and offer to live in the pueblos. The Jesuit superiors of the missions should be consulted on all these things, he says, because the love these fathers have for the Indian is well known.

Such were the wise provisions of the Governor. But it seems evident that, as had been always the case even from the very beginning of the conquest, they were not applied. Decadent Spain was less than ever strong enough in the eighteenth century to enforce her beneficial laws in this far outpost of her empire. Glandorff, therefore, witnessed the ill treatment of his Indians, and the military and the civilian were in one or another instance joined even by the Jesuit.

During the span covered by Glandorff's career in the missions of Alta Tarahumara interesting events were occurring and interesting things were being done in other parts of the Jesuit mission field in this southwestern section of North America. At the very time in which Glandorff came to the missions of Tarahumara the Jesuits with the help of the secular arm were rounding out successfully the spiritual conquest of Nayarit, far to the south, below the present states of Sinaloa and Durango. In the centuries since the conquest these high rocky ridges and the deep barrancas had constituted an island of paganism and abomination in the midst of Christian and civilized Indians, a constant hiding place for rebels of every description. In the early 1720's this country was finally won for Spain and for the Faith.

The missions of Baja California were being augmented in spite of the rebellion of 1734 in which two missionaries fell. Fathers Ugarte, Consag, and Wenceslaus Link were exploring the mountains and the coasts and the islands of Lower California and the Gulf. Ignatz Pfefferkorn was making his important explorations from Sonora north to the lands of the Gila River and beyond, gathering materials for his remarkable description of Sonora, its geography and inhabitants, its minerals, herbs, animals, insects, poisons, and all the rest.[22]

While all of this activity was going on in other fields and while Father Glandorff was moving toward the last decade of his years an important development took place in the south which affected some of the Tarahumara missions: twenty-two Jesuit establishments were given over to the care of the diocesan clergy. From the beginning of the Jesuit mission system in North America it had been the intention of the Fathers General to relinquish the missions to the diocesan bishop whenever the neophytes were thought fit to dispense with the tutelage of the missionaries. In 1746 the Jesuit Provincial of New Spain, Father Cristóbal de Escobar y Llamas, thought this time had arrived for twenty-two missions in the districts of Topia, of Tepehuán, and of some of the country of Lower Tarahumara.

Provincial Escobar suggested the secularization of these twenty-two missions in a dispatch to the King of Spain, Philip IV, early in 1646. In the meantime the King died and there was a delay. Correspondence back and forth continued for several years, the Bishop of Durango, Martín de Alisacoechea, was not overwilling to accept the charge because of lack of men, but a royal cédula from Ferdinand VI to the Viceroy, Francisco de Hüemes y Horcasitas, settled the matter in favor of the secularization of these missions. The twenty-two establishments were definitely handed over to the Bishop of Durango late in 1753 by Father Francisco Pérez de Aragon, representing the Provincial, Father Andrés García. Of the number, only seventeen are listed, and among these are some which have entered into our story of Tarahumara. Santiago Papasquiaro and Zape of the Tepehuán unit went over to the Bishop, and of the Lower Tarahumar pueblos and partidos Las Bocas, San Pablo Ballesa, San Gerónimo Huejotitlán, Santa Cruz, Santa María de Cuevas, and Satevó were relinquished by the Black Robes.[23]

Minute lists of the properties and appurtenances of each of the transferred missions were made for the Bishop of Durango and some of these have been preserved. The mission of Glandorff's at Tomochic would not be so well supplied in properties and belongings as some of the transferred missions. Yet we can gain a fair idea of what Glandorff at Tomochic and the later Tarahumar missionaries at other pueblos possessed for the administration of their respective missions and for their personal support or comfort from the perusal of the inventory of Satevó.[24]

There lived here in the mission pueblo of Satevó the year of the transfer, 1753, 150 families of Tarahumar Indians. They were served spiritually by a good, well-appointed mission church and by a resident Jesuit padre. A one-room house near the church served as residence for the missionary, though a short distance away was another house with a kitchen for guests. A large barn stood near the father's house and a smaller one farther on. There was a well-equipped mill and an orchard with some wild vines and stumps. A truck garden hard by the house served the padre and beyond were fields where grew cotton, lentils, and chick-peas. Near the mill was another piece of ground where kidney beans were grown and pasturage was available. The crop garnered there amounted to two *fanegas* (one fanega being 1.60 bushels). The missionary had bought another field from one Victoriano, which yielded five *almudes* of corn (an almud being a fraction of a bushel). There were two other fields in the vicinity. A small one across the Río Satevó, the yield of which was only a fanega and a half of corn and another on this side the stream which produced one fanega and eleven almuds of the same crop. For the working of the orchard and of the cultivated fields the mission possessed seven yoke of oxen with seven plows. The store of provision at the time was: fifty fanegas of wheat, forty of corn, with one fanega of wheat sown.

But the mission possessed also cattle ranges, for the padre must have his meat for himself and an occasional guest, and on festival days for the extra regalement of his neophytes. The range, called a rancho, grazed cattle, horses, and sheep. It was a gift made a few decades previously by Don Francisco Gonzales Ramírez when Father Domingo Lizarralde was resident priest. There was a string attached to the gift, however. The resident missionary must say twelve Masses a year for the Holy Souls. The ranch gave pasture to a hundred head of branded cattle, a hundred head of sheep, fifty mares, and four riding horses. But there were other head of cattle and horses, being fattened up, it would seem, for the grand repasts of the pueblo on the occasion of the greater feasts. Thus set apart for the coming day of St. Ignatius were twenty-five head of cattle and twenty-five mares, and for the next feast day of St. Francis Xavier, patron of the mission, the padre had on reserve fifty head of cattle and another fifty mares! The Indians of this pueblo of Satevó would eat well, at least on the festivals of the Church.

There is in this record a meticulously minute inventory of the furniture and appurtenances of the church, the sacristy, and of the father's house. At the risk of monotony, but because it seems to hold some historical color we run through it here with a few generalizations where the minutiae become unusually detailed.

The church was of whitewashed adobe, with a nave and two transepts. It had a sturdy façade set off by large solid portals secured by strong locks. The baptistry with the baptismal font was of hewn stone, and there were in the body of the church two other standing containers for holy water made of the same material. There was a wooden pulpit, two confessionals, and six benches for the convenience of worshipers. The main altar was set off by a gilded retable containing three statues: Blessed Mary the Virgin in the center, wearing a silver crown, flanked by SS. Ildefonso and Francis Xavier. The side walls were adorned by sixteen paintings of various saints. In the sanctuary stood an image of the Infant Jesus, which was valued at more than three thousand pesos. There were twenty-three other pictures.

On the gospel side in the nave was an altar dedicated to *Madre Santísima de la Luz*. This side altar was adorned with seven statues of saints, a canopy of wood embossed with silver, and a tabernacle with a silver border surmounted by an image of Our Lady of Sorrows. Another altar stood in the nave on the epistle side of the church, dedicated to Blessed Mary the Virgin. Her statue stood in the middle clothed with a tunic and mantle of gold tissue. This altar was likewise set off by a small gilded retable which contained a statue of the Immaculate Conception, the head wearing a silver crown. Two other statues stood in niches of this retable, one of the Blessed Virgin, the other of St. Michael. Before this altar hung a brass candelabrum. A communion rail closed in the main altar and within the sanctuary thus formed were a bench, three tables for the wine and water cruets, a small stool for the servers at Mass, one large hand bell of bronze and three small ones. The choir loft contained an organ with three stops, a violin, a lyre, a guitar, a harp, a horn, and a drum, and in the church tower were five large and small bells and another hand bell.

Other articles are listed as making up the furniture of the church: four hundred and forty-two pounds and two and a half ounces of ornaments and decorations in silver most of which were gilded, a baldaquin,

two lecterns, one lamp, an aspergillum, two candlesticks, a censor
with boat and spoon, a banner of Christ and a diadem of St. Ignatius;
a statue with halo and palm branch of St. Xavier, a silken streamer
for the crucifix, a silver vase for water near the tabernacle, a missal, a
diadem of St. Joseph, and a bambino with crown and scepter, a banner with embroidered cross and scepter, a lamp vase, three chalices, one
candlestick, a pyx for the monstrance, a halo of Our Lady of Sorrows,
two sets of cruets with the vases, and a ciborium. Such were the articles which stood in the sanctuary of the mission church of Satevó
when the mission was handed over to the Bishop in 1752.

But this is not an end of the details of the inventory. What of the
sacristy, where many other articles pertaining to the altar and its services would be preserved. These too are listed most carefully. First the
room is described. It was large with a domed ceiling of scrolled wood.
It possessed a baptismal font of hewn stone, a basin, surmounted by a
crucifix, for washing the hands. It was enriched by a baldaquin set off
with statues, and there were images in each of the corners. A chest
contained nine bowls, a set of white silken vestments to be used for
High Mass, three bordered altar cloths, and other ornaments. There
were, moreover, in this chest a silken banner of St. Ignatius, various
silken vestments, four missals (each one is described), and many
other vestments of various colors and designs and in this inventory
each one is minutely described.

Also (in or outside the chest), there were thirteen cinctures, eight
albs, two surplices, twenty purificators, six cornualtares, ten corporals,
nine amices, a small cloth of ribbed silk, a baldaquin with drapery, an
altar covering with braided fringe, various cloths and altar coverings,
the colors of which are given, forty-six bronze candlesticks, an old
chalice, three covers for the ciborium, a white veil with key for Holy
Thursday, thirteen coins to give the Indians at their weddings, a
small purple tunic for the Infant Jesus, several other banners (each
described), a copper aspergillum, wooden candlesticks, a tall wooden
cross, some candlestick molds, a statue of the Infant Jesus, some wooden
lions with pedestals of stone for the candlesticks, four large China
vases with lids and a stand for each which cost four hundred pesos, five
colored opas, a large veil of silk for the tabernacle during feasts, and
other coverings, hangings, and ornaments. There were besides all of

this a bed with sheets, a quilt, pillows, and bolster. Perhaps the largest piece in the sacristy was an altar with columns.

But the end is not yet. There were the father's house and two barns. The residence must be described and its furniture and appurtenances inventoried. Only one large and good room made up the dwelling which had a solid roof, doors, and windows, and was connected with the church by a passageway. In the house were two pictures, five tables with three writing desks, six chairs, four benches, one clothes closet, one bookshelf containing two volumes on theology by Doctor Machado, two board beds, a kneading trough, some towels and two small napkins, a metal spoon and fork, a large heavy knife, two frying-pans, a heater, a ladle, two bronze candlesticks, an earthen pan for cooking maize and an iron spit, six plates, six cups, and an axe. At the time of the transfer the dwelling was provisioned with an *arroba* (twenty-five pounds) of beeswax, six bunches of tallow candles, an arroba of butter, a bottle of wine for Mass, an arroba of chocolate, two loaves of sugar, and some medicinal drugs.

Certainly, judging from Satevó, the missionaries lived poorly enough. Glandorff at Tomochic was probably even less well off. But the transfer of these twenty-two missions would release a number of Jesuits who could now serve in Alta Tarahumara, and especially in northern Sonora where the plan was to march farther on, connect the Sonoran with the Lower California missions, cross the Colorado at Yuma, and form a mission unit for Alta California.

But at least more men could now be sent into Alta Tarahumara, and Father Glandorff at Tomochic during the last decade of his long career of forty years may have been released from the care of his more distant visitas and may have lost, perhaps with disappointment, the opportunity of exercising for his neophytes his alleged miraculous endurance and fleetness of foot.[25] Still, the work was vast, for the very year of Glandorff's death, 1763, fifty pueblos in Alta Tarahumara were attended by Jesuits, and in 1767 nineteen fathers were serving nineteen partidos.[26] Little did Bartholomé Braun suspect when he published the sketch of his illustrious subject that within three years of its writing the King of Spain by a stroke of his pen would bring death to all the Jesuit establishments of his vast empire flung over the surface of two hemispheres.

Chapter XXIV

THE LAST REPORT

WHEN FATHER Ignacio Lizasoain was appointed official Visitor to all the Jesuit missions of northern Mexico the superiors were ignorant of the final and fatal blow which was to befall them. Neither did anyone else know what was going to happen, for the veil of the future is, perhaps fortunately, never lifted from before the gaze of human beings. Not even the King of Spain, Charles III, knew in 1761 and 1762 what he was going to do in 1767, because from all available evidence his resolve to suppress the Order in all his dominions and in Spain was suddenly taken. Father Lizasoain visited the missions in the mind that the organization would be enduring and the activities carried on without interruption. There is a dramatic or even a tragic quality, therefore, in the report of his observations made during 1761 and the following year.

We have witnessed and pondered the official visitation to the missions of Father Juan Ortiz Zapata in 1678, we have scrutinized the report of Visitor Juan de Guendulain made for the Provincial of New Spain in 1725. It remains only to look over the last summary which was drawn up and sent to headquarters at the beginning of 1763, less than five years before the whole organization would be completely undone.

Ignacio Lizasoain began his visitation of the west coast missions from the Río Yaqui where the old establishments begun in the early 1600's had for long known an almost continuous happiness and prosperity.[1] On April 4, 1761 the Visitor left Báhcum on the lower Yaqui in order to investigate the missions in that part of Sonora. After examining the condition of Soyopa, Movas, Aribechi, and other centers, he moved eastward toward the divide which connected the missions on either slope of the Sierra Madre. On May 9 he arrived at Yepachic, the most western establishment of the Tarahumar system, from there he rode to Tutuaca and thence over a ridge to Tomochic, Glandorff's mission, and then on over another spur of the sierra to the close set and flourishing centers of the Río Papigochic. He went upstream traveling

[1] For notes to chapter xxiv see page 256.

southwest and then over another divide whence he dropped to the headwaters of the Río Concho, where Sisoguichic and Cárichic were situated. Then the Visitor went on southwest into the plains or over the rolling hills northwest of Parral. The padre moved along on his horse or mule, for within two months he had visited the principal centers of Alta Tarahumara, sleeping sometimes at ranchos, as that of San Joaquín and then traveling over bad trails, *mal camino,* to Nono-ava. There he turned north to San Borja, remarking in his diary the *camino aspero* of some of the journey. Passing through Cusihuiriachic he went on to Chihuahua where he spent the hot weeks from July 2 to August 19.

After his rest in Chihuahua, Lizasoain with a pack train and accompanied by Christian Indians and soldiers threaded far north through Franciscan mission country where he beheld desolation and abandonment of former Christian pueblos owing to Apache raids. Passing through San Buenaventura, almost directly north of Chihuahua, he went on to Casas Grandes, to the royal presidio at Janos near the international border, and many leagues farther north across the Gila into the land and the pueblos of the Moqui Indians. The reason for this northern jaunt the padre does not give, but the Jesuits with royal encouragement had long kept an eye on this region which had been partly ruined by the Apaches. Returning from Moqui, Lizasoain left Janos on September 10, taking a southwesterly direction which would bring him to the missions of Pimería Alta, the land of Kino's missionary activities. He passed slowly through the missions of southern Sonora stopping at most of the establishments to take stock of spiritual and material conditions. Reaching Río Yaqui he went down to its mouth whence he embarked for Baja California. Here he spent the first three months of 1762. On April 1 he was back on the mainland, disembarking at the mouth of the Río Sinaloa. Thence he went up the river, north to Río Fuerte, on to the Mayo, and once again to the Yaqui. But Visitor Lizasoain seemed to like the Tarahumar country, for during the heat of the summer of 1762 we find him back at mission San Borja where he spent August and most of September. On the twenty-fourth he passed west over the great divide into the mountains of Chínipas, then he traveled south to the missions of Sinaloa, crossed the divide once again eastward and arrived on the broad levels of the mesa central and so on to Parras in Coahuila which he reached November 30, 1762. He rested a few days and then started west again, concluding his recorded itinerary on December 14 at a place called Charcos de Selaya. According to his own almost day-by-day reckoning, the padre had covered during the twenty months of his travel 2,059 leagues. It was a notable achievement.

But the end was not yet, for now he went south to Nayarit in order to inspect the small cluster of establishments there. Early in the century the Jesuits, with the help of the military, had "reduced" into the mission system the wild and troublesome Indians of that barranca-cloven land. The padre's visitation did not really end, therefore, until January, 1763, having consumed twenty-one months. His report omits the more southerly establishments of Alta Tarahumara and all the foundations of Baja Tarahumara, for these had been secularized. Nor did he set down, at least in this set of papers, any directions for the discipline or guidance of the missionaries.

The records of Lizasoain are, in some respects, more complete than those of either Zapata or Guendulain. The former gives the number of families and of baptized Christians, the latter the number of families, of unmarried persons, and of boys presumably in school. But Lizasoain records the number of families in each pueblo and visita, the youngsters undergoing instruction, those who had confessed during the last Lenten season, and those who had received Holy Communion. Early in the record he gives the number of widowers and widows in each mission settlement, but these figures are omitted later on. Both Guendulain and Lizasoain give the numbers of livestock in each mission center. Zapata had omitted this, possibly because in his time most of the missions were but a few years old and had not been able to develop flocks and herds. An item appears in Lizasoain's report of 1761 concerning animals which Guendulain in 1725 rarely mentions, sheep and goats referred to as *ganado menor* in distinction to the herds of horses and cattle called *ganado mayor*. Guendulain goes minutely into the number of cattle, horses, mares, mules, burros, pack animals (which he often gives distinct from burros), and oxen.[2] His successor in this traveling and inspecting job, Father Lizasoain, does not descend to such details as the number of the larger animals, but rarely does he omit the ganado menor, from which we draw just one conclusion—the flocks of sheep and goats had been introduced into most of the Tarahumar missions after 1725. According to Lizasoain, Tutuaca on the northwestern fringe of Tarahumara, though a meager population of 80 families lived there, had 161 horses, more than a thousand head of cattle, 49 sheep, and 37 goats. In 1761 Tomochic, where the now aged Glandorff was still residing, had, with its three visitas, 428 head of cattle, 23 horses and mules, 13 burros, and 190 sheep and goats. Thus the record runs along. Of these smaller animals Temósachic had 250 in 1761; Mátachic 173; Papigochic 300; Cárichic 200, and so on with the rest. The first three missions just mentioned, situated as they were in the fertile Valle de Papigochic, watered by its winding stream, had numerous horses and cattle. There on the mission lands of Temósachic grazed 8,500 head of cattle, 300 horses, 93 mules, and 41 burros; San Tomás on the same stream owned 4,000 head of cattle and 300 mares; Papigochic had a herd of 225 head of cattle, a drove of 210 horses and 60 mules. These establishments along the Río Papigochic were the most flourishing in the number of both the larger and smaller animals.

When the figures of both the visitations of the eighteenth century are put side by side there is noticed a decline in the later record both in the number of Christian Indians living in the pueblos and in the livestock grazing on the mission lands. Mátachic had 180 families in 1725, but only 100 in 1761. Cárichic declined during the same period from 264 families to 190, and Tomochic from 300 to 101. In number of domesticated animals it was the same except in sheep and goats, as we have pointed out. The only exception, so far as population is concerned, was Norogachic a few leagues southwest of Nonoava. The families here jumped in numbers, according to this record, from 200 in 1725 to 1,000 in 1761.[3] It appears that the Tarahumara missions had passed their prime.

From the ecclesiastical point of view some details of Lizasoain's report are very interesting. There is the question of the frequency with which the Christian neophytes received the sacraments of the Church. All were expected to confess once a year and the usual time for this was the Lenten season. The neophytes were to receive the sacrament of Holy Communion at or near the same period. From the Visitor's figures we gather that the ideal was rarely reached. The finest record of these sacramental activities was made at Tutuaca. No resident pastor is set down for this mission and Glandorff probably attended it. There eighty families resided, and of these 150 persons confessed and the same number communicated. At Glandorff's own mission of Tomochic during the Lent before Lizasoain's visitation 90 persons confessed and the same number received Communion. It was the same in the three visitas of Tomochic: all those who confessed went also to Holy Communion. But, in most of the other missions, the number of communicants given is surprisingly small. For instance, at Cárichic 190 families resided. Of the individuals comprising these family groups, 156 confessed but only a few, *pocos* the record says, received Holy Communion. At San Tomás on the Río Papigochic at Eastertime 200 of the individuals of 160 families confessed, but no communions are recorded. At Mátachic the hundred families sent 230 to the confessional, but of these few communicated. So it was with Mátachic's visita called Tejologachic. At Papigochic, although the confessions were consolingly numerous, 500 from 200 families, there were only 15 communions. At Sisoguichic and its three visitas, though the confessions were 430, 190, 235, and 150 respectively, the communions amounted to only four in the mother pueblo, and none in the three visitas. The populous Norogachic's record is the same. In the pueblo and its three visitas 2,100 persons had confessed but only two communicated at Norogachic and none in the three visitas. At Nonoava and its visita there were no communions at all on the part of the 420 who went to confession. And so the record runs generally. The report tells the same story for the other mission fields except that of California, where generally most of those who confessed also went to communion.

Visitor Ignacio Lizasoain enjoyed privileges never before conceded in the west coast mission field to a Jesuit Visitor: that of administering to the neophytes the sacrament of confirmation. It was rare that a bishop entered the northern mission field and only a bishop ordinarily is empowered to administer confirmation. In 1611 the Benedictine Bishop of Guadalajara, Juan del Valle, visited the thriving Sinaloa missions and confirmed approximately 8,000 neophytes. The first bishop of the newly erected See of Guadiana, now Durango, the Augustinian Gonzalo de Hermosillo, visited the west coast missions in

1631, confirming 11,000 Indians and ordaining some clerics.[4] These were exceptions. There is no record of a bishop having crossed the gulf to Baja California nor, before Lizasoain's time, of confirmation having been administered there. The Visitor confirmed 332 persons in California and set down illuminating information concerning the missions of the rock-ridden peninsula. Formerly, a few California neophytes on an occasional voyage to the mainland had received the sacrament at the hands of the Bishop of Guadalajara. The Jesuits in the 1630's had requested the Jesuit General, Mutius Vitelleschi, to obtain from the Holy See the privilege of confirming the dusky neophytes of the missions. The General answered with diplomacy that it would be better were this privilege granted through the King or Viceroy.[5] It was, therefore, a novel thing when Lizasoain went the round of most of the mainland missions armed with the privilege and conferring the sacrament. We can well guess, too, who it was who approved these spiritual faculties. Among Durango's greatest bishops, and sixteenth of the see, was Pedro Tamarón y Romeral. Inaugurated in March, 1759, he was particularly interested in the missions of his vast diocese of which Tarahumara was only one unit. It was he, without doubt, who received from higher superiors the power of delegating Lizasoain. Indeed, the Bishop himself went up into the mission field more than once and he has left a minute description of the regions he visited.[6]

The largest number gathered together for confirmation in Tarahumara was at Temósachic where Father Bartolomé Braun, superior of all Tarahumara, presented 1,066 swarthy neophytes to Lizasoain for the reception of the sacrament. Glandorff at Tomochic presented 800 of his Indians and Manuel Vivanco, superior at Nonoava, presented 645. This figure was surpassed at Sisoguichic where Father Antonio Hitl presented 667. The lowest number was at Coyachic where 98 were confirmed. Altogether, in Alta Tarahumara, Lizasoain confirmed 5,888 mission Indians, and in his journeys to all the missions of the mainland he reached a grand total of 18,431.

The same note sounded by Glandorff concerning the dispersal and mistreatment of the mission Indians finds an echo from time to time in Lizasoain's report. For instance, for Temechic the numbers of families are given as 69, 109, 171, and 123 respectively, but they are of former Lenten statistics. "This year," writes the Visitor, "the pueblos

are very small, for the rest have dispersed, of necessity, or have fled."
The necessity was forced recruiting by Spaniards for domestic service
or for mining. So the number of families had been diminished to 30,
45, 86, 59, for each of the four pueblos of this partido of San José
de Temechic. We have the same notice of one of the visitas of Cárichic
where the Visitor deplores the shrunken condition of the pueblo because the Indians are allowed to leave without a written notice from
their padre and were thus recruited by the Spaniards for labor. Some
fled the pueblo for other reasons and were taken by the Spanish residents of the vicinity.

The financial condition of the missions is roughly indicated by
Lizasoain. Besides the livestock, there is occasional mention of good
fields of wheat or corn. Some of the missions were in debt several
hundred pesos. Most of them had loaned money or goods and were
unable to redeem these debits to their account. Cárichic, for instance,
was unable to redeem the 500 pesos formerly given out in loans, nor
was Nonoava able to get back its 2,000 pesos loaned. These figures
are usually below the thousand mark. The debts were small or none
at all. Norogachic had a debt of 224.5 pesos, Nonoava of 460, Coyachic
of 445.6.

An economic report of three residences is given. Two of them, Parral and Chihuahua, belong to our story; the other, Parras, had formerly
made part of the more southern Tepehuán mission system. At Chihuahua the Visitor found a good church and a newly built college and
residence. The establishment was supported by a property called the
Hacienda de Dolores where there was good land for the grazing of
herds and flocks, for sowing wheat and corn, and for the cultivation
of melons and vineyards. The debts were slight. At Parral Lizasoain
found the church small but well adorned and a school and residence
confined in narrow quarters. The Jesuits with their school were here
supported by the Rancho del Salitre which offered sufficient pasturage
for a herd of cattle and a drove of horses, even though it was lacking
in shade. There were two other properties, the Estancia de San Isidro
and the Estancia de los Carrales. Some of the land on these estates was
suitable for raising corn and wheat. The figures on the livestock were:
50 head of cattle; 1,150 sheep and goats; 1,381 horses, of which 232
were tamed; and 411 mules and 41 burros. Seven thousand pesos were

owed in debts, but this was partly balanced by credit to the amount of two thousand. At Parras the Jesuits raised no corn or wheat upon their property nor developed flocks and herds of livestock, but they had their vineyards, the finest in the region, except for those belonging to the Marquesa of Parras. A revenue of 5,000 pesos came from the Black Robes' vineyards, and the cellar was well stocked with wine and brandy.

And so the diligent Ignacio de Lizasoain wound up his visitation of the Tarahumar missions.[7] After that he traveled many leagues south to the region then as now called Nayarit, where early in the eighteenth century the Jesuits with the help of the government and soldiery had "reduced" the Indians to the mission system. For this small and isolated cluster of establishments the padre has left his record and here, too, he confirmed 219 neophytes.

But time was running out for the Spanish Jesuits in America as it had already run out for their French and Portuguese confrères. Expelled from Brazil in 1759 and from France's American possessions in 1762, the Jesuits of the Spanish colonies were aware of much criticism and of acrid enmity working against them. Perhaps, after the calamities which had overtaken their colleagues, Black Robes in New Spain felt a sword of Damocles hanging over their heads. The fathers, aware of a mounting criticism, declined an inheritance of 200,000 pesos bequeathed for the missions of Baja California by the wealthy dowager Doña Josefa de Arguelles y Miranda. Unjust accusations, such as their alleged exploitation of the pearl fisheries of Lower California, were answered with facts and figures of refutation. But the end came nevertheless within five years of the conclusion of Lizasoain's visitation. The calamity to the mission system had its roots in Europe, roots which were intertwined with the religious and secular policies and intrigues of the Bourbon courts. Spiritually, there had been a decline since the vigorous Catholicism of the Counter-Reformation. Old customs had become outworn, old laws had lost their efficacy or proved unsuited to the spirit of the times which had changed. Such a condition added fuel to the anticlericism and secularism of many leaders, political and intellectual, in the Latin countries, especially in France.

The Papacy, moreover, would have been criticized and disliked for its religious dogmas even if its thought had been more advanced and its administration of the Papal States more efficient. Jansenism had divided the Church in France and the weakness of the court, led first by the Duc d'Orléans and then by the sick king—sick with ennui, Louis XV, was no aid to the spiritual uplift of the nation. Many intellectuals began to think and say that the whole regime was rotten and should be overthrown. Voltaire's *écrasez l'infame* rang through the lettered and polished upper classes of Europe. Conditions in France were moving toward revolution. These disturbing winds blew over the Pyrenees and affected such Bourbon ministers of state as the Count of Aranda. The Jesuits were considered props and pillars of papal strength and many points of their activity or prestige began to be resented in Spain by members of the Voltairean school. Their influence at court (they had been the traditional confessors of the Bourbon kings), their intellectual stand against the radical leanings of the secularist school, their real or supposed wealth, their alleged ambition, the success of their missions in America, their protection of the Indian against exploitation, their property holdings in some of the richest parts of the country through the mission system, even a report of hidden treasure in Paraguay and Baja California—all this led to sharp enmity against the corporate body on the part of the "Philosophers" of Spain. It was court favorites and ministers, rather than the kings themselves, who encompassed the ruin of the Order. They were the ones, in Spain, as elsewhere, who plotted for the Society's downfall. Thus it was that the mind of King Charles III, traditionally friendly, was gradually poisoned against the Jesuits and the machinations of Prime Minister Aranda finally induced the King to sign the decree of expulsion. It was a felling blow and was executed in Spain and throughout her dominions by the instructions given out in June, 1767.

EPILOGUE

THE JESUITS MUST GO

O N THE evening of June 24, 1767, the Viceroy of Mexico, Carlos Francisco, Marqués de Croix, summoned to his palace the Archbishop of Mexico, the judges of the audiencia, and other high officials of Church and State. The Viceroy produced a sealed packet which he had recently received from the supreme government in Spain, purporting to contain royal orders of the gravest character. With the surrounding notables witness to his actions Marqués de Croix proceeded to open the regal missive. Beneath the outer envelope was found another upon which were written the following words: "Under penalty of death you will not open this dispatch until the twenty-fourth of June at nightfall." When this inner document was opened the astonished Viceroy beheld and announced to the notables present the catastrophic significance of the royal orders: The Jesuits were to be expelled from all of New Spain!

An inner wrapper contained detailed orders concerning the measures to be adopted in the arrest of the Black Robes and the persons to be confided with the task. "I invest you," wrote the King to the Viceroy, "with my whole authority and royal power that you shall forthwith repair with an armed force to the house of the Jesuits. You will seize the persons of all of them, and despatch them within twenty-four hours as prisoners to the port of Vera Cruz, where they will be embarked on vessels provided for that purpose. At the very moment of each arrest you will cause to be sealed the records of said houses, and the papers of said persons, without allowing them to remove anything but their prayer books and such garments as are absolutely needed for the journey. If after the embarkation there should be found in that district a single Jesuit, even if ill or dying, you shall suffer the penalty of death. I the King."[1] José de Gálves, Visitador General, took charge of the expulsion in Mexico City and it was carried out according to royal instructions.

The Jesuits were expelled from all their houses and colleges in New Spain, including those at Durango, Parral, and Chihuahua which

---

[1] For notes to Epilogue see page 257.

have entered into our story. As for the missionaries in the field, they were called in by their respective superiors to a central place and given the devastating news. Those on the coast, in Sinaloa and Sonora, were summoned to Mátape where on July 25 fifty-one received the death blow to their life's work. Imprisoned for eight months at Guaymas, and all sick with the scurvy from which one of their number died, they were put on ship, were blown by storms onto the coasts of Lower California, and finally were disembarked at San Blas. Their trek overland southeast to Vera Cruz was marked by a strange and mortal sickness which claimed before Guadalajara was reached twenty of the fifty surviving missionaries.[2]

To Don Gaspar de Portolá, famed discoverer of San Francisco Bay, fell the bitter task of carrying out the royal orders in the Jesuit missions of Lower California. Captain Portolá with twenty-five soldiers arrived at the mission of Loreto on November 30. Father Benito Ducrue, the superior, was called in from his mission of Guadalupe fifty miles away to hear the fatal news. It took a long time to gather in the men from the rocky wastes of this thorny cactus patch, but by February 3, 1768, sixteen of the missionaries, Spaniards, Mexicans, and eight Germans, were ready to sail. Reaching San Blas they went overland to Vera Cruz where they arrived March 27. They embarked for Europe April 13.

But what of the missionaries of Tarahumara and the fathers at Chihuahua? They too had to leave forever their missions and residence and make the heart-breaking journey. In these last years of the Jesuit missions a Polish missionary had come to labor in Tarahumara. His name was Antonio Sterkianowski, and he has left us a detailed account of the expulsion from Tarahumara.[3]

The fatal word arrived at the College of Loreto in Chihuahua on June 30. The two or three Jesuits resident there immediately left on their long journey for Vera Cruz. To the lot of Don Lope Cuellar, Governor of Nueva Vizcaya, fell the sorrowful labor of assembling the nineteen missionaries and sending them south.[4] The Governor had no soldiers so that he was driven to impress into his service twelve or fourteen ragged fellows to make a show of authority. He feared nothing, however, for he knew the docility of the missionaries. Governor Cuellar marched to Mátachic where the Visitor, Felipe Ruanova, resided, and broke to him the terrible news. Ruanova immediately wrote to all his men bidding them go posthaste to Chihuahua, taking with them nothing except their breviaries and supplies absolutely necessary for the journey. Ruanova and our friend Bartholomé Braun were the first to arrive with the Governor at Chihuahua on July 17; on the twentieth the last missionary from far-away Tomachic straggled in. As the fathers arrived one by one they learned their fate and that of the missions of Tarahumara.

A few days passed before arrangements could be concluded for the journey south to Vera Cruz. The missionaries were held prisoners in their residence but the Governor treated them with consideration and they were allowed visitors. When the fathers resident in Chihuahua had left on June 30 the townspeople made every effort to hold them. As word sped abroad of the calamity that had fallen on the missions the Indian governor general of the Tarahumares made plans to travel to Mexico City with a delegation of his redmen to plead with the Viceroy to spare their padres. Governor Cuellar asked the Jesuits to dissuade the Indians from such a move, and to prevent a request for their own liberty which was being prepared.

The fathers, heroically, did the one thing and the other. They bade the Indians hold their peace; they persuaded the townspeople to bow to the royal will. The delegation never went to Mexico City and the peace was kept with the residents of Chihuahua. Father Sterkianowski, one of the former missionaries, reflects significantly on the Governor's request to the fathers: "I understand well that it was an extraordinary thing to avail oneself in these circumstances of the help of the Jesuits, they being in so miserable a plight. But I say likewise with the same candor that nothing more comfortable to our desires could have been asked of us. Always have we insisted with the Indians, both by word and example, that they keep the peace and render obedience to the King of Spain. And now at the moment of departure the same principles were inculcated as a last will and testament, that the thing be the more deeply imprinted on their minds."

After ten days of mild retention in Chihuahua the Jesuits departed July 27, led by Cuellar, and trailing after them were the lamentations of the townspeople and the tears of their faithful sons, the Indians of Tarahumara. By the thirtieth they had reached the mission, no longer theirs, of San Javier de Satevó. Continuing south the party skirted Parral, for the orders were to avoid the larger centers. However, the alcalde mayor went over to visit and console the fathers. They were delayed some days by the Río Florido in flood, but on August 16 were finally able to cross. That evening at the estate of the Gorenas family the Jesuit group met a band of Franciscans who were traveling north to take their places at the pueblos. The Jesuits were nobly generous. They imparted what information they possessed concerning the missions that had but so recently been theirs.

At Fresnillo the townspeople gave the Jesuits a warm ovation and lodged them in their own families two by two, nor did the guards stationed at each house prevent the visiting which went on, nor venders from coming in charity to proffer their wares to the padres. At Zacatecas the departing missionaries were lodged in the Franciscan convent lying some distance out from the town. Here Governor Cuellar left them in sorrow, giving place to two other officers of the Crown while the guard was changed. Two of the Jesuit travelers who had fallen sick were left here in this kindly Franciscan hospitality when the group departed on September 1. Passing south through Aguas Calientes they came to one of the oldest and richest estates in Mexico, Ciénega de Mata, where "they received us," wrote Sterkianowski, "with an excess of kindness and hospitality and reverence."

As the party approached Mexico City it veered east to escape the metropolis. The fathers made known a desire to pay a last visit, before their exile to Europe, to the famous shrine of Our Lady of Guadalupe in the northern suburb of the capital. The officers were kind enough to allow one of their number to travel into the city to lay this petition before Viceroy de Croix. The latter had the humanity to accede to the request.

It was midday, September 16, when they arrived. Soon their inn was thronged with visitors. Word spread like fire that the exiled missionaries from the north were there and out from the capital came literally thousands to visit and to speak with the Black Robes. "Who could count the number of those who came!", exclaims Sterkianowski. "I saw the great avenue from Mexico to Guadalupe ... streaming with a thick concourse of people and there seemed to be a continual procession of unnumbered men and women thronging with eagerness as though to gaze upon the most rare and marvelous objects of the world."[5]

There was a press of jostling humanity about the inn, for all wanted to speak with the fathers or at least to see them. The guard was increased, and the Jesuits saw one high-born señora unceremoniously elbow her way through the crowd to the door. As a guard brandished his stick she was struck on the head, but, succeeding in gaining an entrance, she considered this blow, as she told the fathers, a small price to pay for the privilege of seeing and conversing with these confessors of the Faith.

"It was truly marvelous," continues our chronicler, "and the enthusiasm with which those señors came to visit us from Mexico seemed incredible. The thing was so great that did I wish to expatiate upon it I would not be able to describe it; and did I try to exaggerate, I could not. Any attempt of mine would fall short of the reality. After all these years I still marvel in recording the wonder of the enthusiasm with which these people came, a sign of the high opinion and the great esteem they harbored of the Society."

Two days of this and then the Jesuits were off on their journey east, through the divide which passes hard by the glittering crests, the snow-crowned summits of Popocatepetl and Iztaccihuatl, still east through the beautiful vale of Puebla, east again and descending then from the salubrious highlands of Jalapa down into the hot and feverish lowlands near the sea. Here at Vera Cruz they would embark for Spain.

Arriving October 11 the forlorn travelers sweltered a whole month in the heat of that lethal coast and they were devoured by fleas and mosquitoes. They embarked November 10, but a storm held them eleven days in port. Three fathers falling sick were returned to shore, but finally the ships got under way for Havana. Before reaching Cuba five of our Tarahumar missionaries died, among them Father Bartholomé Braun. Tainted food had done its deadly work. Two days before Christmas these Jesuits from the far north of Spain's empire, having been grouped with others of their brethren from the south, from Argentina and Peru, sailed, sick and sad, forever from the West. They left the Americas to live and die in exile far from their beloved missions and their beloved sons and daughters, their neophytes of the wild.

APPENDIX I

EPITOME OF THE REPORT MADE BY FATHER JUAN ORTIZ ZAPATA
AS THE RESULT OF HIS OFFICIAL VISITATION OF
THE TARAHUMAR MISSIONS IN 1678*

Mission La Natividad comprising five partidos:
  San Miguel de las Bocas, 386 persons (Father Pedro de Escalante)
  San Felipe with three pueblos (Father Francisco de Valdes)
    San Felipe, 312 persons
    Santa Cruz, 455 persons
    San José, 101 persons
  San Pablo Ballesa with three pueblos (Father Martín de Prado)
    San Pablo, 380 persons
    San Juan de Atotonilco, 113 persons
    San Mateo, 120 persons
  San Gerónimo de Huejotitlán with three pueblos (Fathers Gabriel de Villar
    and Manuel Gutiérrez de Arteaga)
    San Gerónimo, 320 persons
    San Francisco Javier } 434 persons
San Ignacio
  San Francisco Javier de Satevó with three pueblos (Father Julio Sarmiento)
    San Francisco, 516 persons
    De las Cuevas, 242 persons
    San Lorenzo, 286 persons

Mission San Joaquín y Santa Ana comprising nine partidos:
  San Joaquín y Santa Ana with four pueblos (Father Francisco de Zelada)
    San Francisco de Borja (Tayeguachic), 376 persons
    Santa Ana (Yeguachic), 504 persons
    Nuestra Señora de Guadalupe (Saguarichic), 286 persons
    San Francisco Javier (Purúachic), 150 persons
  Nonoava with two pueblos (Father Francisco de Arteaga)
    Nonoava, 209 persons
    Nuestra Señora de Copacabana (Paguarichic), 113 persons
  Jesús Cárichic with five pueblos (Father Diego de Contreras)
    Jesús Cárichic, 558 persons
    San Luis Gonzaga (Jajirachic), 41 persons
    Concepción de Patzigochic, 87 persons
    San Casimiro de Bacarinachic, 33 Christians
    San Buenaventura (Tequayguachic) ??

* Zapata's report is to be found in *Archiv. Gen. Mis.*, t. 26, fols. 245–249 and
the same has been printed in *Doc. Hist. Mex. Ser.* IV, t. 3, pp. 316ff. Zapata's
inconsistencies in listing the pueblos have been preserved, but the spelling has
been modernized.

El Nombre de María Santísima with three pueblos (Father Antonio de Oreña)
   El Nombre de María Santísima de Sisoguichic, 179 persons
   Asunción de Nuestra Señora (Echoguita), 9 baptized
   Cutego, 182 baptized
San José with four pueblos (Father José de Guevara)
   San José Temechic, 150 persons
   San Marco (Píchachic), 11 persons
   Santa Rosa de Santa María (Pachera), no Christians
   San Juan de Tosaboreachic, 92 persons
San Bernabé with three pueblos (Father José Tardá)
   San Bernabé Cusihuiriachic, 325 persons
   San Ignacio (Coyachic), 473 persons
   San Miguel (Napaheyachic), 92 Christians
La Purísima with four pueblos (Father Nicolás Ferrei)
   La Purísima (Papigochic), 224 persons
   San Cornelio (Paquirachic), 33 persons
   San Tomás de Villanueva (Tojarere), 77 persons
   San Payo de Basuchic, 100 persons
El Triunfo de los Angeles with four pueblos (Father Tomás de Guadalajara)
   San Rafael de Mátachic, 335 persons
   San Miguel (Temósachic), 74 persons
   San Gabriel de Yepómera, 118 persons
   San Pablo (Cocomorachic), 91 persons
Jesús del Monte de Tutuaca with four pueblos (Father Tomás de Guadalajara)
   Jesús del Monte de Tutuaca, 126 persons
   San Julio Evangelista de Tosánachic, 6 Christian families
   Santiago Yepachic, 40 persons
   San Juan Bautista Moaguina, 6 Christian families†

---

† Zapata lists also twenty farms and one mine with 300 persons in all, because these people were attended spiritually by the missionaries. They would be Spaniards with Indian servants, and they lived near the more southern missions.

APPENDIX II

Comparison of some figures as given by Guendulain in 1725 and by Lizasoain in 1761. Both were official Visitors to Tarahumara.

	1725	1761
Tomochic		
families	300	101
cattle	700	428
burros	50	
horses, mules		23
burros		13
sheep, goats		190
Mátachic		
families	180	100
cattle	400	52
sheep, goats	112	173
mares	6	
horses, mules		69
San Tomás		
families	300	160
cattle	1,000	4,000
horses, mules	497	400
sheep, goats	112	
burros		41
oxen	54	
Papigochic		
families	500	200
cattle	1,200	225
horses, mules	380	270
burros	36	
sheep, goats		300

	1725	1761
Cárichic		
families	264	190
cattle	400	420
mules	60	
sheep, goats		200
Sisoguichic		
families	280	140
cattle	290	620
mules, burros	308	
horses, mules		67
Norogachic		
families	200	1,000
cattle	1,000	150
mules, burros	324	52
sheep, goats		44
San Borja		
families	150	110
cattle	180	480
horses, mules	89	256
oxen	26	
sheep		390
Nonoava		
families	234	150
cattle	700	
mules		20
horses, mules	206	
sheep		150

NOTES

ABBREVIATIONS USED IN THE NOTES

Archiv. Gen. de Indias:	Archivo General de Indias
Archiv. Gen. Hist.:	Archivo General, Historia
Archiv. Gen. Mis.:	Archivo General, Misiones
Archiv. S.J. Roman.:	Archivum Societatis Jesu Romanum
Doc. Hist. Mex.:	Documentos para la Historia de México
Ribas:	Historia de los Triumphos...
Alegre:	Historia de la Compañía de Jesús en la Nueva España

Ribas has been cited according to book and chapter; Alegre according to volume and page, and so with the other authors generally, unless otherwise indicated.

CHAPTER I: THE LAND AND ITS PEOPLE

[1] The sources for the contents of this introductory chapter are various. There are the old Jesuit letters and records, including Father Joseph Neumann's famous book the *Historia Seditionum.* . . . These are listed in the bibliography. Among modern specialized studies may be mentioned Ralph L. Beals, *The Comparative Ethnology of Northern Mexico before 1750;* Carl Sauer, *The Distribution of Aboriginal Tribes and Languages in Northwestern Mexico,* and *Aboriginal Population of Northwestern Mexico;* A. L. Kroeber, *Uto-Aztecan Languages of Mexico.* Of great importance for this chapter is the work by Wendell C. Bennett and Robert M. Zingg, *The Tarahumara, An Indian Tribe of Northern Mexico.* Some of the information has been obtained from personal observation in travel through Tarahumar country, excepting, however, the regions of the high sierra.

[2] Usage in spelling has differed. I have followed the practice of Dr. Herbert E. Bolton, editor of this series, as follows: region, Tarahumara; singular noun, Tarahumar; plural noun, Tarahumares; adjective, Tarahumar. The colonial Spaniards added a final "c" to many of the place names, such as Papigochic, although in Tarahumar pronunciation the final "c" was often or always omitted, as in Norogachi. The former usage has here been followed. In actual pronunciation the final "c" is practically silent, and therefore in such place names the accent has been omitted over the penult.

[3] In 1946 eleven Jesuit fathers, six scholastics, and seven brothers were working in six mission centers: Norogachic, Cerocahui, Narárachic, Sisoguichic, Chinatu, and Guadalupe y Calvo. There were organized seven schools for girls and five for boys attended by 500 pupils. The fathers reopened this mission in 1900.

CHAPTER II: THE FRONTIER CREEPS NORTH

[1] Ricard, La 'Conquete Spirituelle' du Mexique, pp. 27ff.

[2] Cf. among numerous instances the letter of Pope Alexander VI to the Spanish sovereigns, quoted by Bertrand and Petrie, History of Spain, p. 243, and the letter of Columbus to the same sovereigns quoted by Helps, The Spanish Conquest of America, I, 111.

[3] Ricard, op. cit., pp. 28ff.

[4] Ibid., p. 112.

[5] The late Archbishop of Bombay, Alban Goodier, S.J., in Why I Am and Why I Am Not a Catholic (ed. Hilaire Belloc), p. 41.

[6] "Many of the mines are still producing, and total production to date of merely the Zacatecas mines exceeds a billion dollars." Caughey, California, p. 45.

[7] Mecham, Francisco de Ibarra and Nueva Vizcaya, pp. 83 and 123.

[8] For an early detailed account of the founding of these missions in the north, cf. Arlegui, Crónica de la Provincia de N.S.P.S. Francisco de Zacatecas, passim.

[9] Cf. Shiels, Gonzalo de Tapia; Bolton, Rim of Christendom; Dunne, Pioneer Black Robes on the West Coast; and idem, Pioneer Jesuits in Northern Mexico.

[10] Cf. Dunne, Pioneer Jesuits in Northern Mexico, chap. iii.

[11] The sources differ as to the year of Fonte's arrival in the missions. Ribas, X, 40, gives 1600. The anua of 1601 gives that year.

CHAPTER III: FONTE, FIRST APOSTLE OF THE TARAHUMARES

[1] Ribas, X, 40. The anua says he came in 1601.

[2] Ibid., X, 10.

[3] Alegre, II, 6.

[4] Francis Xavier had not been canonized, but it was not uncommon at that time, before the publication of the Bull of Urban VIII forbidding it, to forestall the official judgment of the Church and call one a saint even before canonization.

[5] Ribas, X, 40.

[6] Fonte in a letter of May 13, 1603, had already urged the sending of three men to these places. Cf. Jesuit Archives, Ysleta, Texas.

[7] Alegre, II, 6.

[8] Ibid.

[9] Ribas, X, 40.

[10] Archiv. S.J. Roman., Mex. 14, anua of 1610, fol. 577; Ribas, X, 10.

[11] Alegre, II, 44, is mistaken when he says it was Father Martín Peláez. Cf. Archiv. S.J. Roman., loc. cit., fol. 555.

[12] Ribas, X, 10, prints Fonte's account.

[13] Many of this nation still live in these same caves, as may be seen, for instance, in the palisades which stand guard over the higher reaches of the Río Papigochic.

[14] Ribas, X, 11.

[15] Ibid.

[16] Cf. Schetelig, "A proposito de un centenario," *Boletín de la Sociedad Chihuahuense de Estudios Históricos,* III (Oct.–Dec. 1940), 431.

[17] *Anua* of 1612, Archiv. S.J. Roman., Mex. 14, fol. 609.

[18] *Anua* of 1614, Archiv. S.J. Roman., Mex. 14, fol. 639.

[19] Ribas, X, 43.

[20] *Archiv. S.J. Roman., Mex. 15, anua* of 1615, fol. 26.

[21] *Ibid., Mex. 14, anua* of 1612, fol. 633, and *anua* of 1615, Mex. 15, fol. 41; Alegre, II, 54.

[22] *Anua* of 1615, *loc. cit.,* fol. 32.

CHAPTER IV: FONTE IS SLAIN

[1] Ribas, X, 12ff.; *anua* of 1616, Ayer Collection, pp. 71ff.; Alegre, II, 82ff.; *anua* of 1616, synopsis, Archiv. S.J. Roman., Mex. 15, fol. 366ff. The following narrative is from these sources. For a full account, cf. Dunne, *Pioneer Jesuits in Northern Mexico,* chap. xiv, and "The Tepehuán Revolt," *Mid-America,* XVIII (Jan., 1936), 3-14.

[2] Ribas, X, 12.

[3] *Anua* of 1623, Archiv. Gen. Mis., t. 25, fol. 92; Alegre, II, 153. It is possible that these two names refer to the same individual, though the *anua* speaks of them as distinct persons.

CHAPTER V: REBUILDING A BROKEN FRONTIER

[1] Cf. Dunne, *Pioneer Jesuits in Northern Mexico,* chaps. xvi and xvii.

[2] *Archiv. S.J. Roman., Mex.* 15, fol. 45.

[3] Ribas, X, 35, where Lomas' letter is given.

[4] *Anua* of 1624, Archiv. S.J. Roman., Mex. 15, fol. 127.

[5] "Papeles del Almirante Mateo de Vesga, . . . ", Archiv. Gen. Indias, 67-1-4. Cf. Bandelier-Hackett, *Historical Documents Relating to Mexico . . .* II, 118ff.

[6] "Papeles del Almirante Mateo de Vesga, . . .," *ibid.,* p. 125.

[7] *Anua* of 1623, Archiv. Gen. Mis., t. 25, fol. 90; Alegre, II, 144.

[8] "Relación de José Pascual", Jesuit Archives, Ysleta, Texas.

[9] Dunne, *op. cit.,* chap. xviii.

[10] *Anua* of 1624, *loc. cit.*

[11] *Razon y Minuta de los yndios . . .,* Bandelier-Hackett, *op. cit.,* II, 152 ff.

[12] Alegre, *loc. cit.*

[13] "Relación de José Pascual," *loc. cit.;* Alegre, II, 184f.

[14] *Archiv. Gen. Mis.,* t. 25, fol. 92; Alegre, II, 153.

[15] *Archiv. S.J. Roman., Mex.* 15, *anua* of 1624, fol. 127.

[16] *Archiv. Gen. Mis.,* t. 26, fol. 244.

[17] *Ibid.,* t. 25.

[18] *Ibid.;* Alegre, II, 153.

[19] *Anua* of 1626, Archiv. Gen. Mis., t. 25, fol. 164.

[20] Alegre, II, 185; "Relación de José Pascual," *loc. cit.* There seems to be some discrepancy between Alegre and the *anuas* as to the circumstances of the founding of San Miguel de las Bocas.

[21] Ribas, *Corónica y Historia Religiosa*, II, 535ff.

[22] *Anuas* of 1629 and 1630, *Archiv. Gen. Mis.*, t. 25, fol. 227, and letter of Contreras to Ribas, *loc. cit.*, fol. 284.

[23] *Anuas* of 1629 and 1630, *loc. cit.*, fol. 229.

[24] Alegre, II, 190. Allen Chrystelow says the mines were discovered only in 1632, see his "Father Joseph Neumann, Jesuit Missionary to the Tarahumares," *Hispanic American Historical Review*, XIX (Nov. 1939), p. 427.

CHAPTER VI: A NEW MISSION UNIT

[1] McShane, "Hernando de Santarén," MS., p. 200.

[2] Alegre, II, 194.

[3] The first recorded diocesan synod was held in 1635 and among its papers we find the name of the Bishop and of el Canónigo Lic. D. Francisco Rojas de Ayora. Cf. Mendoza y Herrera, *Constitutiones del M. I. y V. Cabildo Metropolitano de Durango*, p. 31, privately printed.

[4] Letter of September 13, 1638, *Archiv. Gen. Mis.*, t. 25, fol. 282 f., where he gives also an account of the trouble. A somewhat fuller story is in Alegre, II, 208 f.

[5] Ribas, "Historia de la Provincia de Cinaloa," Jesuit Archives, Mexico.

[6] Letter of Contreras to Ribas, *Archiv. Gen. Mis.*, t. 25, fol. 285.

[7] This letter is of August 18, 1638, written from Santiago Papasquiaro, and is one of those documents, full of information, which are the delight of the historian. It is found in *Archiv. Gen. Mis.*, t. 25, fol. 284 f.

[8] *Archiv. Gen. Mis.*, t. 25, fol. 285.

[9] Alegre, II, 220.

[10] Colección de Cartas Inéditas, Vitelleschi to Ribas, October 30, 1639.

[11] *Noticias de las misiones sacadas de la anua del Padre José Pascual, Año de 1651*, in *Doc. Hist. Mex.*, 4th ser., III, 169 ff. Cf. Also Chrystelow, *op. cit.*

[12] Alegre, II, 220.

CHAPTER VII: FOUR CACIQUES REBEL

[1] Sauer places the racial Tarahumar border even north of Parral. Cf. Carl Sauer, *The Distribution of Aboriginal Tribes and Languages in Northwestern Mexico*, map, facing p. 1. As a matter of fact in the pueblos lying west and south of Parral Tepehuanes and Tarahumares were sometimes found together. It will be remembered that Fonte induced many Tarahumares to migrate south.

[2] Bancroft, *History of the North Mexican States and Texas*, I, 346, considers it doubtful whether Figueroa was here or twenty-five miles south at Huejotitlán; Alegre (II, 220), states definitely that the padre went to San Felipe; the "Relación de José Pascual" makes it certain. Alegre, however, is clearly wrong when

he identifies San Felipe with the present Chihuahua. Cf. Zapata's report of these missions in 1678, *Archiv. Gen. Mis.*, t. 26, fol. 244.

[3] Alegre, II, 221.

[4] *Ibid.*, II, 236; Bancroft, *op. cit.*, I, 346.

[5] *Anua* of 1646–1647, *Archiv. Gen. Mis.*, t. 26, fol. 1.

[6] *Archiv. Gen. Mis.*, t. 25, fol. 399.

[7] *Anua* of 1646–1647, *loc. cit.*, fol. 25.

[8] *Relación del Padre Nicolás de Zepeda desde el Pueblo de San Miguel de las Bocas, 28 de Abril, 1645.* Cf. *Doc. Hist. Mex.*, 4th ser., III, 130 ff.; Alegre, II, 244 ff.; and Bancroft, *op. cit.*, I, 348 ff.; the accounts of Alegre and Bancroft differ somewhat.

[9] In these depredations the Tobosos were often united with the Salineros and other groups. Cf. Bandelier-Hackett, *op. cit.*, II, 158.

[10] *Doc. Hist. Mex.*, *loc. cit.*, pp. 141 f.

[11] Bandelier-Hackett, *op. cit.*, pp. 160 ff.

[12] *Doc. Hist. Mex.*, *loc. cit.*, pp. 170 f.

[13] *Ibid.*, pp. 172 and 183.

[14] *Noticias de las misiones sacadas de la anua del Padre José Pascual, año de 1651.* Cf. *Doc. Hist. Mex.*, 4th ser., III, 179 ff. There is another unsigned narrative of events written from Parral just as complete as Pascual's and in accord with it entitled, *Alzamiento de los Indios Tarahumares y su asiento, año de 1649, Doc. Hist. Mex.*, *loc. cit.*, pp. 172 ff. The original of Pascual's account is the aforementioned "Relación de José Pascual" in the Jesuit archives at Ysleta, Texas. There is a copy of Pascual's relation in the Archivo General de Indias, as also letters concerning the revolt from Governor Fajardo, Bartolomé Toledano, Rector of the Missions, Diego del Castillo, Juan de Barrasa, and others. These add little of importance to our knowledge. Cf. Archiv. Gen. de Indias, 66-6-17. Cf. also Alegre, II, 365 ff.; Bancroft, *op. cit.*, I, 352 ff.

[15] In the Tarahumar language place names did not end in a consonant, but in a vowel thus: Papigochi, Temechi. We follow the Spanish usage which added a "c" to the final "i."

[16] Archiv. Gen. de Indias, 66-6-17.

[17] *Ibid.*

[18] Bandelier-Hackett, *loc. cit.*, pp. 162 f.

CHAPTER VIII: ANOTHER JESUIT FALLS

[1] Alegre, II, 236.

[2] *Relación de Nicolás de Zepeda, Doc. Hist. Mex.*, 4th ser., III, fol. 178.

[3] *Alzamiento de los Indios Tarahumares, Doc. Hist. Mex.*, 4th ser., III, 177; Bancroft, *op. cit.*, I, 355; Alegre, II, 367.

[4] Report of Zapata, *Archiv. Gen. Mis.*, t. 26, fol. 248; Bancroft, *op. cit.*, I, 355.

[5] *Noticias de las misiones sacadas de la anua del padre José Pascual, Año de 1651, loc. cit.*, fol. 191 ff.; Alegre, II, 366 ff., has a few details omitted in Pascual's *anua*. Bancroft, *op. cit.*, I, 356, briefly sketches events. Ribas, Tanner, Astrain, and Decorme all have substantially the same story.

[6] Ribas, *Corónica y Historia Religiosa*, II, 549.

[7] Cf. *anua de José Pascual, Doc. Hist. Mex.*, 4th ser., III, 179 ff., and Alegre, *loc. cit.*

[8] Ribas, *loc. cit.*

[9] Colección de Cartas Inéditas, Nickel to Rada, May 20, 1651.

[10] Cf. for instance Tanner, *Societas Jesu* . . . II, pp. 543 ff.

CHAPTER IX: APPEASEMENT, NEW REVOLT, MASSACRE

[1] Alegre, II, 370.

[2] *Ibid.* Rocha, "Una Cruel Matanza Tobosos," adds to our knowledge of the details of the campaigns. Cf. *Boletín de la Sociedad Chihuahuense de Estudios Históricos*, III (Oct.–Dec., 1940), 401 ff.

[3] The *anua* of José Pascual (*Doc. Hist. Mex.*, 4th ser., III, 193 ff.) and Alegre, II, 370 ff., give substantially the same story. The *anua*, however, omits Morales' disastrous interference. The figures, as usual, differ somewhat.

[4] Alegre, II, 393.

[5] *Ibid.*, II, 382.

[6] Ribas, *Corónica y Historia Religiosa*, II, 550 ff.

[7] *Anua* of José Pascual, *loc. cit.*, p. 197; Alegre, II, 382. Temechic in the sources is often spelled Temaychic or Temaichic.

[8] The *anua* of José Pascual, *loc. cit.*, pp. 198 ff., gives a detailed account of the beginning of this new uprising. Alegre, II, 392 ff., offers still more details.

[9] José Pascual, *loc cit.*, p. 198, says the attack on the Villa lasted half an hour; Alegre, II, 393, says it lasted three hours.

[10] Ribas, *loc. cit.*; Alegre, *ibid.*

[11] Ribas' account (*loc. cit.*) differs slightly from that of the *anua* of José Pascual and of Alegre. According to him some of the soldiers held out in the fort for three days and two nights. Father Antonio Montero, superior of the mission, says Basilio was slain within the church and his body then taken out and burned. Cf. Decorme, *La Abra de los Jesuitos Mexicanos*, II, 273 ff., who gives Montero's account. Ribas, *loc. cit.*, prints a variation of the same. We have followed Pascual's narrative. No one probably knew exactly what happened. Cf. also Tanner, *op. cit.*, II, 546, and Astrain, *Historia de la Compañía de Jesús en la Asistencia de España*, V, 350, who follow Pascual.

CHAPTER X: THE PURSUIT OF CHIEF TEPORACA

[1] Alegre, II, 395; Bancroft, *History of the North Mexican States and Texas*, I, 358, where Alegre is cited. The names of the Franciscan missions as given by Alegre and Bancroft are Santiago, Santa Isabel, San Andrés, San Bernabé, San Gregorio, San Diego, and San Bernardino. Yaguna of Bancroft is the same as San Gregorio.

[2] Alegre, II, 393, gives the whole story. Bancroft, *op. cit.*, sketches it from Alegre. Pascual's *anua* of 1651 gives substantially the same account, emphasizing certain minor details.

[3] The sources cited in note 2 agree on the foregoing story. Bancroft makes the slight mistake of considering Tepóraca still a pagan.

[4] Letter of Pascual from San Felipe to Governor Fajardo, September 10, 1652. Cf. Archives of Parral, "Informaciones hechas por el Governador Diego Fajardo."

CHAPTER XI: JURISDICTIONAL DIFFICULTIES

[1] Dunne, *Pioneer Black Robes on the West Coast,* chap. xv.

[2] Ribas, III, 16.

[3] *Anua* of 1623, *Archiv. Gen. Mis.,* t. 25, fol. 93; Ribas X, 38; Alegre, II, 153.

[4] Mendoza y Herrera, *Constitutiones del M. I. y V. Metropolitano de Durango,* p. 3.

[5] Colección de Cartas Inéditas, Nickel to Calderón, December 12, 1652.

[6] *Ibid.,* Nickel to Real, October 30, 1656.

[7] The sources for this period are full of the monotonous documents of this quarrel and of the litigation which ensued. For a running account of events cf. Dunne, Andrés Pérez de Ribas, chap. xx.

[8] Mendoza y Herrera, *op. cit.,* p. 6.

[9] Archiv. Gen. de Indias, 66-6-17.

[10] Alegre, II, 244.

[11] *Ibid.,* II, 389.

[12] *Ibid.,* II, 366.

[13] Alegre, II, 389 ff., gives the document as issued from the chancery of the *audiencia* of Guadalajara. Repercussions of these disturbances appear in the letters of the Jesuit General to the Fathers Provincial. General Goswin Nickel in a letter of December, 1652, to Provincial Rada comments on the Bishop's action and goes at length into the consideration of what the Mexican Jesuits' policy ought to be in such circumstances. Cf. Colección de Cartas Inéditas, letter of December 12, 1652.

[14] Colección de Cartas Inéditas, letter of March 30, 1644.

[15] Cf. Nickel's letter to Rada, June 20, 1652, and Nickel's letter to Calderón, December 12, 1652, Colección de Cartas Inéditas. The name *doctrina* it seems is more often applied to the instruction in the catechism of a group of Indians not necessarily belonging to a mission system *entre infieles.* Such was the doctrina of Tepotzotlán concerning which there was much controversy. For a more detailed study of this whole question cf. W. Eugene Shiels, S.J., "The Legal Crisis in the Jesuit Missions of Hispanic America," *Mid-America,* XXI (Oct., 1939), 253-276.

[16] Colección de Cartas Inéditas, Nickel to Rada, May 20, 1651. Cf. also, *loc. cit.,* Caraffa to Velasco, February 20, 1649.

[17] *Ibid.,* Nickel to Calderón, December 12, 1652.

[18] *Doc. Hist. Mex.,* 4th ser., III, 210 ff.

[19] Mendoza y Herrera, *op. cit.,* p. 6.

[20] Colección de Cartas Inéditas, Nickel to Real, January 24, 1655.

CHAPTER XII: RECOVERY

[1] Colección de Cartas Inéditas, letter of August 20, 1651.

[2] *Ibid.*, letter of August 20, 1658.

[3] *Ibid.*, letter of September 30, 1649.

[4] One of these reports is dated from San Pablo, June 8, 1662; the other likewise from San Pablo, November 14, 1668. The first is entitled: *Puntos de añua de esto diez años que he asistido en este partido de San Pablo de la mision de Tarahumares y Tepehuanes (de unos y otros hay) desde el año de 1652 hasta este de 1662 sumariamente lo que a pasado quanto a lo espiritual.* This is printed in *Doc. Hist. Mex.*, 4th ser., III, 217 ff. and is in MS in the collection entitled, *Documentos para la historia eclestiaca y civil de la Nueva Vizcaya* (Mexico, 1849), pp. 245 ff. The second report is entitled: *Puntos de añua de esta mision de Tarahumares de la Compañia de Jesus de estos años proximos pasados, hecha a catorce de noviembre de 1668.* Gerónimo de Figueroa. Cf. *Doc. Hist. Mex.*, *loc. cit.*, pp. 223 ff. and *Doc. Hist. Viz.*, pp. 251 ff.

[5] Figueroa's *Puntos de anua, Doc. Hist. Mex., loc. cit.* pp. 217 f.

[6] Quoted by Ludwig von Pastor, *History of the Popes*, XIX, 4.

[7] Colección de Cartas Inéditas, Vitelleschi to Díaz, April 4, 1631; Caraffa to Velasco, June 21, 1646.

[8] Alegre, II, 441.

[9] Figueroa's relation of 1668, *Doc. Hist. Mex.*, 4th ser., III, 227; Alegre, II, 444 ff.

[10] Figueroa's *Puntos de anua, Doc. Hist. Mex., loc. cit.* p. 225.

[11] Alegre, II, 441.

[12] *Carta escrita al Sr. Gobernador y Capitan General de este reino por D. Antonio de Sarria, Alcalde Mayor y Teniente de Gobernador, Capitan General de las Provincias del Saltillo y Valle de Parras, fecha 3 de septiembre de 1669.* Cf. *Doc. Hist. Mex.*, 4th ser., III, 269 ff.; Alegre II, 447 f., who gives the year as 1669. This date is confirmed by the *anua* of 1669 which contains a detailed account of the celebration written by the Jesuit Provincial, Pedro de Valencia. This document is in the archives of Parral and a copy of it was kindly given to the writer by Sr. José G. Rocha, archivist and historian of Parral. This *anua* says that three Jesuits preached on three successive days.

[13] *Mandamiento del Señor Virrey, Marques de Mancera, sobre las doctrinas de Casas Grandes que estaban en los Yumas, jurisdiction de San Felipe del Parral, Doc. Hist. Mex.*, 4th ser., III, 230.

[14] *Puntos de anua, catorce de noviembre, 1668, Doc. Hist. Mex., loc. cit.*, p. 229; Alegre, II, 441.

CHAPTER XIII: TARAHUMARA SPREADS ITS MISSIONS

[1] Alegre, II, 451 and 463.

[2] *Ibid.*, II, 463.

[3] *Ibid.*

[4] The old missionary may not have realized that he was delivering the message of a dead man, for Provincial Cobián passed away the previous June, to be

succeeded as Provincial by Father Manuel de Arteaga. Cf. Alegre, II, 462; Schmitt, *Synopsis Historiae Societatis Jesu*, col. 556.

[5] Alegre, II, 464.

[6] *Ibid.*

[7] We have only a secondhand account of this scene in Alegre, *loc. cit.*

[8] Alegre, II, 465; Astrain, *op. cit.*, VI, 478 ff.

[9] Cf. Bannon, "The Jesuits in Sonora," MS., chap. vi.

[10] Colección de Cartas Inéditas, letter of December 20, 1649. Cf. Shiels, "The Critical Period in Mission History," *Mid-America*, XXI (April 1939), 97-109.

[11] Huönder, *Deutsche Jesuitenmissionäre des 17. und 18. Jahrhunderts*, p. 21, where Oliva's letter is quoted.

[12] Cf. Astrain, *op. cit.*, VI, 514 ff., where the document itself is given.

[13] Cf. Almada, *Apuntes Históricos de la Región de Chínipas*, chap. vi.

CHAPTER XIV: TWO GREAT APOSTLES

[1] Alegre, II, 469 f.

[2] Sometimes spelled Cuciguarachic or Cuciguriachic.

[3] *Archiv. Gen. Mis.*, t. 26, fol. 213, where a letter of Tardá to his Provincial is given.

[4] Report of Tardá, *ibid.*; Alegre, II, 470.

[5] Report of Tardá, *Archiv. Gen. Mis.*, t. 26, fol. 213.

[6] *Archiv. Gen. Mis.*, t. 26, fol. 216 ff. This report is printed in *Doc. Hist. Mex.*, 4th ser., III, 272 ff. Cf. Alegre, II, 472, and III, 10 ff.

[7] Letter of Tardá and Guadalajara to the Provincial, February 2, 1676, *Archiv. Gen. Mis.*, *loc. cit.*, fol. 216.

[8] *Ibid.*, fol. 217. This portion of the report is incorporated with the longer document dated February 2, 1676.

[9] *Ibid.*, fol. 218.

[10] *Relación de las Misiones . . . que hizo el P. Visitador Juan Hortiz Zapata*, in *Archiv. Gen. Mis.*, t. 26, fol. 248.

[11] *Ibid.*, fol. 249.

[12] Letter of Tardá and Guadalajara, *loc. cit.*, fol. 220.

[13] *Relación de las Misiones . . . que hizo el P. Visitador Juan Hortiz Zapata*, *loc. cit.*, fol. 249.

[14] The missionaries seem at this time to have applied the term Tepehuán to large and undefined groups in this section, the mountainous border between modern Durango and Sonora. Here, *Archiv. Gen. Mis.*, t. 26, fol. 222, Tardá and Guadalajara in 1675 use the term Tepehuán and three years later Visitor Juan Zapata, *ibid.*, fol. 249, calls even Tutuaca a Tepehuán pueblo.

CHAPTER XV: NEW MISSIONS IN ALTA TARAHUMARA

[1] Thus Father Joseph Neumann describes the dwellings. Cf. letter of February 2, 1682, of which a copy is in the Bolton Collection, University of California.

[2] Cf. Bolton, *Rim of Christendom*, p. 8 and note.

[3] Letter of July 29, 1686, Bolton Collection, University of California.

[4] Letter of February 2, 1682, *loc. cit.*

[5] Letter of Tardá and Guadalajara, February 2, 1676, *loc. cit.*, fol. 224.

[6] *Archiv. Gen. Mis.*, *loc. cit.*, fol. 224. Cf. also *Doc. Hist. Mex.*, *loc. cit.*, pp. 292 f., where the Visitor's letter is given.

[7] Arlegui, *Crónica de la Provincia de N.S.P.S. Francisco de Zacatecas; Doc. Hist. Mex.*, 3d ser., *passim*. Cf. also Bancroft, *History of the North Mexican States and Texas*, pp. 116 ff., and Dunne, *Pioneer Jesuits in Northern Mexico*, chap. iii.

[8] Tomás de Guadalajara writing from Mátachic to his Provincial, July 20, 1677, gives a full account of the dispute. Cf. *Archiv. Gen. Mis.*, *loc. cit.*, pp. 237 ff.

[9] Cf. above, p. 43.

[10] Guadalajara to Altamirano, July 20, 1677, in *Archiv. Gen. Mis.*, *loc. cit.*, pp. 237 ff.

[11] *Ibid.*, fol. 240.

[12] *Ibid.*

[13] *Ibid.*

CHAPTER XVI: ZAPATA VISITS TARAHUMARA

[1] The old spelling is Hortiz.

[2] *Relación de las Misiones que la Compañia tiene en el Reyno y Provincias de la Nueva Vizcaya en la Nueva España, echa el año de 1678 con ocasion de la Visita General dellas que por orden del P. Provincial Thomas Altamirano hizo el P. Visitador Juan Hortiz Zapata de la misma Compañia.* A manuscript copy of this report exists in the *Archiv. Gen. Mis.*, t. 26, fol. 246-273, and a printed copy in *Doc. Hist. Mex.*, 4th ser., III, 301-419.

[3] This figure falls far short of the numbers given for the famous Paraguay missions at their height. There the numbers of Indians under the care of the Jesuits at one time reached the total of 143,000, and through decades of their history these missions or reductions averaged from 120,000 to 140,000. Cf. Astrain, *op. cit.*, V, 537.

[4] For the west coast missions of Sonora at this time, cf. Bannon, "The Jesuits in Sonora," MS.

[5] *Archiv. Gen. Mis.*, t. 26, fol. 244 ff.

[6] *Ibid.*, fol. 244.

CHAPTER XVII: NEUMANN BEGINS A CAREER

[1] Neumann, *Historia Seditionum*, chap. ii.

[2] Bolton, *Rim of Christendom*, p. 14. Bolton here (note 1) gives the names of eighteen of these travelers. They were Fathers Calvanese, Borgia, De Angelis, Manker, Borango, Gerstl, Tilpe, Strobach, Neumann, Cuculinus, Klein, Christman, Ratkay, Revel, Fischer, Kerschpamer, Kino, and Brother Poruhradiski.

[3] Neumann, *loc. cit.*; Bolton, *loc. cit.*

[4] For interesting details concerning Jesuit travel to America cf. Treutlein, "Jesuit Travel to New Spain," *Mid-America*, XIX (April 1937), 104-123.

[5] Letter of Father Victor Walter to the Rector of the Jesuit College in Munich from Mexico early in 1723. Cf. Hauptstaatarchiv, Munich, Jesuitica, MS 294. Transcript in Bancroft Library, University of California.

[6] Christelow, "Father Joseph Neumann, Jesuit Missionary to the Tarahumares," *Hispanic American Historical Review*, XIX (Nov. 1939), 425.

[7] Quoted in Bolton, *op. cit.*, p. 67.

[8] The details of this journey from central Europe to Mexico City were written by Ratkay himself in this letter. The whole missive is found in Joseph Stöcklein, *Der Neue Welt-Bott, mit allerhand Nachrichten dern Missionariorum Soc. Jesu*, P. I, no. 28 (Augsburg and Gratz, 1726). Bolton, *loc. cit.*, weaves the contents of this letter into a racy narrative.

[9] Neumann gives a detailed account of his long missionary career in a splendid history written by request for the instruction of his brethren in Europe. It is entitled *Historia Seditionum quas Adversus Societatis Jesu Missionarios, eorumq. Auxiliares Moverunt Nationes Indicae ac Potissimum Tarahumara in America Septentrionali, Regnoque Novae Cantabriae, jam Toto ad fidem Catholicam propemodum redacto, Auctore P. Josepho Neymanno Ejusdem Societatis Jesu in Partibus Tarahumarorum Missionario* (Pragae, Typis Univers. Carolo-Ferd. Soc. Jesu. ad S. Clem.). There is no date on the title page. The preface is dated April 15, 1724. The Bohemian Jesuit, Father Joseph Vrastil, kindly procured at the request of the writer a photostatic copy of this rare work which in 1933 was lodged in the Bibliothek des Jesuitenordens at Prague. In quotations from Neumann's work and letters the writer has used the excellent, but as yet unpublished, translation from the Latin by Dr. Marion Reynolds for the Bolton Collection.

[10] Regulations issued by the Visitor Hernando de Cabero, in 1662, give the number of mules or horses a traveling missionary may have for a journey. Those traveling from the missions to Mexico City could have from six to eight animals; those leaving Sonora ten or twelve. This allowed for the death of some of the beasts. Cf. "Ordinaciones comunes para todo los PP. misioneros que hizo el P. Visit. Hernando de Cabero," num. 3, Jesuit Archives, Ysleta, Texas.

[11] Letter to Jesuit in Bohemia, January 15, 1681.

[12] Neumann, letter of January 15.

[13] Neumann to Bohemian father, February 2, 1682.

[14] Astrain, *op. cit.* IV, 543 ff.

[15] Neumann, *op. cit.*, chap. ii.

[16] Copies of six letters of Joseph Neumann belong to the Bolton Collection. One of them, however, that of July 29, 1686, to Father Stowasser may be found in Joseph Stöcklein, *op. cit.*, Pt. I, no. 32.

[17] These and the following details from Neumann's letter to an unknown Jesuit of Bohemia, dated February 2, 1682.

[18] Letter of February 2, 1682.

[19] *Archiv. Gen. Mis.*, t. 26, fol. 247.

[20] Cf. John F. Bannon, S.J., "The Conquest of the Chínapas," *Mid-America*, XXI (Jan. 1939), 3-31.

[21] Letter of February 2, 1682.

CHAPTER XVIII: A KALEIDOSCOPIC TWELVEMONTH

[1] Neumann, *op. cit.*, chap. ii.
[2] *Ibid.*
[3] Neumann to Stowasser, July 29, 1686.
[4] *Ibid.*
[5] *Ibid.*
[6] Letter of February 20, 1682.
[7] *Relación de la Nueva Entrada de los Padres de la Compañía de Jesús a las Naciones de Chinipa, Varohios, Guailopas, Guasaparis, Temoris y Otras,* in *Doc. Hist. Mex.,* 3d. ser., pp. 779 ff. Cf. also Almada, *op. cit.,* chap. vi ff., and Bannon, "The Conquest of the Chínipas," *loc. cit.*
[8] Neumann, letter of February 2, 1682.
[9] Letter of February 2.
[10] Letter of February 20, 1682.
[11] Neumann, letter of February 2, 1682.
[12] *Ibid.*
[13] *Ibid.*
[14] Cf. Astrain, *op. cit.,* VI, 479 ff., where Rolandegui's report of February 14, 1682, is offered in part. The missionary gives 8,000 as the number of baptized at the time of his visitation.
[15] Neumann, *op. cit.,* chap. iii.

CHAPTER XIX: STORM, TREASON, AND REVOLT

[1] Neumann, *op. cit.,* chap. iii.
[2] Cf. the historical sketch in manuscript of the foundation of this church and college in the library of Sr. José Rocha, Parral. After many vicissitudes subsequent to the expulsion of the Jesuits in 1767 most of the old shell was finally destroyed and at the end of the nineteenth century a theater was built on the site which later was occupied by the *ferretería* of Jorge Pérez. The name of the street today is significantly Calle del Colegio. The shop was consumed by fire in January 1941. In the rear an ancient wall of the church still stands looking on the Río del Parral, and the destruction of the ferretería laid bare the thick side walls of the old structure.
[3] Letter of July 29, 1686.
[4] *Ibid.*
[5] *Ibid.*
[6] Neumann, *op. cit.,* chap. iii. The present narrative is all taken from this source, which gives Diego as Foronda's surname. Decorme and Astrain differ slightly in their accounts of the two deaths.
[7] Decorme, *La Obra de los Jesuitas Mexicanos,* II, 297, following the *Informe de 1691* of Father Juan de Estrada, says Foronda was martyred in Nahuarachic.

CHAPTER XX: THE UPRISING OF 1697

[1] Letter of September 15, 1693.

[2] Letter of January 15, 1681.

[3] Bandelier-Hackett, *op. cit.*, II, 391.

[4] *Ibid.*, II, 305.

[5] *Testimonio de Cartas y ynformes sobre los Presidios del Reino de la Vizcaya Escritas por el Maestre del Campo Don Joseph Francisco Marin, Cavallero del Orden de Santiago y Otras Personas expertas, e ynteligentes Remitidas al Excelentisimo Señor Virrey Conde de Galve. 3 de Agosto hasta 30 de Septiembre de 1693.* Cf. Bandelier-Hackett, *op. cit.*, II, 391.

[6] Bandelier-Hackett, *loc. cit.*

[7] *Testimonio de los auttos hechos sobre las Providencias dadas en tiempo de Don Gabriel de el Castillo Governador de el Parral Sobre operaciones de Guerra y otros puntos. 31 de Mayo de 1691 hasta 9 de Febrero de 1694.* Cf. Bandelier-Hackett, *op. cit.*, II, 290 ff. Cf. also *Respuesta Fiscal Sobre Diferentes Puntos de Guerra con los Yndios Enemigos del Reyno del Parral Motibados de Diferentes Ynformes del Virrey de Mexico Conde de Galve...*Madrid, 1 de Abril de 1698. *Op. cit.*, pp. 418 ff. and pp. 423, 461.

[8] Don Joseph Francisco Marín, *Testimonio de Cartas...*, Bandelier-Hackett, *op. cit.*, II, 401.

[9] Letter of September 15, 1693.

[10] *Ibid.*

[11] Neumann, *op. cit.*, chap. iv.

[12] *Ibid.*

[13] *Ibid.*

[14] *Ibid.*

[15] *Ibid.*

[16] In the Archiv. Gen. de Indias, 67-4-99, is a report of September 1, 1698 on the movements against the rebels: "Respuesta fiscal dada en las dependencies del Reyno de el Parral su fecha 1 de Septiembre de 1698."

CHAPTER XXI: PRECARIOUS APPEASEMENT

[1] Neumann, *op. cit.*, chap. iv.

[2] *Ibid.*

[3] *Ibid.*

[4] *Ibid.*

[5] *Ibid.*, chap. v.

[6] *Ibid.*

[7] *Ibid.*

[8] *Ibid.*

[9] *Rim of Christendom*, p. 22.

[10] *Ibid.*

[11] Neumann, *op. cit.*, chap. v.

[12] *Ibid.*

[13] But a new scourge, even in Retana's time, was beginning to advance out of the north: the Apaches! They were soon to commit robberies, murders, and depredations as far south as Parras and the Valle de San Bartolomé near Parral, opening a trail that would be trod throughout more than a century of blood. Cf. *Informe Acerca de los Presidios de la Nueva Vizcaya. Doc. Hist. Mex.*, 2d. ser., I, 168 ff. and 181 ff.

[14] Archiv. Gen. de Indias, 67-5-15.

[15] *Ibid.*

[16] Neumann's letter of April 15, 1724 to the Provincial of the Bohemian Province.

[17] Decorme, *La Obra de los Jesuitos Mexicanos*, II, 302.

CHAPTER XXII: TARAHUMARA'S NORTHERN HOME

[1] Schetelig, "El Colegio de Jesuitas," in *El Heraldo*, Chihuahua, issue of September 8, 1940, p. 5.

[2] Neumann, *op. cit.*, chap. v.

[3] Schetelig, *loc. cit.*, where portions of some pertinent documents are printed. The principal documents are published by León Barri, Jr., in the *Boletín de la Sociedad Chihuahuense de Estúdios Históricos*, II, nos. 2, 3 and 4 (July–Sept., 1939), from manuscripts in his own possession.

[4] The published title of this work was *Florelegio Medicinal* (Mexico, 1712). That same year it was published in Amsterdam, again in Mexico, 1719; in Madrid, 1732; and finally a third time in Mexico, 1889. Cf. Sommervogel, *Bibliothèque de la Compagnie de Jésus*, VII, 1537.

[5] Neumann, *op. cit.*, chap. v; Sommervogel, *loc. cit.*

[6] Decorme, *op. cit.*, II, 235. The title of Guadalajara's grammar and dictionary runs in part thus: *Compendio del Arte de Lengua de los Tarahumares y Guaza-pares....Contiene cinco libros de la Gramatica, un Vocabulario, que comienza en Trahumar [sic], y otro en Castellano, y otro de nombres de parentesco,* (Puebla de Los Angeles por Diego Fernandez de Leon, Año de 1683). Cf. Sommervogel, *op. cit.*, III, col. 1897.

[7] Neumann, *loc. cit.*

[8] The second use of this word appears as Pamachis.

[9] Neumann, *loc. cit.*

[10] This document is in manuscript in the bound volume entitled, *Documentos para la Historia Ecclesiastica y civil: Nueva Vizcaya*, pp. 484 ff. and printed in the *Doc. Hist. Mex.*, 4th ser., IV, 23 ff.

[11] *Doc. Hist. Mex., loc. cit.*, p. 26.

[12] *Ibid.*, p. 32.

[13] "Instrucción del P. Prov. Joseph de Arjó al P. Juan de Guendulain y despues al P. Joseph de Echeverría para la visita gral. de las Misiones....1722–5, in the Jesuit Archives, Ysleta, Texas.

CHAPTER XXIII: THE LAST GREAT APOSTLE

[1] Cf. *Carta del P. Bartholomé Braun, Visitador de la Provincia Tarahumara, a los PP. Superiores de esta Provincia de Nueva España, sobre la Apostólica Vida, Virtudes, y Santa Muerte del P. Francisco Hermano Glandorff* (Mexico, 1764). Silvestre Terrazas has an enthusiastic article on the famous missionary in the *Boletín de la Sociedad Chihuahuense de Estúdios Históricos*, II and III (July–Dec., 1940), pp. 375 ff., entitled *El Gran Sabio y Santo Padre Glandorf en Chihuahua.*

[2] Terrazas, *loc. cit.*

[3] Cf. Jesuit Archives, Ysleta, Texas.

[4] Letter of January 18, 1752, from Tomochic to Father Sixtus Hesselmeier wherein he says it is now thirty years and more since he began to live among the Indians. Cf. Haupstaadtarchiv, Munich, Jesuitica MS 283. Transcripts in the Bancroft Library, University of California.

[5] "Anua misionis Tomochensis" written by Glandorff himself under date of August 16, 1730; in the Jesuit Archives, Ysleta, Texas.

[6] Cf. Bolton, *Rim of Christendom*, p. 22, for a racy sketch.

[7] Braun, *op. cit.*

[8] Hauptstaadtarchiv, Munich, Jesuitica MS 294. Transcript in Bancroft Library, University of California.

[9] Letter to Father Sixtus Hesselmeier, Hauptstaadtarchiv, Munich, Jesuitica MS 283. Transcript in Bancroft Library.

[10] Letter of October 4.

[11] *Ibid.*

[12] Letter of January 18.

[13] *Ibid.*

[14] "Anua misionis Tomochensis"; letter to Hesselmeier.

[15] There are extant Glandorff's official report or *anua* for Tomochic, dated August 16, 1731 and seven letters to his superiors written between 1746 and 1749. These are to be found in *Archiv. Gen. Hist.*, t. 309-333. Transcripts made by Father Mariano Cuevas rest in the Jesuit Archives, Ysleta, Texas.

[16] Colección de Cartas Inéditas, *passim*, Jesuit Archives, Ysleta, Texas.

[17] Letter to the Visitor, Juan Manuel de Hierro, from Norogachic, February 2, 1747.

[18] Letter from Tomochic to the Provincial, Andrés Xavier García, September 15, 1749.

[19] Letter of February 2, 1747.

[20] The final parts of this letter are lost and there is no date.

[21] *Consulta al Señor Virrey del Governador de Chihuahua sobre la moderacion de los mandamientos*, San Felipe el Real, Sept. 1, 1744. Cf. *Doc. Hist. Mex.*, 4th ser., IV, 39 ff.

[22] Cf. Ignatz Pfefferkorn, *Beschreibung der Landschaft Sonora samt andern merkwürdigen Nachrichten von den innern Theilen Neu-Spaniens und Reise aus Amerika bis in Deutschland* (Köln am Rheine, 1794). A fine account of this old work is given by Dr. Theodore E. Treutlein, "Father Pfefferkorn and His Description of Sonora," *Mid-America*, XX (Oct., 1938), 229-252, and

"The Jesuit Missionary in the Role of Physician," *ibid.*, XXII (April, 1940), 120-141.

[23] Alegre, III, 287 and 289; Bancroft, *History of the North Mexican States and Texas*, I, 587. Concerning details of the transfer of the missions there exists an interesting document in the Jesuit Archives of Ysleta, Texas, entitled: "Copia de una instruccion del Sr. Obispo de Durango al Sr. Vicario Visitador Ochoa, Cura del Parral quien viene a recevir por la Mitra las Misiones q cede la Compañia." The purport of the various items is that the Jesuits in leaving the ceded pueblos may not take with them stores of grain, herds of sheep or cattle, or articles which belong to the furniture of the priest's dwelling. And the curate is to have the first bid on articles which the departing missionary might wish to sell.

[24] Archiv. Gen. de Indias, Aud. de Guadalajara, 67-4-2.

[25] In 1705 seventy-one pueblos in Nueva Vizcaya had been under Jesuit charge. In 1751 sixteen Jesuits were serving in the colleges of Parras, Parral, and Chihuahua and thirty-five in the mission units of Topia, Tepehuanes, and Tarahumara. Cf. Bancroft, *op. cit.*, I, 588.

[26] *Ibid.*

CHAPTER XXIV: THE LAST REPORT

[1] *Noticia de la visita general de P. Ignacio Lizasoain.* . . .

[2] Guendulain reporting on the livestock of Norogachic gives the following figures: 1,000 head of cattle, 300 pack animals, 24 mules, and 124 goats. For San Tomás he has the following: 1,000 head of cattle, 146 mares, 110 horses, 131 mules, 54 oxen, 110 burros, 112 sheep and goats.

[3] See below, Appendix 2 for a comparison of figures.

[4] Cf. Dunne, *Pioneer Black Robes on the West Coast,* chap. xiv and pp. 196 f.

[5] Colección de Cartas Inéditas, Vitelleschi to Provincial Luis de Bónifaz, October 30, 1638.

[6] Cf. Pedro Tamerón y Romeral, *Demonstración del vastísimo obispado de la Nueva Vizcaya* (Mexico, 1937). Bancroft, *History of the North Mexican States and Texas,* pp. 595 ff., offers a multitude of statistics taken from Tamarón and other sources.

[7] Lizasoain visited first Tutuaca and Yepachic which had no resident missionary. Then in the following order he lists the head pueblos of a partido with resident missionary: Tomochic (Purísima Concepción), Herman Glandorff; San Tomás, Blas de la Palmas; Temósachic, Bartolomé Braun; San Rafael de Mátachic, Phelipe Ruanova; Nuestra Señora de la Concepción de Papigochic, Isidro Sabera; San José de Temechic, José Michio (superior of Alta Tarahumara); Jesús de Cárichic, Luis Angel; María Sisoguichic, Antonio Hitl; Nuestra Señora del Pilar de Norogachic, Ildefonso Vorro; Nuestra Señora del Pópulo de Gueguachic, Antonio Sterkianowski; San Juan Bautista de Tomachic, Juan Trujillo; Nuestra Señora de Monserrate de Nonoava, Manuel Vivanco; Nuestra Señora del Pilar de Bacagueriachic (a possible future mission where lived 200 Christian Tarahumares); San Francisco de Borja de Tehuacachic, Gregorio Javier Vargas; San Ignacio Coyachic (no missionary). The padre of most of the above cabaceras administered to three visitas each given a pious name prefixed to the Tarahumar appellation.

EPILOGUE

[1] Quoted in Bancroft, *History of Mexico*, III, 438 f.

[2] Cf. Dunne, "Expulsion of the Jesuits from New Spain," *Mid-America*, XIX (Jan., 1937), 3–30.

[3] Antonio Sterkianowski, "Destierro de los Jesuitos Missioneros," MS. The original is in Florence, but a photostat copy of this splendid source is in the Bolton Collection, University of California. Prior to this find the details of the expulsion from Tarahumara were unknown. Bancroft says: "Of the circumstances connected with the expulsion from Chihuahua nothing whatever is known," *op. cit.*, I, 588.

[4] Sterkianowski, *loc. cit.*, who says there were eighteen missionaries. But Rafael de Zelis, *Catàlogo de los sujetos de la Compañía de Jesús que formaban la provincia de México el dia del arresto, 25 de Junio de 1767*, avers there were nineteen.

[5] *Ibid.*

BIBLIOGRAPHY

MANUSCRIPTS

Jesuit annual reports *(anuas)* in six collections:
  The Roman Jesuit Archives of Europe.
  The National Archives of Mexico.
  The Jesuit Archives of Mexico.
  The Bancroft Library.
  "Memorias para la Historia de la Provincia de Sinaloa."
  The Herbert E. Bolton Collection, University of California.

Letters and Reports, Archivo General de Indias, Bancroft Library, University of California.

Letters and Reports, Archivo General y Público de la Nación, Mexico City.

Letters and Reports, Archives of Parral.

Letters and Reports, Jesuit Mexican Archives, Ysleta, Texas. This collection consists of correspondence between the Jesuit General and the provincials of New Spain. It is referred to as Colección de cartas inéditas.

Letters and Reports, Bancroft Library Collection. This includes the collection of transcripts entitled *Documentos para la historia eclesiastica y civil de la Nueva Vizcaya*, Mexico, 1849.

Letters of Joseph Neumann, S.J. Bolton Collection, University of California.

Lizasoain, Ignacio. "Noticia de la visita general de P. Ignacio Lizasoain Visitador General de las Missiones de esta Prov. de Nueva Espana q. comenzio dia quarto de Abril de 1761 ans. y se concluye a finis de Henero de 1763 con algunas notas y addiciones q. pueden servir pa. el conocimiento de estas Missiones y Provincias de ellas." W. B. Stevens Collection, University of Texas Library.

Pérez de Ribas, Andrés. "Historia de la Provincia de Cinaloa," Jesuit Archives, Mexico.

Sterkianowski, Antonio, S.J. "Destierro de los Jesuitos Missioneros," Bolton Collection.

McShane, Catherine M. "Hernando de Santarén" (recent).

Bannon, John F., S.J. "The Jesuits in Sonora" (recent).

Dunne, Peter M., S.J. "Andres Pérez de Ribas" (recent).

Note: Most of the manuscripts of the Bancroft Library and of the Bolton Collection above referred to exist as transcripts or photostats.

PRINTED SOURCES AND SECONDARY WORKS

Alegre, Francisco Javier, S.J. *Historia de la Compañía de Jesús en Nueva España.* 3 vols., Mexico, 1841.

Almada, Francisco R. *Apuntes Históricos de la Región de Chínipas*, Mexico, 1937.

Arlegui, José. *Crónica de la Provincia de N.S.P.S. Francisco de Zacatecas*, Mexico, 1737.

Astrain, Antonio, S.J. *Historia de la Compañía de Jesús en la Asistencia de España*, 7 vols., Madrid, 1902.

Bancroft, Hubert Howe. *History of Mexico,* 5 vols., San Francisco, 1883.

————*History of the North Mexican States and Texas,* 3 vols., San Francisco, 1884.

Bandelier, A. F. and Fanny R. *Historical Documents Relating to New Mexico, Nueva Vizcaya and Approaches Thereto, to 1773,* 3 vols., ed. Charles Wilson Hackett, Washington, Carnegie Institution, 1923 ff.

Beals, Ralph L. *The Comparative Ethnology of Northern Mexico before 1750,* Univ. Calif. Publ. Ibero-Americana, 2, Berkeley, University of California Press, 1932.

Belloc, Hilaire, ed. *Why I Am and Why I Am Not a Catholic,* New York, The Macmillan Co., 1930.

Bennett, Wendell C., and Robert M. Zingg. *The Tarahumara, an Indian Tribe of Northern Mexico,* University of Chicago Press, 1935.

Bertrand, Louis, and Charles Petrie, tr. W. P. Wells. *History of Spain,* New York, Appleton-Century Co., 1934.

Bolton, Herbert Eugene. *Guide to the Materials for the History of the United States in the Principal Archives of Mexico,* Washington, Carnegie Institution, 1913.

————*Rim of Christendom,* New York, The Macmillan Co., 1936.

Caughey, John Walton. *California,* New York, Prentice-Hall Publishing Co., 1940.

Cuevas, Mariano, S.J. *Historia de la Iglesia en México,* 5 vols., El Paso, Revista Catolica Press, 1928.

Decorme, Gerardo, S.J. *La Obra de los Jesuitas Mexicanos Durante la Epoca Colonial, 1572–1769,* 2 vols., Mexico, 1941.

Documentos para la Historia de México, 20 vols., Mexico, 1853–1857.

Dunne, Peter M., S.J. *Pioneer Jesuits in Northern Mexico,* Berkeley, University of California Press, 1944.

————*Pioneer Black Robes on the West Coast,* Berkeley, University of California Press, 1940.

Guadalajara, Tomás de, S.J. *Compendio del Arte de la Lengua de los Tarahumares y Guazapares...*Puebla de Los Angeles por Diego Fernandez de Leon, Año de 1683.

Helps, Arthur. *The Spanish Conquest of America,* 4 vols., London, 1855.

Huonder, Anton. *Deutsche Jesuitenmissionäre des 17. und 18. Jahrhunderts,* Freiburg-im-Breisgau, 1899.

Jacobsen, Jerome V., S.J. *Educational Foundations of the Jesuits in Sixteenth-Century New Spain,* Berkeley, University of California Press, 1938.

Kroeber, A. L. *Uto-Aztecan Languages of Mexico,* Univ. Calif. Publ. Ibero-Americana, 8, Berkeley, University of California Press, 1934.

Mecham, J. Lloyd. *Francisco de Ibarra and Nueva Vizcaya,* Durham, Duke University Press, 1927.

Mendoza y Herrera, Francisco. *Constituciones del M. I. y V. Cabildo Metropolitano de Durango,* Durango, 1920.

Neumann, Joseph, S.J. *Historia Seditionum quas Adversus Societatis Jesu Missionarios, eorumq. Auxiliares Moverunt Nationes Indicae ac Potissimum Tarahumara in America Septentrionali, Regnoque Novae Cantabriae, jam Toto ad fidem Catholicam propemodum redacto, Auctore P. Josepho Neymanno*

Ejusdem Societatis Jesu in Partibus Tarahumarorum Missionario, Pragae, Typis Univers. Carolo-Ferd. Soc. Jesu. ad S. Clem.

Pastor, Ludwig von. *History of the Popes*, 32 vols., London, 1899 ff.

Pérez de Ribas, Andrés. *Corónica y Historia Religiosa de la Provincia de la Compañía de Jesús de México en la Nueva España*, Mexico, 1896.

————*Historia de los Triunfos de Nuestra Santa Fee entre Gentes los mas Barbaros y Fieras del Nuevo Orbe*, Madrid, 1645.

Pfefferkorn, Ignatz. *Breschreibung der Landschaft Sonora samt andern merkwürdigen Nachrichten von den innern Theilen Neu-Spaniens und Reise aus Amerika bis in Deutschland*, Köln am Rheine, 1794.

Ricard, Robert. *La 'Conquête Spirituelle' du Mexique*, Paris, Institut d'Ethnologie, 1933.

Sauer, Carl. *The Distribution of Aboriginal Tribes and Languages in Northwestern Mexico*, Berkeley, University of California Press, 1934.

————*Aboriginal Population of Northwestern Mexico*, Univ. Calif. Publ. Ibero-Americana, 10, Berkeley, University of California Press, 1935.

Schmitt, Ludovicus, S.J. *Synopsis Historia Societatis Jesu*, Ratisbon, 1914.

Shiels, W. Eugene, S.J. *Gonzalo de Tapia*, New York, The United States Catholic Historical Society, 1934.

Sommervogel, Carlos, S.J. *Bibliothèque de la Compagnie de Jésus*, 11 vols., Paris, 1890.

Steinheffer, Johann, S.J. *Florelegio Medicinal*, Mexico, 1712 ff.; Amsterdam, 1712; Madrid, 1732.

Stöcklein, Joseph. *Der Neue Welt-Bott, mit allerhand Nachrichten dern Missionariorum Soc. Jesu*, Augsburg and Gratz, 1726.

Tanner, Mathias. *Societas Jesu usque ad Sanguinis et Vitae Profusionem Militans in Europa, Asia, Africa et America contra Gentiles Mahometanos, Judaeos, Haereticos, Impios pro Deo, Ecclesia, Pietate*, Pragae, 1675.

Zelis, Rafael de. *Catàlogo de los sujetos de la Compañía de Jesús que formaban la provincia de México el dia del arresto, 25 de Junio de 1767*.

PERIODICAL LITERATURE

Bannon, John F., S.J. "The Conquest of the Chínipas," *Mid-America*, XXI (Jan. 1939), 3-31.

Barri, León, Jr., "Documentos Sobre la Fundación del Colegio de los Jesuitos en Chihuahua," *Boletín de la Sociedad Chihuahuense de Estúdios Históricos*, II (July–Sept. 1939), 48 ff.

Chrystelow, Allen G., "Father Joseph Neumann, Jesuit Missionary to the Tarahumares," *Hispanic American Historical Review*, XIX (Nov. 1939), 423-442.

Dunne, Peter M., S.J., "The Expulsion of the Jesuits from New Spain," *Mid-America*, XIX (Jan. 1937), 3-30.

————"The Tepehuán Revolt," *Mid-America*, XVIII (Jan. 1936), 3-14.

Rocha, José G. "Una Cruel Matanza de Tobosos," *Boletín de la Sociedad Chihuahuense de Estúdios Históricos*, III (Oct.–Dec., 1940), 401 ff.

Schetelig, Lorenzo Arellano, "El Colegio de Jesuitos," *El Heraldo*, Chihuahua, Sept. 8, 1940, p. 5, and Sept. 15, 1940, p. 3.

Shiels, W. Eugene, S.J., "The Critical Period in Mission History," *Mid-America*, XXI (April 1939), 97-109.

———"The Legal Crisis in the Jesuit Missions of Hispanic America," *Mid-America*, XXI (Oct. 1939), 253-276.

Terrazas, Silvestre, "El Gran Sabio y Santa Padre Glandorf en Chihuahua," *Boletín de la Sociedad Chihuahuense de Estúdios Históricos*, II & III (July–Dec. 1940), 375 ff. and 408 ff.

Treutlein, Theodore E. "Father Pfefferkorn and His Description of Sonora," *Mid-America*, XX (Oct. 1938), 229-252.

———"The Jesuit Missionary in the Role of Physician," *Mid-America*, XXII (April 1940), 120-141.

———"Jesuit Travel to New Spain, 1678–1756," *Mid-America*, XIX (April 1937), 104-123.

INDEX